THE SSAC
INTRODUCTORY DIVE TRAINING MANUAL

KV-015-553

THE SSAC INTRODUCTORY DIVE TRAINING MANUAL

1st Edition

1991

THE SCOTTISH SUB-AQUA CLUB

GLASGOW

Published by The Scottish Sub-Aqua Club
40 Bogmoor Place, Glasgow

ISBN 0 904419 04 5

This edition published in Great Britain. 1991.

Printed in Scotland by W. M. Bett Ltd., Tillicoultry

Foreword

Last year the Scottish Sub-Aqua Club published *The Advanced Dive Training Manual.* Preparation of this Introductory Manual has taken longer because of the very thorough revision of training methods that the National Diving Council has undertaken. As a consequence the Introductory Manual differs considerably from its precursor, the first half of the old Dive Training Manual. Much new material related to new training methods and to newer types of equipment as well as details of the various SSAC extra (endorsement) courses is included. The opportunity has been taken to increase the amount of illustration.

I am grateful to all those members who have helped with this new edition, especially Peter Armstrong, the NDO for 1990 and 1991, Alasdair Porter for some of the new drawings. Peter Collings for the cover photograph and Ian Ramsden for other illustrations.

Adam Curtis
Editor

Contents

Chapter 1

Learning to dive

Diving, both snorkelling and aqualung diving, is a sport which is non-competitive but which requires a good deal of training to master because you are going to enter a fascinating different world which works in a very different way from land-based life. This manual is about that training and about carrying out diving safely.

There are a number of types of diving. The simplest is breath-holding diving, which evolved in the 1930s by adding fins, mask and snorkel into snorkelling which requires simple training. The next more complex stage is sports diving with air breathing equipment carried by the diver, known as Scuba (Self-contained underwater breathing apparatus) or aqualung diving. The term Sports Diving is rather imprecise but covers both snorkelling and aqualung diving. This book is about snorkelling and aqualung diving. Of course the term Scuba can also be used to cover other types of self-contained equipment such as oxygen rebreathers, Nitrox sets, etc. but these are outwith the normal use of amateurs.

This book takes snorkelling and aqualung training to the fairly advanced level termed Second Class Diver. The companion volume, *The SSAC Advanced Training Manual* provides information about more advanced aspects of sports diving.

There are two training routes in the SSAC. Most people will want to proceed directly to aqualung training. This leads to the first milepost, the Third Class Diver qualification via a small amount of snorkel training: you should use Chapters 1, 2, 4, 5 and 6 from this book. But you may wish to follow a different track and concentrate on snorkelling. If so, read Chapters 1, 2 and especially Chapter 3. Or you may wish to become expert in both types of diving in which case the whole book is for you.

If you are fifteen or over you may choose either route but if you are under fifteen you are allowed, for medical reasons, only to undergo snorkel training. If you are under fifteen years of age you should join the Club as a Junior Snorkeller.

The various stages and routes of training in the SSAC are shown in Fig.1.

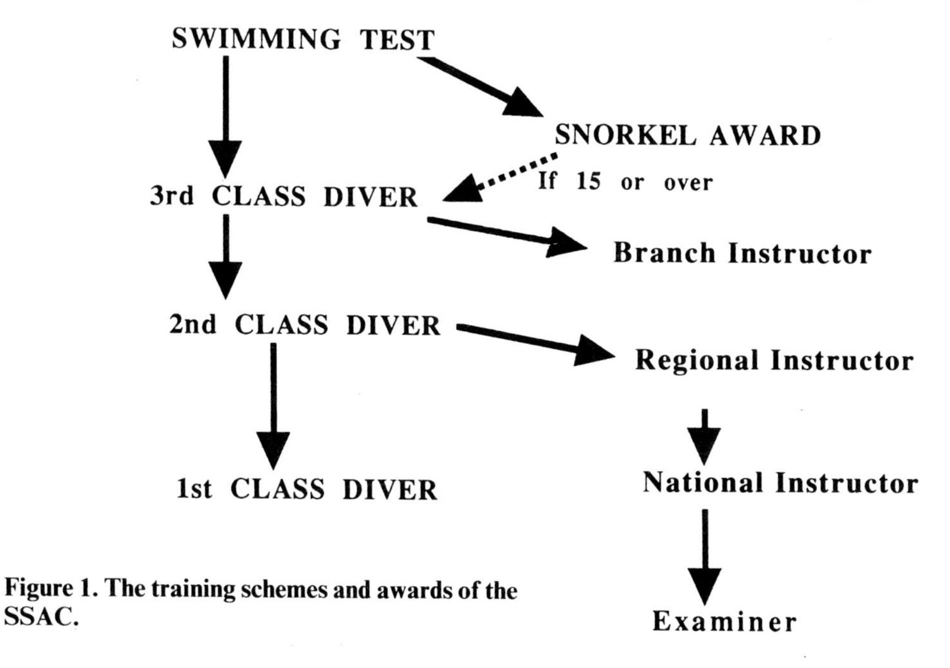

Figure 1. The training schemes and awards of the SSAC.

The Club

The SSAC was founded in the early months of 1953 and was the first Sub-Aqua Club in the UK and one of the first in the world. It has grown and prospered since then and has been responsible for developing many of the aspects of sports dive training to be found in many other training schemes of other groups. It has, true to its name, remained a Scottish-based organisation though its influence has spread to some parts of England. The Scottish base has meant that because of the relatively small population of Scotland the SSAC has never grown to a vast size. The Club started with a Glasgow group based at Ibrox Pool. Hamilton Branch was then formed and by 1961 the Club had grown to twelve branches. In 1990 it has eighty branches.

The Club has had a very good record of safe diving and very very few serious or fatal accidents have occurred in its diving but remember that careless, thoughtless, uninformed and reckless diving practices are potentially dangerous. This book emphasises the need for thought, sense, knowledge and care to prevent accident and the fact that these qualities also contribute to the enjoyment of diving.

Diving in Scotland can be amongst the best in the world because the underwater life is varied and colourful. The underwater terrain is often impressive with big underwater cliffs and the water is often clear. On the west coast underwater visibility is usually 10 metres and can be as good as 30 metres. The water is cold but modern dry and wet suits keep you remarkably warm. There are also a vast number of wrecks.

How it operates and how you can get the best out of it.

Why you should have a Club at all and why you might want to belong to it.

The Club provides a recognised source of expert training for diving and also a means of running dives so that they are safe and enjoyable and not too expensive.

Training is not simply a matter of passing a certain number of tests and then just diving in. The Scottish Sub-Aqua Club, like nearly all diving clubs, has found that there is a certain amount of practical work and theory that you must know before you dive underwater but that training does not end there. In part, training is simply experience plus diving regularly (say at least twice a month) but there is also further formal training which you can and should go on to. The basic training leads to the 3rd Class Diver award.

So once you've joined and trained you can get out to dive with your Branch of the Club in the open water (sea or freshwater). Very soon you'll find that diving is really fascinating, simply being where air-breathing humans are not supposed to be, moving underwater almost weightlessly rather like a bird. For some people these are the fascinations of diving that never leave you. For others a more objective interest such as marine biology, photography, wreck surveying and salvage, underwater archaeology, and a little food collecting is required.

Who can join the Club?

Anyone who is over the age of 14. If you are younger you can join as a Junior Snorkel Diver, either through your school, youth group, or by visiting a Branch of the Club that is running a course for Junior snorkellers. Some people think that because they are in their fifties they are too old to learn to dive but provided they are in reasonable health there is no problem. In fact diving, provided it can be carried out in unstrenuous conditions, can be a pleasant and healthy exercise both for those who are no longer young and for those who are physically handicapped in certain ways. The Club makes special arrangements for those with physical disabilities (contact headquarters). The minimum age for aqualung training or diving is 15.

The Club expects you to be able to swim when you join; maybe not rapidly or elegantly but with a certain strength and without panic. The reasons for this are described in Chapter 2 but in essence you must be at home in the water to be able to train to dive. The only other requirement, other than of course paying the joining fee and subscription, is that you should obtain a certificate from your doctor stating that he or she has examined you and passed you fit for diving (see also training schedule). We do not insist on your producing this certificate the moment you start but we do insist that you produce the certificate before you proceed to aqualung training. Basically, so long as you are not suffering, or have suffered, from a serious respiratory or circulatory system disease, are not overweight (appreciably), are not an insulin-dependent diabetic nor an epileptic, you are probably fit to dive.

How do you join?

First discover where and when the Branch which you want to join meets (usually at a swimming pool in the evening for a training session). You may get information at your local swimming pool or through divers you might meet, but you can always get it from our Head Office. Most branches are Ordinary branches and are open to any person of, or over the age of, 14, but some branches, usually attached to schools, universities or various firms, are Special branches and are only open to members of certain groups. Go along to the session and make yourself known to the persons in charge. It may be useful to have contacted the Branch Secretary beforehand to discover just where they are meeting and so that they know you'll be there. Or go to an 'open night', perhaps advertised locally, and 'try a dive'. The main branch committee officers who are likely to be around are the Treasurer, Secretary (these two can usually tell you how to join), the Chairman, the Diving Officer, and (in some branches which have them) the Training Officer. The last two will tell you how to start your training.

Most branches like to let you look at what is going on and try some swimming and snorkelling exercises or the Swimming Assessment. If you are unable to complete some exercises, do not worry, lots of others have failed the first time and have gone on to pass it later and become good divers. So the branch of your choice will probably let you come for one or two sessions without joining, though you may have to pay the baths charge levied by the baths' authorities. A BI (Branch Instructor) will supervise your training and all subsequent tests you take.

There will be local pool rules set up by the branch to run training safely and to satisfy the pool authorities: make sure that you find out what they are.

If you like what you've seen, and want to join, get a membership application form from a Branch Official and either get him to send it in with your money to the Head Office, or post them off to the Head Office, or take them there when it is open. If you are under 18 you will need the counter-signature of a parent or guardian.

What happens when you join?

As soon as your entry form and entry fee and first subscription are received at Head Office you are a member of the Club. On joining you will be sent:

1. A membership certificate for a twelve month period.
2. A Training Schedule, which is a description of the tests and becomes a record of the tests you have passed during your training (see below for further details).
3. A Logbook in which to record dives (see below).
4. A wallet for training schedule and logbook.
5. A medical certificate form to take to your doctor.
6. A copy of the Club's constitution.
7. A copy of the Training Manual (both volumes) and
8. A copy of the current issue of the *Scottish Diver* magazine. You will receive further copies of the magazine throughout the twelve month period of your subscription. At present the magazine is issued bi-monthly.

The Club likes to keep details of its members on a computer database but asks for your agreement, to your details being entered into the database, on the joining form. If you do not agree, no details will be put into the database. The Club does not make any details from the database available to any outside sporting, commercial or other organisation. If you wish to receive a printout of your personal details as held on the database please contact Club HQ.

Renewing your membership

Memberships are renewed twelve months after the last subscription. A month before your membership renewal falls due you will be sent a reminder that your subscription is about to fall due. Bear in mind that you cannot vote or be voted into office either in the Club AGM or in your Branch AGM if you are not a current member. If you fail to renew your membership within a stated period after it falls due, but then wish to rejoin, you may be charged a rejoining fee. The amount of this fee and the period of grace after expiry of your membership that you will be allowed, are determined by the Club and details can be obtained from the Administrator.

All subscriptions for members of Ordinary branches are handled by the Club Headquarters, and not by branches, though as a matter of helpfulness some Branch Treasurers send in the membership forms and subscriptions for groups of their members. Bear in mind that a substantial part of the subscription from each member is returned to the Branch to help its funds. Special branches normally send in details of members and their pooled subscriptions from time to time. Members of Special branches pay a slightly lower subscription than Ordinary members but Special branches do not receive a proportion of the subscriptions.

Using the training schedule

The training programme is set out in the Training Schedule. The Club has a standard training schedule so that we can be sure that someone who has reached a particular level has the same capabilities as another with the same level of training. In effect we might sum this up by saying that any 3rd Class diver is able to look after him- or herself in most situations in the water but cannot be expected to do more than look after his or her diving partner. A 2nd Class diver should be able to look after a group of divers in most situations while a 1st Class diver is able to do anything that any compressed air diver might be expected to do. The instructional qualifications add the knowledge (and assurance to others) that you can also train others to dive. The 3rd Class diver qualification is recognised nationally and internationally as proof that you are safe to be let into the water with an aqualung, while the higher qualifications show that you can do more than this alone. However, if you went along to dive with a group who did not know you, they might well ask to see not only your Training Schedule but also your Logbook as well, since this would show whether you were keeping your experience up by diving recently. Official proof of this is also contained if you have been signed up annually as an Active Diver in your training schedule, but to get this you need to keep a good Logbook.

So, as you train and pass tests, make sure that the person who trains you – who should be one of the Branch Instructor (BI) or your Branch Diving Officer (BDO) – signs the appropriate part of your training schedule. The BI should report to the BDO that you've passed such and such a test so that this fact can be entered in the training records of the Branch. These records provide a source of information should you, for instance, lose your training schedule.

When you've reached the 3rd Class level your Training Schedule should be sent or brought before the Regional Coach for signature and entry of your qualification in Club records. If you are posting the Schedule send it recorded delivery to Club Headquarters. Make sure that you get your signed and officially stamped training schedule back again within a few weeks.

As we said above, the Training Schedule completed to 3rd Class diver or beyond is virtually a licence to dive, and you should expect to have to produce it and be accepted as a diver by it if you visit any other SSAC Branch and those of other clubs. Occasionally, particularly if you have been off diving for some time, a Diving Officer of your own, or of some other Branch might ask you to show something of your ability in either the pool or the sea. He or she should not ask you to do all the tests again but merely to show that you can carry out some of the harder procedures in perhaps a single dive. This is a reasonable request because it is surprising how fast you can forget underwater skills that you learned in the pool and the sea. However, it would be unreasonable to start by asking you to take all the tests again unless you have shown, which we hope you don't, that you are really out of practice.

Your rights as a member

These are set out in full detail in the Constitution but since that takes some reading, here is a summary:

1. The right to receive training not only up to 3rd and 2nd Class level in your Branch but also to higher levels with courses organised either regionally or nationally. Training at higher levels includes Sub-Aqua life saving classes, training for the 1st Class diver and various Instructor qualifications, and various specialist courses such as those on marine biology, underwater photography etc. Use of aqualung, cylinder charged with air, a regulator, weight belt, and lifejacket is provided for each trainee by many Ordinary Branches at no charge until the trainee has completed 3rd Class.

Most trainees begin to buy their own cylinder, regulator, lifejacket etc, once they have started diving in the open water (sea or freshwater loch) but many Branches will hire this equipment at a small charge to members after they have completed 3rd Class.

Special training courses or accelerated 3rd or 2nd Class training courses may charge a fee but the Club keeps these charges as low as possible. Usually the fee covers accommodation and a part of the cost of providing equipment (i.e. hire) and travelling and accommodation costs for instructors. Instructors receive no payment. The only exception to this is that Regional Coaches receive a small annual honorarium.

2. The right and encouragement to attend Branch and General Committee meetings at which you may speak but have no voting rights (unless you are an elected representative). The right to attend, speak and vote at Branch and Club AGMs and, if they happen, Extraordinary AGMs.

3. The right to use the Club library at the headquarters of the Club; to obtain information on equipment, training methods, insurance, starting Branches, expeditions, holidays, diving sites etc, from the relevant officers of the Club, and the right to obtain facilities of the other organisations to which the Club is affiliated.

4. Insurance cover as a member of the Club. The Club insurance cover indemnifies you as an individual member against claims by others, including other members of the Club, arising from your own, or your Branch or Club diving activities. It does not cover personal claims from you for loss of equipment, injury to yourself resulting from your own negligence, carelessness or bad luck. Nor does it cover claims by your dependents for accidents or loss resulting from your own error. Branch or Club equipment should be covered separately against theft, fire, etc. Further information on insurance cover can be obtained from the Club Treasurer or the Honorary Insurance Adviser (address through the Club headquarters).

Your part in the Club and Branch

We've told you so far of all the good things that you can get from the Club. What do you have to put in, other than the subscription? Obviously a reasonable keenness to want to dive and of course a reasonable attitude to rules. The rules are there for the enjoyment and safety of your own as well as everyone else's diving, so they should be treated seriously but not slavishly or imposed so heavily that the joy goes out of diving. The Club insurance policy, the good reputation of your Branch and the Club, but above all your own safety require that you obey Club diving and training rules when diving with the Club: it is also a very good idea to obey them even when you are diving with groups outwith the SSAC. We don't want to be stuffy about the rules but failure to obey Branch or Club diving rules whilst diving with the Club could be, if proved and of a serious nature, grounds for suspension or other disciplinary measures, as well as loss of insurance cover for the incident involved. All that sounds horrible but nearly everyone does obey the rules so all these terrible threats have hardly ever had to be used.

The diving rules are to be found in the Club Constitution, Training Schedule and Logbook, but for convenience the major ones are set out below:

1. Do not dive with an aqualung without having passed a medical examination including a full plate chest X-ray, preferably recently, that you are fit to dive. If you have been seriously ill, or have not dived for a year, the Club requires you to pass a medical examination again before aqualung diving.

2. Do not dive if feeling unwell or inexplicably apprehensive. It's normal to be a bit worried by a dive, particularly your first few, but if you are unreasonably worried do not dive.

3. Never dive alone unless you are roped to a surface attendant, with both you and the attendant conversant with the rope signals and with a standby diver ready to dive if anything goes wrong. In some situations voice communication with the surface by telephone etc, may take the place of a signal line but you must still have a way of being hauled up. Even if you are the best diver in the world you might be taken unwell without warning, or suffer unpredictable problems with equipment: a fellow or 'buddy' diver can really look after you if either of these things happen. So always dive in pairs or maybe threes and have someone on the surface (Club diving makes this a rule) who knows exactly when you went in and roughly where you are. Commercial and some scientific diving sometimes requires diving alone but then you are roped to the surface (or to an underwater habitat) attendant and are usually in voice communication with the attendant. Moreover, such diving usually involves wearing a full face mask which gives added protection from drowning should you become unconscious.

The Club permits a member to dive alone on a Club dive if he or she is roped to the surface with a surface attendant and a fully kitted standby diver ready to come to your aid, and if diver and attendant have passed tests in the use of rope signals. While learning rope signals, dive in pairs.

There is one exception to this rule: when

you have to rescue someone, an attempt to save life should not be delayed while a second diver is being got ready.

4. Always obey the rules laid down by the Dive Marshal (beachmaster) and Expedition Officer while on a dive. Let them or their appointees know when you are about to dive and when you surface. They must have exact timings for your dive so that:

(a) They will know whether or not you are overdue in surfacing. You and they will have planned your dive duration taking the probable depth of the water, the volume of air supply you have at the start of the dive, and the need to avoid decompression stops or risk of decompression sickness. If you are overdue in surfacing by five minutes a standby diver will be sent down to find you. If he has to go down for no good reason he or she will not be pleased.

(b) They will know when you surface whether you have a decompression problem.

5. Always wear a lifejacket, preferably an Adjustable Buoyancy lifejacket (ABLJ) or Stab Jacket which should have a supply of breathing air, and know how to use it. Wear it underneath any breathing equipment or weight belt. Lack of a lifejacket has been a very frequent cause of fatal diving accidents. Wear it immediately over your suit or swim trunks or costume or bikini (if water is warm enough in the three last cases) and under your aqualung or weight belt so that if you have to dump your aqualung or weight belt you still have a lifejacket. If you are using a type of lifejacket with which you are unfamiliar, practice with it before starting your dive.

6. Always keep adequately warm while diving. Hypothermia (pp. 33) is a great risk. Once you start shivering it is time to come out. Once you have reached that colder stage when you no longer shiver then your are at great risk.

7. Never hold your breath on ascent when using an aqualung. If you do hold your breath you may have a serious or fatal barotrauma accident (pp. 12). The faster you ascend the more rapidly you must breathe out but always try to limit your ascent rate to 15 metres per minute.

All that sounds very formal and a little frightening to a beginner. So once again we say, to dive safely you must obey some rules and follow some standard procedures, but in fact these are easily mastered. Otherwise we want the discipline to sit lightly on you.

Sources of information: how do you find out what is going on?

Information on what the Club is doing comes partly to you by direct mail, partly in the form of announcements in the Club magazine, partly by announcements sent to Branch Secretaries and Branch Diving Officers and partly by information sent to Regional Coaches. Unfortunately it is very expensive to mail every member so that the only things sent to every member, apart from the Club magazine, are announcements of the AGM and any EGM of the Club and of course a renewal of membership form. So information on diving and special courses is published in the *Scottish Diver* and also sent to Branch Diving Officers and Regional Coaches, while information on general Club matters is sent to Branch Secretaries. Thus these two officers and sometimes your Branch Chairman and other Branch Committee members should know everything – do they? Do they appear at Branch activities? Is there a Branch notice board? It is also up to these officers to let their Regional Coach or headquarters know of any sudden changes in their address or telephone number. If you change your address or telephone number let Club headquarters know as soon as possible. Regional Coaches (addresses in *Scottish Diver* or from headquarters) know a lot about what is going on, as does the National Diving Officer. The General Committee tries hard to keep you informed about what is going on without spending too much of your subscription but it does need a bit of effort from you to keep yourself informed. Similarly if you find out something that might be of interest to the Club, like new training methods, good lecturers, restrictions on diving being introduced at some site, a desire to start a Branch somewhere etc, or are puzzled about Club policy, make sure that the General Committee knows. Ring them up or invite them to come along to your Branch.

What equipment shall I need to buy?

The only equipment we ask you to buy while you're going through pool training is the basic equipment of mask, fins and snorkel. You will need to have these once you start training. If you visit any competent dive shop you should receive good advice about the types to buy.

The following suggestions may be of value.

All equipment should fit you comfortably. Any mask you buy should be fitted with safety glass so that shattering is very unlikely. A test to find a mask which fits is to hold the mask to your face and to suck in through your nose. The mask should hold onto your face without any air sucking in round the edges. So while you're sucking in the mask should not fall off your face into your hands. Check that the mask has a reasonably large field of view. Most divers like a mask with a relatively small air space inside it so that it will be easy to clear of water should it flood while you're diving. If you have a thin face you may find that only a few makes of mask fit you, usually those with a double 'skirt' edge. Drain valves are fitted to some masks: they are not a good idea. Though the drain valve is supposed to help in clearing they eventually get sand jammed in them and then leak water into your mask throughout a dive. Some good masks are sold with sealed up drain valves which you could cut open later. If you like these masks buy them but do not open the drain valve. If you need to wear spectacles you can either buy a large mask which will take your spectacles (minus the side arms) inside it or you will want to buy a specialised mask with separate glasses for each eye which can be replaced by lenses. A few firms will grind prescription lenses into the glass plate of an ordinary mask but this tends to be an expensive process.

Snorkels should be made from softish plastic or rubber so that they have no hard edges to cut you or others. Fins always present a problem to trainees. When you start training in the pool you will not be using a suit and its accompanying bootees (soled neoprene socks), but once you snorkel or dive in the sea you will want to wear a suit and bootees. If your fins fit your naked feet well you'll find that they are too small once you are wearing bootees. Short of buying fins for the pool and another pair for the sea you'll need to adopt one of the three following solutions: first, buy a pair that will fit over bootees and also a pair of fin grips that will keep your fins in place on naked feet; second, buy fins with heel straps (adjustable) and a pocket type space for the foot, so that you can adjust your fins to fit you with or without bootees; third, buy bootees and fins that fit over them right at the start and wear the bootees for pool training. Make sure that fins fit you well. Don't buy fins with very large blades unless you know that you've strong leg muscles.

Once you start snorkelling or diving in the sea you will need to buy a wet or dry suit, a weight belt with extra weights and a knife. Lifejackets, regulators and cylinders (tanks or bottles) can be bought later but can usually be borrowed or hired for your first dives in the sea.

Training will teach you to master equipment and sea conditions.

Enjoy your diving.

(See Fig. 2 for details of equipment.)

As soon as you go into the water, even in the pool, you must know two standard signals, the OK signal and the distress signal. See Fig. 3. You should give them as you surface, you should give them in response to an OK signal from

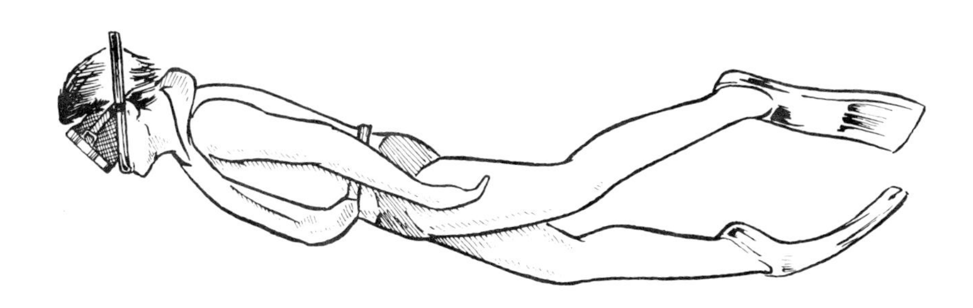

Fig. 2. Equipment for diving.

a. Basic equipment for snorkelling. Note that the snorkeller is shown dressed for pool or warm-water snorkelling. The basic equipment is mask, snorkel, fins and lifejacket. For serious snorkelling in the sea it may be essential to wear a weight belt and carry a diving knife.

somebody else, for that means not only 'I am OK' but also 'Are you OK ?' If you see a Distress signal and are not yet trained far enough to know what to do to attract the attention of others for further help. You give 'OK' signals underwater and as a response to other signals to show you have understood them and will act on them. A stop signal, simply a hand held up, palm outwards, just like those given by traffic policemen to stop traffic means 'You don't agree, or can't do it or must wait or 'stop moving'. A 'dodgy' signal means that you are not happy about something. See p. 66, Fig. 50.

When you surface from a dive, snorkel or aqualung, approach the surface gently with an arm outstretched above you. Look up to see what is there. You do not want to collide with another diver, a boat or a floating plank! Your outstretched arm can be used to give an OK signal with outstretched arm the moment you surface.

Bear in mind that it is good practice for all kinds of reasons detailed later in this Manual to make a slow approach to the surface through the last few metres. Learn to surface slowly and cautiously even when you are snorkelling.

Fig. 3

The OK signal.

'I am in distress.' Hand at shoulder level. Immediate assistance needed.

The Distress signal.

'Distress at surface: come and get me.' Hand waved from side to side until acknowledged. Boat or snorkeller or other diver on surface must pick-up, tow or support victim.

Chapter 2

Getting Started

TRAINING SCHEMES AND READING THE MANUAL

The usual root for most trainees is to proceed to the Introductory Training which is composed of three parts:

A short set of training and tests usually in a swimming pool, which ensure that you know how to use mask, fins and snorkel.

The use of the Aqualung. The training and testing of this section should normally certainly start in the pool and in some groups may be continued and completed in the pool but we emphasise the desirability of moving to safe, confined open-water for the latter parts of this training. Those groups who wish, or who are constrained in their use and access to a pool may prefer to do most or even all of the training in the openwater. Eventually, whatever your approach, this training takes you to openwater, sea or/and freshwater and you develop all the skills you really need to dive safely in a group of two in the openwater within the safety organisation set up by diving in a Branch Expedition. In a sense once you have completed this training you can look after yourself and your buddy in most ordinary diving situations but you should remember that the newly qualified 3rd Class Diver has not got the experience to tackle difficult, deep dives or rough water or decompression dives or dives in wrecks or caves.

A knowledge of the simple theory of diving, acquired usually from lectures given by the Branch, followed by a test of their knowledge.

See below for advice on this training.

But some readers will prefer to proceed to Snorkel Diver Training before going on to Aqualung Training either because they have a clear interest in Snorkelling or are too young to start aqualung training (under fifteen years of age). If so they should read the detailed section on Snorkel Tests (pages 28-33). Those who are primarily interested in Aqualung training should not skip these pages but realise they refer to a fuller training in snorkelling than they will receive. However, the Third Class training does require a knowledge of basic snorkelling skills so that the reader should follow the other and more general parts about snorkelling and related skills.

Note that the material to be given in Lectures is set out in some detail in this section of the Manual. Each section of theory is identified with the Lecture number (see Training Schedule) it deals with.

Essential preparation, confidence and competence

Training is an essential part of the preparation for diving. However, training should not be regarded as a very serious problem to strive against but rather as an enjoyable way of preparing yourself for aqualung diving. The initial training has two aims: first, that you should be able to dive with enjoyment and without undue apprehension; and second, that you develop a sensible awareness of the dangers of diving and the methods of minimising these dangers. The good diver is always gently and carefully analysing his or her own performance in and under the water and becoming more and more aware of how to handle diving more and more effectively.

Confidence and competence the key factors

Testing your training is essential in order that others who may dive with you, or supervise your dives, shall also have confidence in your ability. The 3rd Class award can be regarded as a licence to dive and the 3rd Class diver is a person who can look after him or herself when diving with another person. The schedule is a list of tests but the important parts of learning generally come while you are preparing for a test or even failing a test rather than while you are passing one. The important thing is that you should ensure that you get good training; testing only finds out whether you are well trained. Don't worry about failing a test, but do worry if you don't know why your doing something or why you failed. Try and work it out yourself and then confirm your diagnosis with your training officer. Every aspect of the testing schedule has its reasons and many of these are outlined below. But remember that the aim is not the test but the training: the training described below is hung on pegs, each labelled 'a test', but don't let that make you believe that tests are the aim.

LECTURE 2

THE BASIC PHYSICS OF DIVING

If you understand some of the simple physical laws underlying diving you will find it easier to understand features of the training programme. The main relevant law is **Boyle's law.** This states that the volume of a certain mass of gas is inversely proportional to the pressure. Thus if you double the pressure of a given mass of gas its volume halves. A mathematical way of stating this is that if P is pressure and V volume, $P\alpha\frac{1}{V}$. The pressure at sea level, due to the column of air above (right up to the edge of space) is defined as 1 BAR (equivalent to 1 atmosphere, or 14.7 lbs per sq.in. (psi)). Water is much denser than air so that a column of water of 10m depth and cross section 1 cm^2 weighs approximately 1 kilogram, in other words the pressure such a column exerts is 1 kg. per cm^2 = 1 BAR. Thus the total or absolute pressure at 10m depth is 2 BAR (derived from 1 BAR of atmospheric pressure above the water, and 1 BAR of pressure due to the water). At 20m depth the pressure has risen to 3 BAR, and at 30m to 4 BAR. Boyle's law allows us to predict the volume of the air space in a snorkeller's lungs as he or she carries out a breath-holding dive. At 10m depth the air space in the lungs will have half the volume it had at the surface, and at 40m (rather a remarkable snorkel diver) one-fifth it had at the surface, see Fig. 4 for a graphical representation.

The body of the snorkeller is not damaged because flesh and body fluids, like water, are virtually incompressible. The soft tissues of

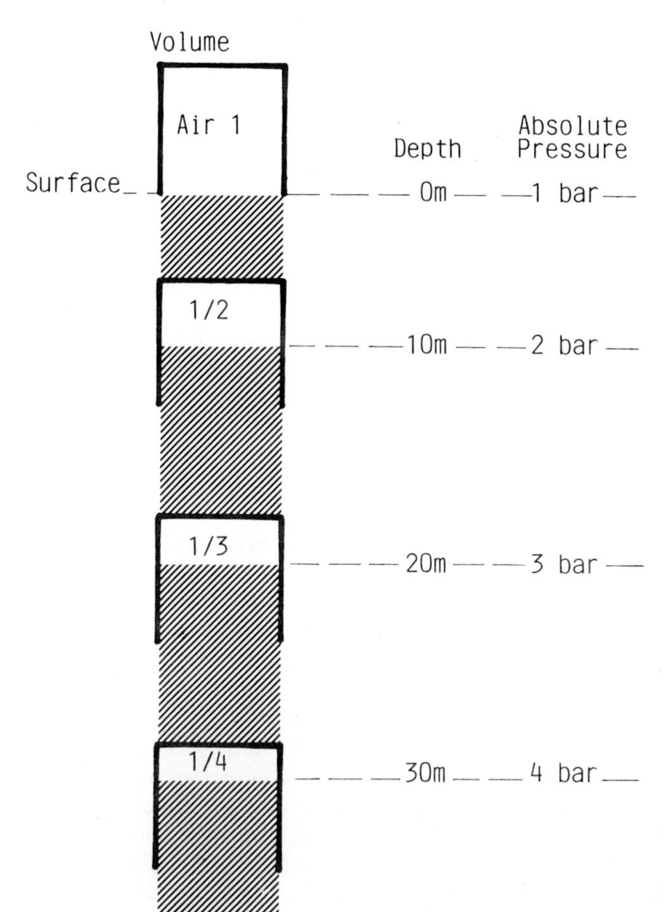

Fig. 4. A graphical illustration of Boyle's law. A volume of air, shown enclosed as it were by an inverted box (heavy line), is taken from the surface to increasing depths of 10, 20 and then 30m. The volume of air in the box diminishes to half the surface volume at 10m, one-third at 20m and one-quarter at 30m. The absolute pressure at the various depths increases linearly with the increasing depth, as the pressure rises so the volume falls, according to the inverse law (Boyle's law).

the body are deformable, however, and the space occupied by the air space of the lungs is replaced by movement of soft tissues into the rib cage. Incidentally this explains why obese divers have much better figures when they are seen at the bottom of a snorkel dive. It is because the soft tissues are deformable but incompressible that the air spaces in the lung can change to match the outside pressure so that pressure does not damage the body.

However, there are a few parts of the body which contain compressible air spaces surrounded by undeformable bone so that they have problems in adapting to increases in pressure. The simplest situation, in terms of understanding, is that caused by a poorly filled cavity in the teeth. Such a situation may cause the painful event called **Dental Barotrauma.** As the diver descends the increasing water pressure acts through the soft tissues to compress the air space in the tooth. However, the hard material of the tooth cannot deform so that the soft tissue at the base of the tooth is pushed into the cavity. The deformation causes pain as the nerve at the base of the tooth is affected by the change in shape of the tissue. Sometimes the pain is felt only on ascent as the pressure decreases. The explanation in that event is as follows. During the descent air flows into the cavity from the mouth as the pressure increases so that the volume of the cavity does not change. However, in such cases the filling may act like a one-way valve so that as the air inside the cavity expands (as the diver ascends) the air cannot escape. As a consequence it pushes on the soft tissue at the base of the tooth causing pain. In extreme cases the air expansion may actually shatter the tooth.

Another part of the body which may demonstrate the effects of pressure in a painful way, **Sinus Barotrauma,** are the set of sinuses in the face. These are blind ended air spaces branching off the nose and the air space above the palate, see *Advanced Dive Training Manual* for diagrams. If your sinuses are clear of mucus diving presents no problem since they fill with air from the nose as you descend to maintain a constant volume and similarly release air to the nose as you ascend. However, if there is appreciable mucus in the sinuses, a condition which you may have if you have a cold or certain types of allergic condition, the mucus may block off parts of the sinuses so that you cannot equalise the air pressure as you descend or ascend. In such cases pain and maybe bleeding from the sinuses may occur. The moral is 'do not dive with a cold'.

However, the parts of the body which are most likely to be affected by changes in pressure are the ears, **Aural Barotrauma**. The middle and inner ears (see *The Advanced Dive Training Manual* for diagrams) are largely surrounded by bone so that you have, in effect, a tube surrounded by a wall of bone. The tube is blocked by the ear drum at the junction of the outer and middle ear. Normally the middle ear connects to the throat by the Eustachian tube, and if this tube is open there is no problem as the diver descends or ascends. If, however, the Eustachian tube is blocked by mucus, air cannot enter the middle ear as pressure increases to maintain its volume. As a result the eardrum is forced inwards by the pressure acting from outside, with painful results. It may even break if you insist on descending. There are various practices for 'ear clearing' which allow you to open the Eustachian tube so that you can equalise the pressure inside the middle ear with that in your mouth and around you in the water. These will be explained to you by your BTP, or read *The Advanced Dive Training Manual*. On occasion you may descend with little or no problem only to find that your Eustachian tube will not allow air to escape as it expands during ascent. This causes the eardrum to bow outwards and possibly break. Slow ascent or descent together with good earclearing prevents these problems. But if you have heavy mucus discharges, as for example with a cold, do not dive, if only because of the risk of Aural Barotrauma on descent or ascent, as well of course as the risk of Sinus Barotrauma.

As a trainee snorkel diver you will find that the increase in pressure even in the small depth of 2m, as at the bottom of a pool, may be sufficient to cause you to experience any or all of these effects in small measure. So you need to learn about ear clearing as soon as you start to snorkel. You may also find that pressure affects your body because of the use of a mask. The air space in the mask is of course just as susceptible to volume changes as you dive as any other gas space. If you take no precautions the result will be that the mask will be forced painfully down onto your face and your eyes may be pushed outwards to some extent towards the mask space. You may acquire a 'pop-eye' appearance as a result for a few days. The solution is very simple, allow air to pass through your nose into the mask as you descend. Of course if you simply use swimming goggles you cannot equalise pressure in this way and you will become 'pop-eyed' if you use them for diving. In practice if you fail to equalise the pressure in your mask as you descend you will find that the most usual event is for water to trickle into the mask to do so for you.

Another consequence of the effect of pressure is on the buoyancy of the diver. As we stated above, a snorkel diver finds that his or her lungs diminish in volume as you descend, though of course there is no direct awareness of the fact. As a consequence the snorkel diver has less buoyancy. You will find that even in a snorkel dive of 3-4m you will lose about 1 kg. of buoyancy. Similarly the air space in a dry suit will diminish as you descend with a consequent loss in buoyancy. The gas bubbles in the foam neoprene of a wet suit (or a neoprene dry suit) will diminish in volume as pressure increases with depth. Your training with ABLJs (Adjustable Buoyancy Lifejackets or Stab Jackets) or with dry suits will teach you to take measures to compensate for this loss of buoyancy.

The aqualung diver, who, of course, breathes air at the same pressure as the water around his mouth (ambient pressure), naturally tends to keep his or her lungs at the same volume as at the surface by taking in extra masses of gas during descent. This compensates for any loss of buoyancy of the type that a snorkel diver would experience but of course the aqualung diver still may have buoyancy problems with his or her dry suit (see above).

The fact that the aqualung diver breathes in air under pressure and fills his lungs, places him or her in potential risk of **Pulmonary Barotrauma** during ascent. If the diver breathholds during ascent the air in the lungs expands as the pressure is reduced. As soon as the lungs are expanded beyond their normal maximum expansion, there is a risk of the air breaking through the tissues lining the lung. This is very likely to cause **Air Embolism,** if the air enters the blood stream; a condition which is usually rapidly fatal. Alternatively, the air may collapse one or both lungs as it escapes (**Pneumothorax**) or escape into the tissues (**Emphysema, Cutaneous** or **Mediastinal**). See *Advanced Dive Training Manual* for a full description of these conditions. However, **Pulmonary Barotrauma** is very easily avoided by the aqualung diver. The simple rule is never to hold your breath during ascent and ascend at a rate not exceeding 15m per minute.

An appreciation of Boyle's law will, in addition, help you to understand the use of aqualung cylinders, the operation of a regulator (demand valve), air endurance during a dive and the further physics required for understanding the problems, risks and procedures associated with decompression sickness and inert gas narcosis. These topics will be dealt with later in the Manual. The contents of this section provide that basic information which a trainee starting snorkel dive training should have, and form a basis for the 'Effects of Pressure' lecture.

SWIMMING ASSESSMENT

The main purpose of this group is to establish that you are at home in the water and that you are strong enough to support yourself at the surface for a short time when conditions are slightly adverse. When you come to dive, you will find yourself in conditions of temporary negative buoyancy for short periods before you have had time to adjust your equipment; and inability to prevent yourself sinking or to prevent yourself panicking places you at risk. Thus these tests also establish that you do not panic when negatively buoyant: the swim with the weight belt and supporting yourself with forearms clear of the water establish strength and freedom from panic. Style or speed is not very important, though the whole test must be completed without more than a momentary rest between stages (except of course for the five minutes float which is a delicious pause) so that it is clear that you are capable of a fairly sustained effort.

The training personnel must not place excessive weight on you when you swim with a weight belt. A guide for persons of average buoyancy might be:

under 8 stone	2½ kg	6 lbs
8-10 stone	3 kg	8 lbs
10-13 stone	4 kg	10 lbs
13 stone and over	5 kg	12 lbs

Very overweight persons will probably have been refused a Medical Certificate in any event. The careful Training Officer will also look at your body build – don't be worried by this – slight and thin people tend to be of fairly low buoyancy, muscular big-boned people of negative buoyancy, fat people with large lungs positively buoyant to a marked degree. No one in this test should be more than 1 kg. (2 lbs) negatively buoyant – this means that in such a situation you have to use muscular effort equal to more than 1 kg. force to keep afloat and still more to have your mouth above water: after all your head has weight. If in real doubt about your buoyancy, put on a weight belt of known weight, large enough to sink you when you are motionless and get someone to weigh you in the water with a spring balance. The balance hook could be fixed to a line fitted with a snap clip (carabineer) attached to a shoulder harness. Make sure that you are entirely submerged when weighed. To find your buoyancy subtract the weight of the weight belt (weighed in water) from the reading on the spring balance. If the answer is negative you are positively buoyant. Hard to do but interesting. Remember to do it both with full and empty lungs. A simpler test is to see if you can lie, kneel or stand on the pool bottom, fully submerged, with full or empty lungs. But this merely tells you that you are or are not positively buoyant.

Training personnel must know that their trainee can quickly release the weight belt if necessary.

The duck dives should establish that you keep your eyes open underwater – an essential ability for divers. The underwater swimming reinforces this point, shows that you have some breath-holding ability and that you can control your buoyancy enough to get underwater fairly easily. Don't take a big breath and then duck down, your buoyancy will be too great and your endurance poor. Take a half-lungful. Most trainees have not swum with their forearms clear of the water previously – training personnel should demonstrate.

Remember that keeping your lungs very full helps your positive buoyancy.

Fig. 5. Weight belt releases (buckles). a. The 'flick' type, in which the action of lifting the metal (or plastic) lever releases its grip on the belt so that the free end can slide through the buckle as you remove the weight belt. b. The 'Spirotechnique' type. Two diagrams are included to show how the end of one side of the belt is inserted from behind (inner side as you wear it) through the widest part of the slot (following the arrow in the diagram) and turned back (see below) to hold the belt in place. Releasing the buckle simply requires the reverse movement. The lower 'hook' is widely used in parts of Europe when a jock-strap is worn as part of the harness holding the aqualung. This type of harness is rarely used in the UK or USA. The left-hand buckle holds any loop etc, inserted into the 'hook' in place until the release is undone.

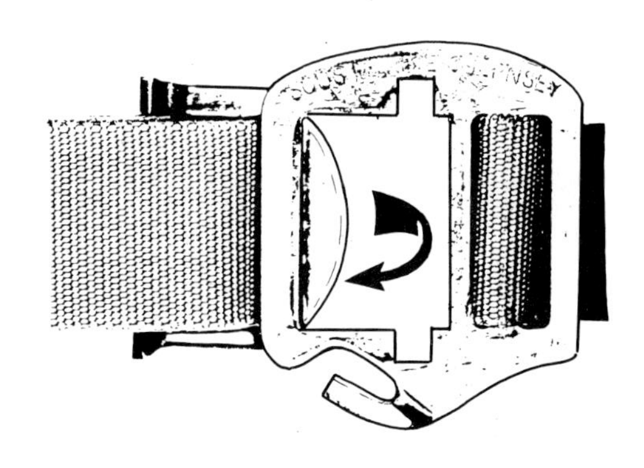

The need for buoyancy control

This section of the book is only advisory. You will find that you have to achieve a fair measure of control of your buoyancy in order to pass the various pool and open water tests but you may well work out your own effective method of learning about it. Once you're diving you will realise consciously, and your body will learn almost unconsciously, about buoyancy control. But it is very desirable to learn about it as soon as possible because you can have fairly spectacular accidents if you cannot control your buoyancy. The accidents where you sink rapidly because you are negatively buoyant can by and large be avoided if you can drop your weight belt quickly, but of course this presumes that you will not panic. The earlier you realise that you are sinking the sooner and more effectively you can deal with the problem. So buoyancy control is partly a matter of learning to sense that you are rising or sinking as well as a matter of learning how to actually control the matter.

The problem of being too buoyant is harder to deal with if you have emptied any buoyancy aid such as a lifejacket (surface, adjustable buoyancy or stab) of all its gas or air. But remember that you have the following ways of controlling buoyancy, some being only for aqualung dives.

(a) *Breath control.* If you keep your lungs very full and only momentarily exhale small volumes of air, you will be some 1-2 kg. more buoyant than the situation in which you keep your lungs as empty as possible. This technique works well on the surface and when snorkel diving. However, this can be a dangerous practice when using an aqualung if you start ascending rapidly, because you are nearer a pulmonary barotrauma accident than when you breathe in and out deeply. See *Advanced Dive Training Manual* for a description of pulmonary barotrauma ('burst lung').

(b) *Use of fins.* Provided that your fins are the right size for you and your finning is a good stroke with no cycling, you ought to be able to get somewhere between 1.5 and 3 kg. thrust over long periods, and this can be used to keep you in an upright position in the water.

(c) Judge *the weight to be put on your belt* taking into account the increase in buoyancy as your air is used up from your bottle, and the loss of buoyancy in the suit at the planned depth of the dive. This of course only applies to aqualung divers. Buoyancy varies between seawater and freshwater.

(d) *Use of ABLJs* (Adjustable Buoyancy Lifejackets) or Stab Jacket as a buoyancy aid. Note the risk in doing this, namely that if you then lose your weight belt you may become so buoyant that you end up in a fast ascent with a risk of barotrauma, if you are using an aqualung. Training in the use of ABLJs Stab Jackets starts in snorkel training.

(e) *Use of dry suits.* Inflating or deflating the air held inside the dry suit allows control of buoyancy.

(f) Use of *extraneous objects such as rigged lines*, objects on the bottom etc. This may be useful but always presents a degree of risk.

All this will become more real to you as you start diving in the sea. But you can start acquiring a knowledge of whether you are slowly sinking or rising in the pool, and you can also start learning how to control it. Some of the tests are designed in such a way that good buoyancy control is necessary if you are to pass them.

Buoyancy exercises – should be a pleasure

Here are two suggestions about exercises that, amongst other things, will help you to improve your buoyancy control. Other exercises could be used as well.

1. *The 'bottom of the pool' exercise*

You put on a weight belt sufficient to make you clearly, though not enormously, negatively buoyant. Enter the pool and, after taking a moderate breath, allow yourself to sink to the pool bottom at about 2m depth. Lie face down on the bottom for 15 seconds; then take the belt off and control your buoyancy by breathing out, so that you lie on the bottom for another 15 seconds. Then surface. This exercise improves your breath-holding capacity and your buoyancy control. Training personnel should make sure that you can quickly release your weight belt before trying this exercise and that someone watches you all the time you're doing it just in case you have trouble with belt release.

2. *Emptying lungs exercise*

The main point of this exercise is to give you a feeling of what it's like to have empty lungs. Take a fullish breath and climb down the pool steps or ladder until you are about 2m underwater. Then breathe out as much as possible.

When you are sure that you have done this, let go of the steps gently and see if you sink or float. If you sink, swim up to the surface, if you float you will know that, provided you really emptied your lungs, you have a buoyancy control problem.

There are many other exercises either in use or easily thought out which will achieve the aims of improving your buoyancy control and breath-holding ability as well as your agility in the water. All such exercises are well worth trying out. Basic equipment is needed for the first exercise set out above, nothing is needed for the lung emptying at 2m.

Basic Snorkel Skills for all Divers

The aim of this set of tests is generally to prepare you for aqualung training and to provide a number of skills basic to diving. Before you start training, good and bad points of various types of mask, snorkel and fins should have been explained to you, see also Chapter 1.

If you have not had the appropriate lectures by the time you are training for this make sure you know about the dangers of hyperventilation, the causes and recognition of hypoxia and drowning and the simple physiology of EAR (Expired Air Resuscitation).

1. *Sinking and fitting equipment.* The test shows that you can collect and refit a number of items of basic equipment while in the water and unable to stand on a solid surface. Thus it simulates refitting displaced or exchanging equipment while in open water. The test can be carried out in several ways. Above all the refitting should be done efficiently, calmly and quickly.

Mask clearing is tested underwater. It is very important that you should be able to clear a mask underwater both for snorkelling and for aqualung diving. First, you should not panic if water fills or starts to fill your mask. Second, it is a great advantage to be able to regain clear vision. You should be allowed to fit all equipment on the surface and then to duck dive, flood mask and clear it, but if you're able to clear the mask just after you've picked it up and while you're still underwater you are clearly skilled. Remember that the principle of mask clearing is to allow air blown gently out of your nose to force water downwards and out of the mask. So to do this you must hold your head so that the normal bottom of the mask is really at the bottom. If you start with your body upright and then tilt your head back a bit you get the mask into the right position. Using both your hands push the top of the mask against your forehead and pull the bottom of the mask very slightly away from the base (nostril end) of your nose. This stops air escaping from the top and allows water to flow out from the bottom. Then blow gently through your nose into the mask. Don't waste air. A good mask clearer can clear the average mask two to four times on one breath, see Fig. 6.

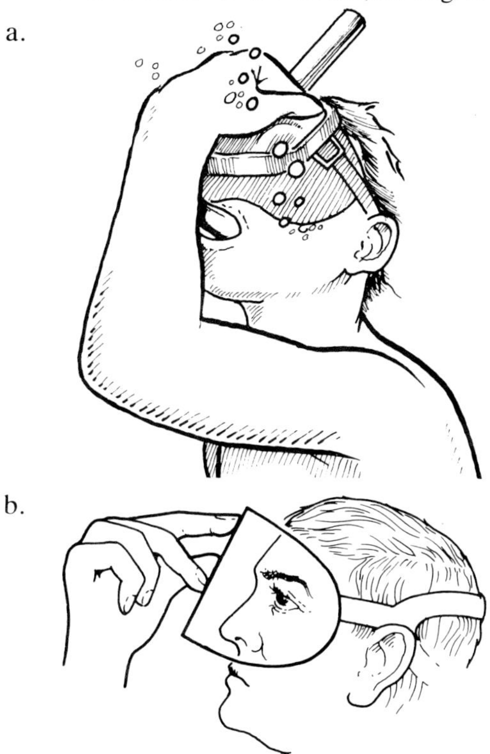

Fig. 6a. Mask clearing. Note that the head is tilted back so that the forehead is only slightly higher than the nose. The top of the mask is held against the forehead by one hand while water and some air escapes from under the 'skirt' of the mask just above the mouth. Normally the diver will be tilted slightly forward in the water. b. Sideways view of diver clearing mask, mask shown diagrammatically.

The Training Schedule asks that you clear the mask just under the surface, using air breathed in through the snorkel for clearing the mask. This simulates the situation in which you breathe in air from the aqualung and use it to clear your mask. You should be tested in this manner. But note that it is good practice to be able to clear the mask underwater using air from your lungs while breath-holding because this simulates and teaches you to cope with the problem of flooding your mask while snorkel diving.

2. *Finning and snorkel diving while under way.* Here they should be testing that you fin well and strongly (no leg cycling, i.e. marked bending at the knee), ideally your legs should be a straight line from the hip, though not stiff (a little flexing cannot be prevented). They should also note that you have no trouble with use of snorkel (particularly with clearing it) and mask. A weak finner will be unable to get through later tests unless marked improvement comes. A weak finner, or someone nervous with their mask and snorkel, is at risk in open water. The BTP will expect you to keep your arms against your side except possibly in the initial stages of the duck dive or if your mask has to be cleared. Why?

3. *Breath-holding.* Efficient snorkelling and aqualung training requires that you can hold your breath for at least 30 seconds. Well, can you? Most people have some trouble with breath-holding at first. Don't either take and hold a large breath, or clear your lungs right out before starting the breath-holding. Either of these extremes will probably shorten your time. Half-full lungs are just about right. Easy to practice on shore before the session. Never hyperventilate (repeated deep breathing) before breath-holding, you can kill yourself even on dry land by doing this.

You are asked to carry out the relevant test without wearing mask or snorkel. This may seem a trifle difficult but it is good practice for the stage in aqualung training when you learn to refit your set underwater.

LECTURE 3

LIFEJACKETS

The purpose of a lifejacket is simply to provide enough buoyancy to ensure that a person floats with either the mouth and nose clear of the surface even when unconscious or to give them enough buoyancy to rise from depth to the surface and then adopt that position. The diver has special need of the second feature of lifejackets. The statement 'floats with either the mouth and nose clear of the surface even when unconscious' is of paramount importance. The enfeebled or unconscious human can do little or nothing to control their attitude in the water so that the buoyancy device, the lifejacket, must hold them in the correct attitude. Not all lifejackets do this. It is important to appreciate that the unconscious person normally lets their mouth fall open so that the mouth must float clear of the surface. The diver ensures that he or she has little or no positive buoyancy at the surface so that diving is easy and does not require muscular effort to fight against buoyancy. Consequently the properly equipped diver is less buoyant at the surface than most surface swimmers. In turn this means that the diver needs a lifejacket in emergency to a greater extent than many other water users such as yachtsmen. It is true that the diver should release his weight-belt in emergency to gain buoyancy but the confused and enfeebled divers may forget or be too weak to do this. Study of fatal diving accidents shows that the failure to wear a lifejacket has been a fairly frequent cause of death. Some divers think that a dry suit can provide enough buoyancy to replace that of a lifejacket but this is not true in all situations. Anyhow the ABLJ/Stab Jacket provides an additional line of defence – something that is always needed.

Lifejackets used by divers are of two main types : the ABLJ (Adjustable Buoyancy Lifejacket) and the Stab (properly known as the Stabiliser Lifejacket), Figs 7 and 8. Some divers in other countries use the very simple surface lifejacket, which is better than nothing and effectively very like those provided by airlines under your aircraft seat, or Buoyancy Compensators which come in varying models the most complex of which is equivalent to the Stab Jacket.

Both the ABLJ and the Stab Jacket can be used (1) for surface support (2) for adjustment of buoyancy underwater and (3) for emergency breathing air supply underwater. Surface lifejackets can only do the first of these things, Buoyancy compensators in their simpler form can do the first and second but cannot do the third. Note, however, because of looseness of terminology some people refer to Stab Jackets as Buoyancy Compensators. The main difference between ABLJ and Stab Jacket is that the ABLJ is worn separately from other equipment while the Stab Jacket carries the main breathing air cylinder attached to it. Thus when you put on the Stab Jacket you also don the cylinder, presumably with regulator attached. One of the attractions of doing this is that in one action you put on the major part of your diving equipment or take it off. It is also thought by most users to be more comfortable than the separate ABLJ and air cylinder system.

Physically the Stab Jacket looks rather like a waistcoat with the air cylinder at the back, while the ABLJ covers the front of the torso, and both have a collar going round the back of the neck. Both consist of:

1. One or more airtight buoyancy bags providing about 17 to 20 kg. of buoyancy when fully inflated. This means that though a diver in the water should be close to neutral buoyancy when all the rest of his or her equipment is properly adjusted there is an appreciable reserve of buoyancy to be used in emergency by inflating the jacket. But two consequences flow from this:

(*a*) the diver should never overweight him or herself and rely on dry suit inflation to balance the effect of the weight belt because if the dry suit is damaged the diver may become too negative even for the buoyancy of the inflated jacket.

(*b*) the properly weighted diver is at risk of an overfast ascent if the jacket is inflated and no immediate adjustment is made to set the buoyancy right by air dumping.

2. A protecting cover usually made of tough fabric.

3. An inflation/deflation breathing tube attached to the buoyancy bag. The tube is provided with a simple breathing valve and mouthpiece so that air can be orally blown into the bag (for oral inflation), so that air can be drawn out of the bag when you inhale, and exhaled into the sea when you breathe out and so that air can be dumped from the bag. The valves usually fitted are called AP valves (a type commonly seen in this country) or in another type the Air 2 valve. Abroad you may meet rather more primitive valve systems.

4. A means of inflating the bag rapidly using a small attached air emergency cylinder or/and a direct feed which takes air from the regulator.

5. Most ABLJs and Stab Jackets are fitted with a 'dump valve' which allows rapid venting of the air in the buoyancy bag.

6. All ABLJs and Stab Jackets also have an overpressure relief valve so that you cannot overinflate and burst the bag by letting too much air into it from the direct feed or from the attached air cylinder.

7. A drain valve may be fitted to remove water that has entered the buoyancy bag during the dive or which has been used, as it should, to rinse the inside of the bag after a dive.

8. Some measure of harness to hold the ABLJ or Stab Jacket onto your body when you've donned it. The ABLJ will usually have a strap running from the back of the collar through the crotch to the lower part of the front of the jacket and also a waist strap. Both should be worn fairly but not ridiculously tight. You should check out your own jacket on purchase on land discovering how it feels both empty of air and fully inflated. People with really large torsos may need specially large sizes of jacket. The jacket should not ride up when the jacket is partially inflated. The Stab Jacket has often got quick releases on one or both shoulders and a breast strap or zip joining the two 'wings' of the jacket together and a waist strap which carries much of the strain of having a full sized air cylinder on your back. Other exciting things like D rings to attach torches, gauges, tools etc. are often fitted, or pockets for hiding goodness knows what from the eyes of goodness knows whom.

If you use an ABLJ make sure when you put it on that the vertical strap is fitted first so that the waist strap holds the vertical strap in. Otherwise there is a risk that the vertical strap can get wrapped around pillar valves, or even your arm when you try to take the aqualung off, which is sort of embarrassing or even downright dangerous in some emergencies. The Stab Jacket usually does not have this sort of problem.

Using the ABLJ and Stab Jackets

1. As a surface buoyancy aid. Learn how to inflate the jacket (and your buddy's) orally through the mouthpiece. Usually you need to press a button in the centre of the exhale part of the valve or on its side to do this. Remember to take your finger off the button while you take the mouthpiece out to get a fresh breath of air otherwise the air you have just put into the jacket will escape. Try to become familiar with a variety of jackets you are likely to meet. The diver you have to rescue may not be your buddy but someone else's.

2. As a surface buoyancy aid filling the jacket from the direct feed or from the small emergency cylinder. Learn how to do this and how to do it with models other than your own. The jacket should hold the victim on his or her back at the surface ready for EAR or/and tow.

3. As an underwater buoyancy aid to get neutral buoyancy. The jacket is either orally inflated or inflated by using the direct feed or emergency cylinder. Oral inflation is done underwater by taking a full breath from your regulator, taking out the regulator mouthpiece, putting in your jacket mouthpiece and breathing into it (usually with the button in the end of the mouthpiece pressed) and then replacing your regulator mouthpiece.

In ordinary diving with a dry suit do not inflate your ABLJ but adjust your buoyancy by inflation or deflation of your dry suit. If you have air in both your ABLJ/Stab Jacket and your dry suit you have two separate lots of buoyancy to control. Wet suited divers will of course have to fill or dump air from their ABLJ or stab jacket. Bear in mind that oral filling or dumping of air will almost always allow some water to get into the lifejacket. It is considered a good idea always to keep a very small amount of air in your lifejacket from the start of the dive. If you suck the buoyancy bag empty of air before a dive a slight negative pressure can develop in the bag as you dive which can allow water to be sucked into the breathing hose during the dive. Try to keep your skill at controlling buoyancy of the jacket by oral inflation in good repair since you should really keep the air in the emergency cylinder for real emergencies only.

The wet suit diver uses oral inflation to keep his or her buoyancy close to neutral at any depth. During descent oral inflation will have to be used to restore buoyancy while during ascent it will be essential to dump air from the jacket to prevent your becoming overbuoyant as the air in the jacket expands as the ambient pressure drops. There will also be changes in the buoyancy of the wet suit with depth which accentuate the changes in the buoyancy of the jacket itself.

4. As a buoyancy aid to obtain positive buoyancy for rescue of self or another.

Because Stab Jackets and ABLJs can provide from 10 to 15 kg of positive buoyancy it is possible to make an exceedingly rapid ascent from depth with the risk of pulmonary barotrauma if the jacket is inflated appreciably. Thus though they can be inflated underwater to rescue yourself or another, bear in mind that the ascent needs careful control by dumping air. This skill should be practiced starting with ascents from very shallow depth, with an instructor at hand to stop your ascent very rapidly if things get out of hand. When you have mastered the skill you should ascend at the recommended rate continuously, and stop for a simulated decompression stop, all ideally without finning. You should also practice inflating your buddy's jacket and bring-

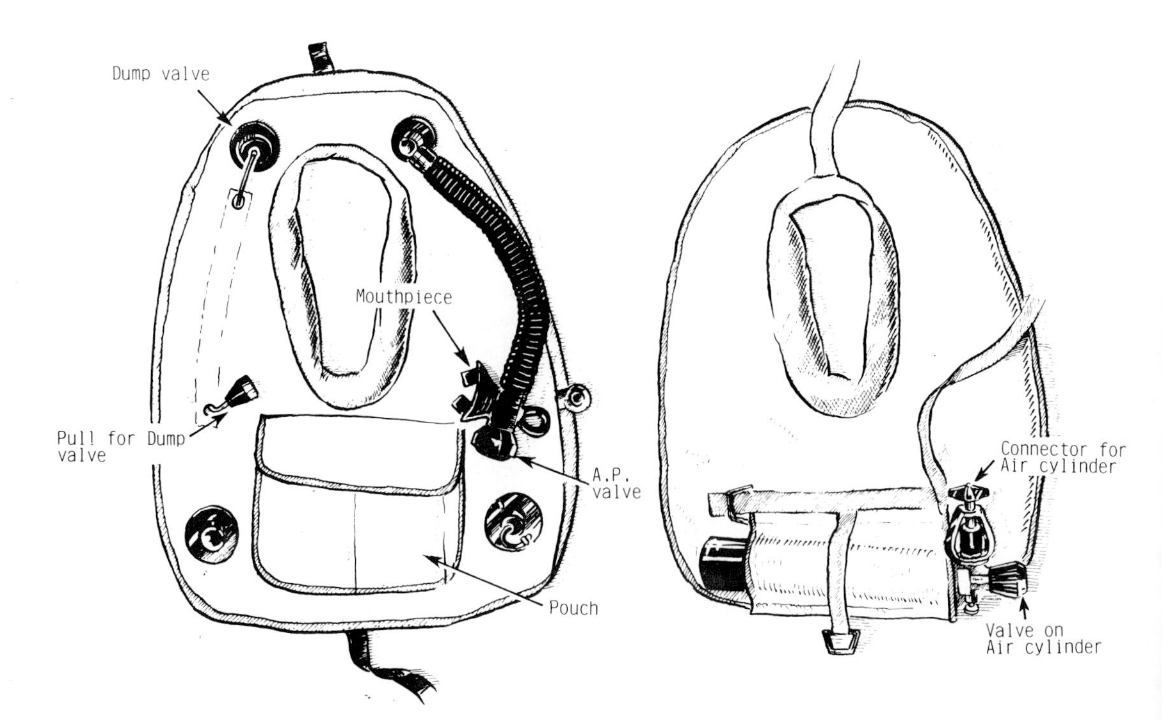

Fig. 7. Lifejackets. The ABLJ viewed (left) from in front and (right) from the side which faces the body. Surface lifejackets are very similar except that no air bottle is fitted though there is a much smaller carbon dioxide cylinder and the dump valve is omitted while the inflation tube is shorter and simpler than the AP valve and mouthpiece. The straps which hold the ABLJ to the body are not shown fully. Some ABLJs use direct feeds from the first stage of the regulator, see also Figs. 16a, b and c.

ing them up at the correct rate. Of course in an emergency to your buddy you would inflate their jacket to bring them up, not your own. The reason for this is that if you inflate your jacket to counteract their possibly negative buoyancy you may all too easily lose your grip of them so that they sink and you ascend out of control – a good prelude to a fatal accident or even two fatal accidents!

The recommended ascent rate depends on the decompression tables or meter you are using but should not be faster than 15 metres per minute, see p. 6 and p. 62.

5. As a source of emergency breathing air using either your emergency air bottle or direct feed. In the early days of ABLJs mastering this breathing skill seemed to be really difficult but modern types of mouthpieces make it relatively easy to use the jacket in this way. Bear in mind that when you put the jacket mouthpiece into your mouth the first inhalation may well be of water, because a small amount has got caught in the breathing hose but air will very soon be available so long as you have remembered to put at least a breath's worth of air into the jacket first. This is perhaps the main skill that you have to learn, namely how much air to put into the jacket and when. You should remember that the air enters the jacket usually near its bottom and so will take a short time to rise up into the collar region where the breathing tube leaves the jacket. This also means that you should try breathing in the 'head-up' position. If you try to breathe with your head well below your chest you will find you get no air until the jacket is quite full of air and that any water in the jacket will have to be drunk before you get to the air. Anyhow in the emergency situation you should be 'head-up'.

How much air do you valve in from the bottle or direct feed and when for each breath? You will learn from practice in the pool just how long you need to turn or press the valve to get a breath. You should refill the jacket while you are breathing out : this ensures that your buoyancy remains almost constant. If you overfill the jacket even very slightly every time you bleed air in you will become more buoyant, maybe too buoyant. This effect will also be accentuated by ascent. But you may need the buoyancy for lift. So you must watch your depth and take an extra breath or two between inflations to keep the buoyancy constant. In the ABLJ/Stab Jacket Endorsement see page 102*ff* you will be required to demonstrate that you can carry out controlled breathing and ascent from the jacket.

Some special points about Stab Jackets

Though we feel that Stab Jackets are on the whole more comfortable in use than ABLJs and hold you in a better position in the water there are some points to note about Stab Jackets.

(i) in some of the earlier models the inflated jacket is not certain to hold you in a head-up position on the surface so that if you are unconscious or semi-conscious there is more risk of drowning.

(ii) some of the earlier models have their auxiliary air bottle placed with the valve to turn the bottle on- or off at a position rather behind you where little strength can be exerted to turn the valve and indeed some people cannot reach it.

(iii) with many stab jackets if you have to remove your tank, eg. to get into a boat, or in emergency, you remove your main emergency buoyancy aid. This defect probably represents a very small increase in risk but if you are in charge of a dive boat or a shore dive where the exit from the water is difficult watch those divers with stab jackets as they take off their tanks (and jackets) with extra care just in case they start to get into trouble. If they are using membrane type dry suits and these have flooded they must remember to remove their weight belts before taking off their jackets. They probably would have to anyhow! However, some Stab Jackets hold the cylinder in a cam action band which can be easily released even by the diver provided that people in the boat or water are at hand to take hold of the cylinder as it comes off. With this system you can keep the Stab Jacket in place for surface lifejacket use.

Bear in mind that most stab jackets make it rather difficult for you to put most or all of the weight on your weight belt on your back. Thus quite a lot of your weight is at the front and thus apt to hold you face down on the surface. So it is even more important with stab jackets not to dive overweight. Remember that if you are diving with a dry suit it is very questionable indeed if you are using more than 28 lbs (11 kg) of weight unless you are really outsize. Most manufacturers recommend weightings of around 18 lbs for normal or even well-built people!

Don't forget to have your ABLJ or Stab Jacket cylinder tested and inspected at least as frequently as the main cylinder. Though the small cylinders fitted to jackets are outwith the cylinder testing regulations this is really just a legal oversight. Small cylinders are just as likely to corrode and effectively are just as dangerous as large ones.

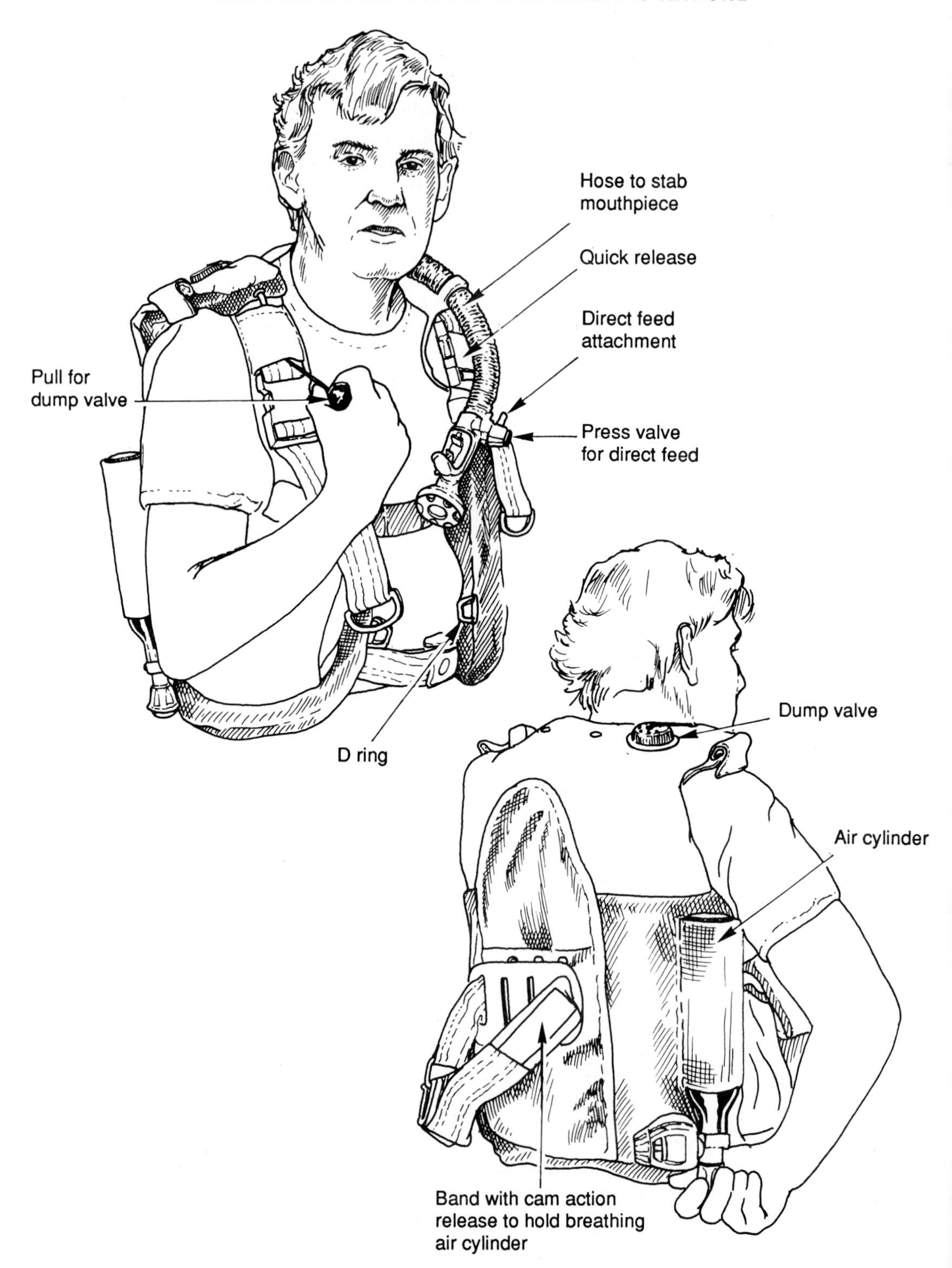

Figure 8. A Stab Jacket showing its various parts. Normally an aqualung cylinder with regulator is fitted at the back, held in place by the band at the back. The auxiliary air cylinder is shown on the right-hand side.

Dry suits also provide a means of buoyancy control so long as oral or direct feed or bottle inflation is fitted. However, though you may well adjust the inflation of your dry suit for buoyancy control during a normal dive, do not rely on it as a source of breathing air or buoyancy in an emergency. If your dry suit is holed or if the zip is damaged, you may not be able to attain enough buoyancy with the dry suit alone. Always wear a lifejacket, preferably an ABLJ, for possible emergencies.

(*End of Lecture 3.*)

(See Advanced Training Manual for contents of Lecture 4, p. 12 Pulmonary Barotrauma.)

LECTURE 5

RESPIRATION, DROWNING AND EXPIRED AIR RESUSCITATION

Respiration

Since much of the training at this stage involves rescue procedures, it is essential that you understand the underlying physics and physiology of drowning. Respiration can be viewed as the whole set of processes involved in transporting oxygen to the cells of your tissues and removing the carbon dioxide formed by metabolism from the body. The process takes place in two differing physical environments. Oxygen in its *gaseous form* is breathed in from the air or air supply. Approximately 21% of the air breathed in is oxygen, 78% of the remainder being nitrogen and the remaining 1% other gases. The inhalation of air involves the use of the breathing muscles (the diaphragm and the intercostal muscles of the chest) to enlarge the air space in the lungs, Fig. 9. Note that the air travels to the lungs through the mouth, nose pharynx, epiglottis, larynx, trachea, bronchi and bronchioles to the alveoli. Oxygen in its *dissolved* state, that is dissolved in the fluids of the body, or in its *combined* state, combined with the haemoglobin of the red cells of the blood, are the other physical environments in which oxygen is transported. Oxygen dissolves in the fluid on the surface of the alveoli, is transported through the cells of the alveolar lining to the pulmonary capillaries. There it enters the blood cells and combines with the haemoglobin. The red cells then move in the blood into the pulmonary venules and pulmonary vein (the only vein containing oxygenated blood) to the heart. From the heart the oxygenated blood travels to the aorta and thence to the arteries, arterioles and finally to the capillaries in the tissues. There the haemoglobin releases its oxygen into solution where it travels to the cells, which metabolise the oxygen. The oxygen is reduced to water and the reduction is linked to the production of carbon dioxide by the cells. Thus we can write in a simplified way:

Food plus Oxygen = Carbon Dioxide plus Water plus Released Energy.

The carbon dioxide leaves the cells partly in solution and partly in the form of bicarbonate. Some is transported in the plasma of the blood and the remainder in combination with proteins of the red blood cells. The carbon dioxide laden blood leaves the tissues via the capillaries, which flow into the venules and thence to the veins. The veins feed into the Venae Cavae, which feeds blood to the right auricle of the heart. It then flows from the right auricle, through the pulmonary artery (the only artery carrying deoxygenated blood) to the lungs. In the alveolar capillaries, the carbon dioxide leaves the blood, diffuses through the alveolar cells and is released into the lungs in gaseous form. It then is breathed out via the bronchioles, bronchi, trachea, glottis, pharynx and mouth or nose.

The stimulus to breathe: hyperventilation

The stimulus to breathe is produced by the carbon dioxide level in the blood reaching a certain level. Lack of oxygen does not produce any stimulus to breathe. When the carbon dioxide level in the blood reaches 0.06 Bar the breathing reaction overwhelms all other controls and an expiration occurs, followed by a quick inspiration. Thus if you are exercising heavily and producing a lot of carbon dioxide, you find you have to breathe frequently in order to keep the blood carbon dioxide level from rising to a very high level. If you hold your breath, the rising carbon dioxide level will force you to breathe after a few minutes, if not earlier. If a diver loses his air supply and is unable to surface or share a regulator with another diver, or otherwise obtain air, he will, as the carbon dioxide level in his blood rises, be forced to inhale. Inhalation of water leads to drowning, see below.

If the snorkeller hyperventilates, i.e. takes

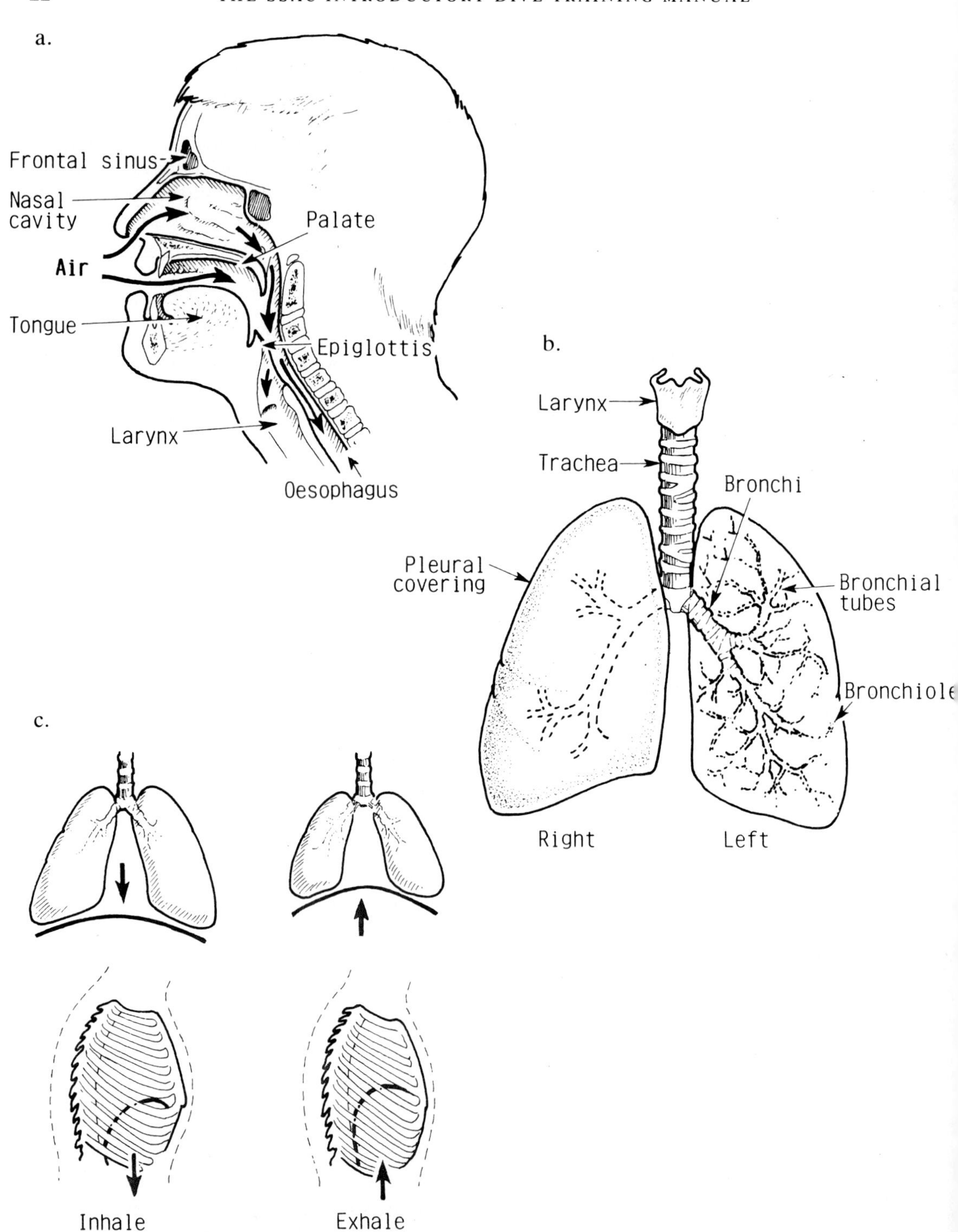

Fig. 9. Respiration. a. The routes by which air enters (and leaves) the body. A section through the head shows the routes to the junction of the larynx and the oesphagus at the epiglottis. Air can, as the arrow in the oesphagus shows, be drawn into the stomach by this route and this may happen in incorrectly applied EAR. b. The structure of the lungs, bronchi and trachea. c. Inhalation (left) and expiration (right) showing the role of the diaphragm (heavy line), in enlarging and diminishing the volume of the lungs.

at least a few very deep breaths, he lowers the carbon dioxide level in the blood. Thus he or she could hold his breath for a longer period than normal after hyperventilation. However, there are great risks in doing so. After a period of hyperventilation, followed by breath-holding, the diver may become markedly hypoxic before the breathing reflex, due to carbon dioxide, becomes overwhelming. Hypoxia, see below, may lead to fainting and inhalation of water and thus drowning.

Anoxia and hypoxia

If insufficient oxygen reaches the tissues, **Hypoxia** sets in. The symptoms are dependent on the extent and duration of hypoxia. Conscious persons with hypoxia experience dizziness, greying and 'tunnel' vision. Detachment is another subjective response. Objectively, the lips, finger-nail beds and ear lobes appear blue in colour, 'cyanosed'. As hypoxia develops, unconsciousness results, with marked pallor, a fast rate of breathing (as long as the airway is not obstructed) and a rapid pulse rate. Hypoxia develops into **Anoxia** in the absence of a supply of oxygen. Anoxia for a period of about six minutes may cause death and will almost certainly cause brain damage. Death will result after about ten minutes if oxygen does not reach the tissues.

The treatment for either anoxia or hypoxia is to restore a supply of adequately oxygenated air. If the symptoms are slight and the victim conscious, it may be sufficient to remove the supply of oxygen-impoverished breathing gas and replace with normal air. If the victim is unconscious and either not breathing, or breathing very slightly, it will probably be necessary to provide **Expired Air Resuscitation** (EAR), or some other form of Artificial Respiration. Methods are described below. Hypoxia and anoxia in divers usually develops as a result of drowning, but there are other causes, see Fig. 10. All readers of this Manual, whether divers or not, should be aware of the main features of anoxia and hypoxia explained in this diagram.

Laryngeal Spasm

Inhalation of water, even in small amounts in droplet form may cause the glottis to go into spasm and seal off the airway to the lungs. If the victim is at the surface and can be removed from the water or is on land, he or she is relatively safe. Signs of hypoxia will appear and the victim will make attempts to breathe with an accompaniment of distressing noises. As hypoxia becomes more marked, the spasm will probably relax and breathing will be resumed.

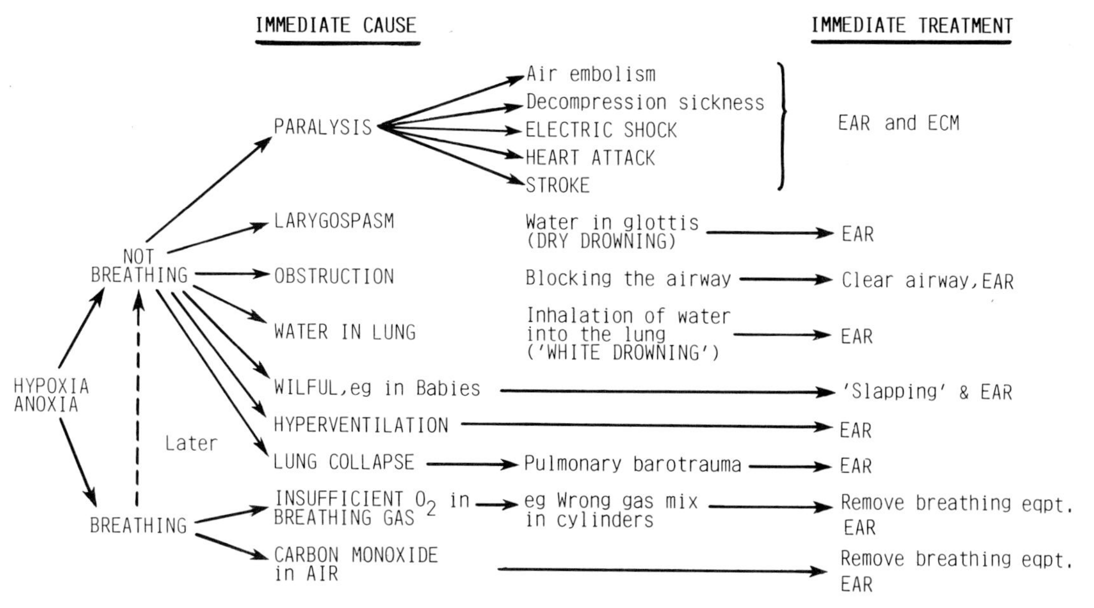

Fig. 10. Anoxia and hypoxia. A line diagram to illustrate causes and treatment. In all cases immediate treatment should be followed by examination by a medically qualified person as soon as possible.

Drowning

There are two types of drowning. The first type, often called 'blue drowning' or 'dry drowning' occurs when water is inhaled as far as the glottis, where it causes a glottal spasm which in turn stops water entering the lung. Anoxia then develops. Exactly similar symptoms will develop if the airway becomes blocked, either by the victim's tongue or an inhaled object. If water has been inhaled, this may reach the stomach. This type of drowning can often be treated successfully by EAR or/ and by removal of any object blocking the airway. Indeed, merely placing the victim in the EAR position, see below, may clear the airway and allow spontaneous recovery.

The second type of drowning, sometimes called 'white drowning', occurs when water enters the lungs. This type of drowning is much more rapidly fatal than 'dry drowning'. If fresh water enters the lungs, water will be absorbed into the blood. The resulting haemodilution may cause bursting of the blood cells and heart fibrillation (an arhythmic ineffective beat). If sea water enters the lungs, water will be absorbed from the blood, causing haemoconcentration which in turn may strain the heart. The effects of haemodilution are more damaging than those of haemoconcentration. Thus death from drowning occurs most rapidly when fresh water enters the lungs, rather less rapidly when sea water enters the lungs and least rapidly when no water enters the lungs. However, the rescuer will usually be totally unable to make an accurate diagnosis as to the actual cause of drowning, so he or she should always consider that there is hope of resuscitating the victim, unless expert medical advice is to the contrary. Thus the rule is that EAR should be continued until expert advice suggests that EAR should be abandoned, or until the victim recovers.

Once water has entered the lungs, it is likely that laryngeal spasm will stop further entry, though the spasm may relax after a while and permit further water entry.

You should note that even though a victim may make a rapid and apparently total recovery, he or she still needs care. The absorption of even small amounts of water into the blood may cause physiological disturbances which may not develop until later. Pneumonia may be a late consequence of water entry into the lungs. The victim who has apparently recovered should be accompanied for the next few hours and taken for medical examination if this is at all possible.

Expired Air and other forms of Resuscitation

In essence, the various forms of resuscitation simply serve to provide a supply of oxygenated air to the lungs and, in the case of External Cardiac Compression, a stimulus to the heart action. Reference to Fig. 10 should suggest that:

1. Providing a clear airway to the lungs is an essential feature of resuscitation. This is simply achieved by the relative positions of the head, neck and trunk. Providing the correct clear airway may be enough in itself to produce recovery.

2. Helping or replacing breathing activity by some external means to ventilate the lungs with air, is likely to be of great help.

3. If heart action has stopped, it is essential to restart the heart to transport oxygen from the lungs to the other parts of the body. This is done by external cardiac compression.

Providing a clear airway. This is done by (i) clearing any obstructions from the mouth or throat and by (ii) positioning the head so that the pharynx and larynx are in a straight line with the back of the throat. This is best done by placing the head as shown in Fig. 11.

The very worst thing to do is to bend the head forward onto the chest. This can stop breathing in an unconscious subject.

Ventilating the lungs. In essence, only two methods are now in use: Expired Air Resuscitation (EAR) and the Silvester-Brosch method. Expired Air Resuscitation is either carried out in the Mouth-to-Mouth (operator's mouth to victim's mouth) or Mouth-to-Nose method (operator's mouth to victim's nose) mode. Either EAR method may be used on land, while Mouth-to-Nose EAR is preferred in the water. The Silvester-Brosch method can only be carried out on land and is only to be used when EAR cannot be carried out, e.g. with severe facial damage, so that no effective sealing of the operator's mouth can be made onto the victim.

In Mouth-to-Mouth resuscitation, the operator seals his lips over the victim's mouth and closes the victim's nose, see Fig. 11. He then exhales into the victim's mouth fairly gently but firmly if the victim is adult, less vigorously the smaller the victim. If the victim's airways are clear, the chest should rise slightly. The operator then removes his mouth

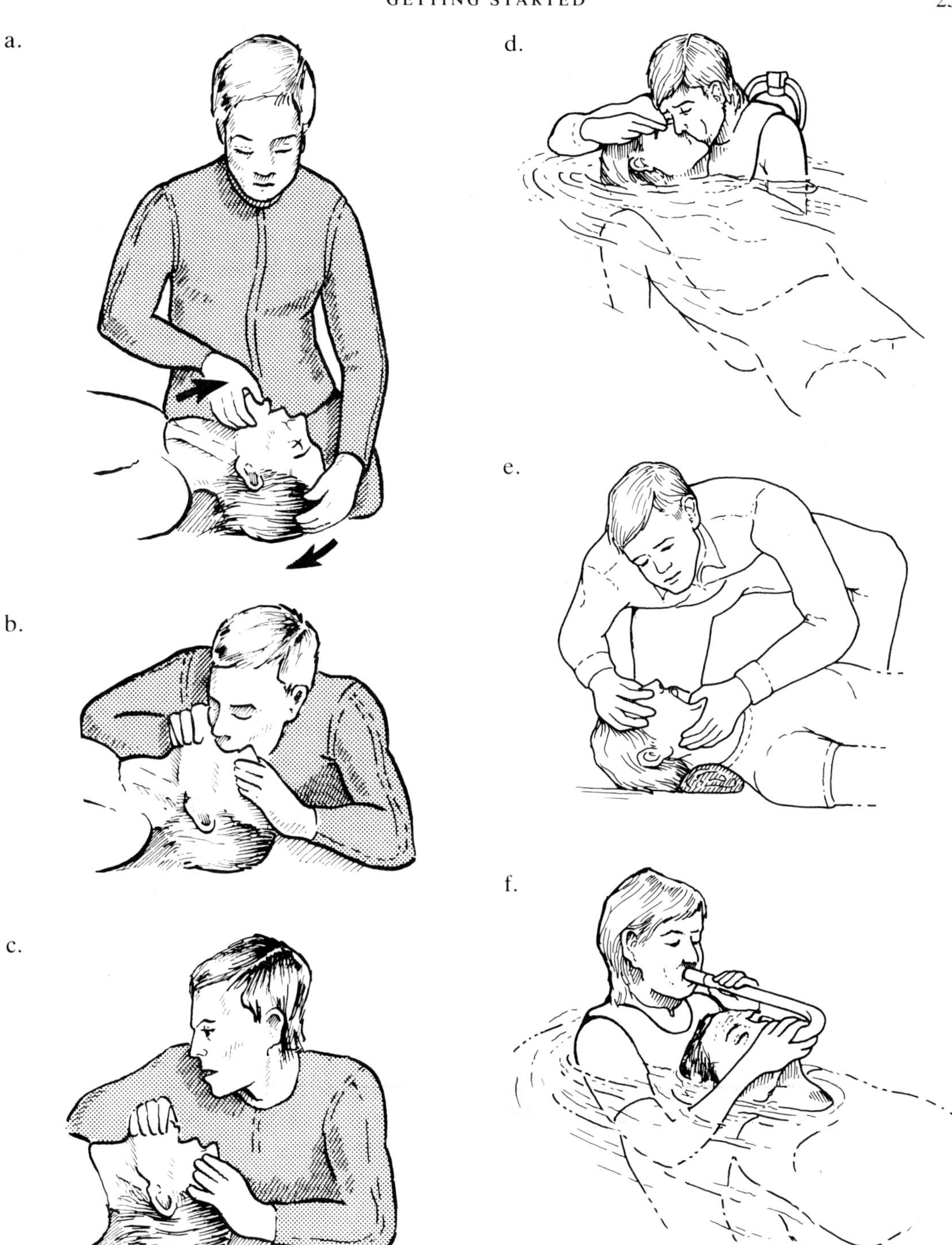

Fig. 11. Expired air resuscitation (EAR). a. Placing the head in the correct attitude. b. Filling the victim's lungs by the mouth-to-mouth route. c. Allowing the inspired air to escape from the victim prior to repeating b. Note in c that the rescuer is watching for lung movement or for air filling the stomach. Air must not be allowed to fill the stomach.

Figure 11d. Mouth to nose EAR in the water. The rescuer usually finds it easier to do this from one side of the victim. The rescuer is using his right-hand to pull the victim's head back into the EAR position. 11e. Starting to clear obstructions from the mouth of a victim. 11f. A method of EAR in the water which can be used but it is difficult to hold the snorkel in place in the victim's mouth.

and lets the air escape from the victim. He should observe the chest falling. He then gives another breath. Initially, four or five quick breaths should be given and then one breath every five or six seconds. The operator should check that he or she is not inflating the stomach; if this happens, gently press the air out of the stomach. The inflation should be fairly slow, taking about three seconds to inflate the lungs. Mouth-to-Nose resuscitation is carried out in much the same way, except that the mouth is sealed with one hand, usually by closing the lips, the operator's lips being applied to the nose. See Figs. 11 and 12 for details of EAR and the Silvester-Brosch method.

External Cardiac Compression (ECC)

If the victim develops cardiac arrest (loss of heart beat) you have a short time in which to act to save him. In diving situations it is likely that drowning or near-drowning will be associated with cardiac arrest but there are other reasons for this condition such as heart attack.

The emergency treatment to restart the heart is External Cardiac Compression : however, if the heart is beating, though perhaps weakly, it is better not to give this treatment because of injury that may be caused. You should have a theoretical knowledge of the procedure but should not practice it.

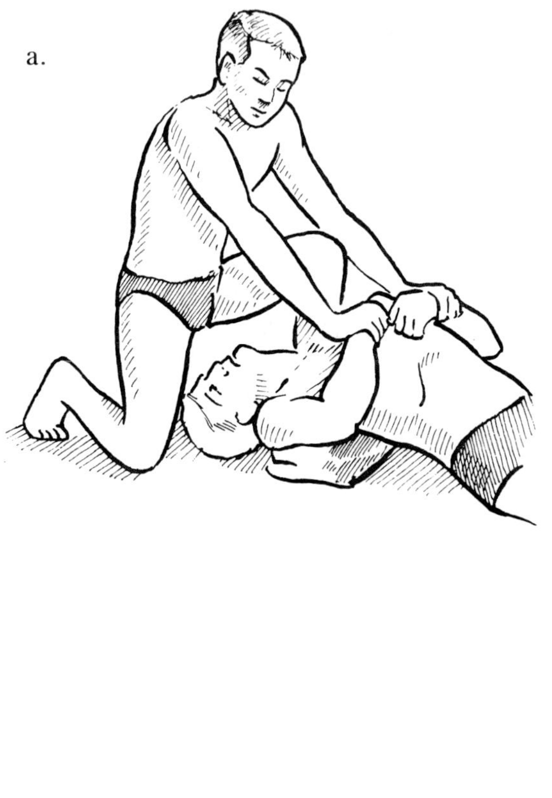

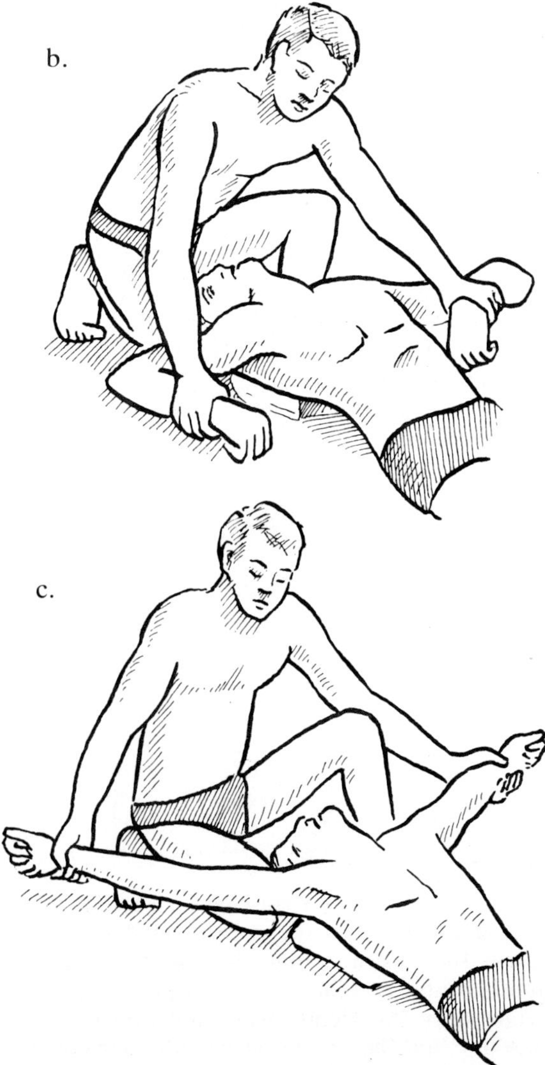

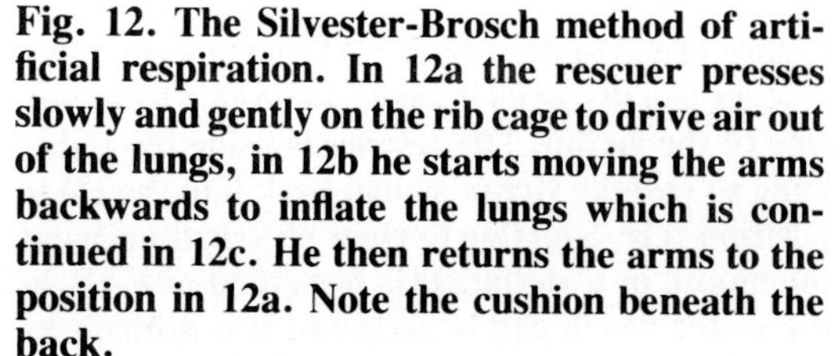

Fig. 12. The Silvester-Brosch method of artificial respiration. In 12a the rescuer presses slowly and gently on the rib cage to drive air out of the lungs, in 12b he starts moving the arms backwards to inflate the lungs which is continued in 12c. He then returns the arms to the position in 12a. Note the cushion beneath the back.

Since heart arrest will stop supply of oxygenated blood to the tissues the victim will appear pallid or even slightly blue in colour. The same appearance of course happens with obstruction to or failure of lung function but a heart beat may persist through resuscitation or restart spontaneously while the first stages of EAR are being given. So how do you know that the heart has failed?

If EAR is being done efficiently and the lungs are being ventilated and yet no improvement in the appearance of the victim occurs you must begin to suspect heart failure. You now need to look for a pulse. The carotid pulse detectable on the side of the neck or in the mouth, see Fig. 13 is usually the most easily felt. Wrist pulses may be so weak and difficult to detect in unconscious divers who are also probably very cold so that you could easily be fooled by the lack of a pulse in the wrist. Dilation of the pupils may be a sign of lack of heart beat but is not a totally reliable sign.

External cardiac compression consists of squeezing the heart between the breastbone and the spine so that blood is forced into the arteries. When you release the pressure the heart automatically refills from the main veins. Repeating this about 65 times a minute approximates to keeping the heart beating artificially and if you are lucky the heart may restart spontaneously after a while.

Normally ECC should be combined with EAR to give what is termed Cardiopulmonary Resuscitation : this requires one person to give EAR and one to give ECC. You should if possible go on a specific training course for ECC because pressure improperly applied to the chest can cause severe internal damage.

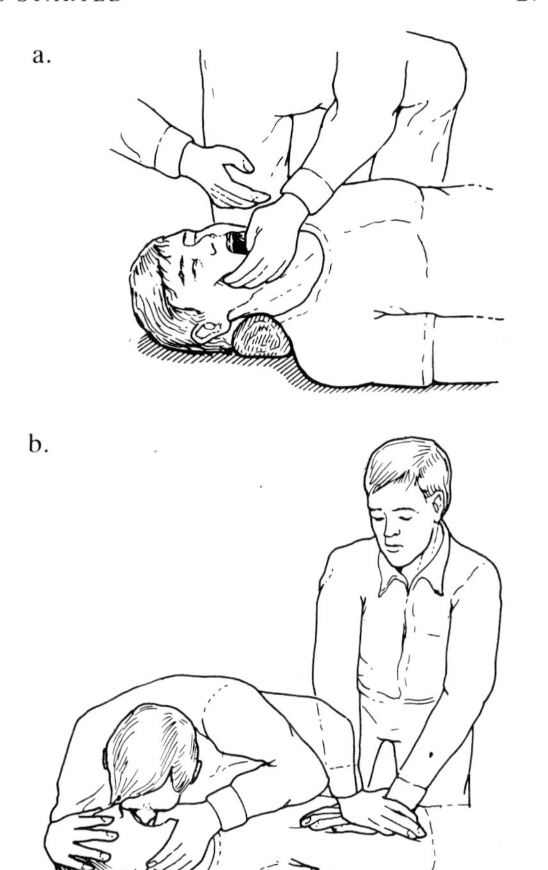

Figure 13a. Finding a pulse inside the mouth prior to External Cardiac Compression. Figure 13b. Combined EAR and External Cardiac Compression.

(*Aqualung trainees may now, if they wish, proceed to p. 33.*)

Chapter 3

Snorkelling

DETAILS OF SNORKELLING AWARD TESTS

The training is divided into two stages, Basic and then Advanced Snorkel Training. Please note that you should be trained for each test group for several sessions before testing. Some Branches find it well worthwhile training people for both tests before actually testing either. Ask your BTP (if he or she doesn't tell you) when they think you'll be ready for test.

Tests 1, 2 and 3 are just the same as those set out above. See p. 15-16.

BASIC SNORKELLER TRAINING

4. *Tow.* Obviously an essential part of rescuing someone. In the Advanced Snorkel Test you will use the skills of towing that you should master at this stage together with skills of resuscitation but at this stage you are learning how to handle towing. If the victim is just tired, or even panicky, or injured towing is all that is needed so long as they are able to breathe easily. Know how to recognise distress in a diver on the surface even if he fails to signal distress. Most rescuers find this test difficult at first because they tend to tow the victim, lifting too much of his head etc, out of the water. This may be nice for the victim but will probably exhaust you. All that is necessary is to keep his mouth and nose just clear and even short submergences of these parts would probably not be harmful in most victims. You should know the various types of tow (see Fig. 14) and why they are used. Basically the reasons are as follows:

Overhead tow. This relatively new type of tow is now thought by many to be the best type of tow as it allows speedy movement through the water together with easy mouth-to-nose resuscitation without stopping the tow. In essence the rescuer uses one hand on the chin and the other holding the back of the head to hold the head in the correct tilted back position. The rescuer fins on his back and, when giving Expired Air Resuscitation, fins himself up so that his mouth is over the victim's nose. See Fig. 14. The tow gives relatively good control of the victim in rough water.

Chin-tow. Good control of victim but in wrong position to give EAR (Expired Air Resuscitation) in the water quickly. Use in rough water and with panicky victim. Fig. 14c shows extended chin-tow.

Cross-chest tow. Not an appropriate to for a diver equipped with fins. See RLSS handbook for details if knowledge of this tow is required.

Methods No. 1 and No. 2. These tows are described in earlier dive literature but have largely been abandoned because of their relative ineffectiveness. See early editions of the BSAC Dive Manual for details.

5. *Rolls.* A test of agility, grace and happiness upside down in the water. An ability to roll forwards or backwards is of great value in snorkel diving if you are diving amongst rocks. A roll is also a rapid way of reversing direction. You should be able to do very tight rolls, which are almost like somersaults, and large radius rolls in which you fin through a circle. The most important feature is that you should not fall to one side or another during the roll. If you do tend to fall to one side the most probable explanation is that you are using your arms to pull you round and are pulling harder with one hand than the other. At least you should learn to balance your arm pulling. Finning into the roll and using your impetus and buoyancy control to continue the turn will give a neat roll. Ideally you should learn to pivot about your middle and gently fin yourself over keeping your body in a straight line. This is quite hard to achieve.

6. *Finning 20m underwater.* Simply a test to ensure that your finning techniques and buoyancy control add up to a technique which will allow you to snorkel dive in the sea. Remember, no 'cycling' in your finning, hands by the side. At last you're 'diving' for the first time.

If you have not had the lecture on ears and eustachian tubes by this time find out about ear-clearing methods and relevant theory.

7. *Finning in upright position with forearms clear of water for 1 minute.* A development from the swimming test but with fins. Should show you how much better fins are for moving around and holding yourself up in the water. Practically used, for example, as part of getting into boat or in any place where you want to get hold of something maybe as much as a metre above the surface, or as part of support of the victim during a rescue.

Note that you are asked to start learning how to use a lifejacket during the Basic Snorkel Training even though there is no specific exercise with the equipment. You

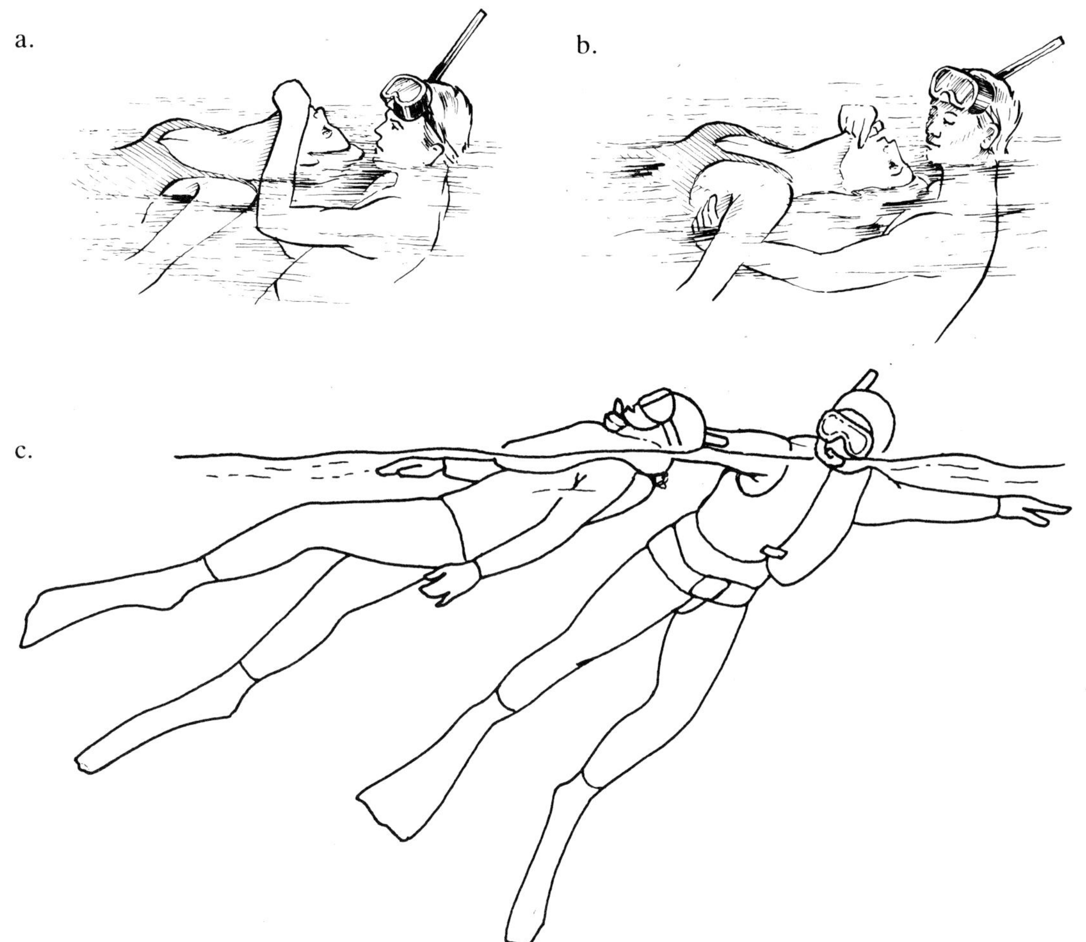

Fig. 14a. Overhead tow. The rescuer holds the victim by the chin, as in the chin-tow. His right arm will hold the hair on the back of the head so that the head is pulled back. His right elbow may be used to support the back of the neck. He fins on his back. Note that the rescuer's mask and snorkel should be lifted off the face to ease breathing and allow giving of EAR if necessary. b. Chin-tow shown in the closed-up mode in which one hand is used to grip the victim under the armpit. c. The extended chin tow. The rescuer may prefer to fin on his back but the position shown allows him to get a better idea of the direction to tow. The rescuer and victim will normally keep their masks on only in fairly rough water. Note that victim's head is placed well back so that the airway is clear, that the victim's body is nearly horizontal so that towing presents little difficulty because the body is well-streamlined by its position. The picture shows rescuer and victim with their masks on but this would normally only be done in moderately rough water. In calm conditions they would push their masks back so that speech and just possibly EAR would be easy. The extended tow does not work well in very rough turbulent conditions because the rescuer's hold on the victim is not very strong. In rough water the rescuer should close up on the victim.

should have learned how to fit the lifejacket and should have become fairly happy finning while wearing it. In the Advanced Snorkel Training you will learn how to use the lifejacket both for your own safety and in rescuing others.

ADVANCED SNORKEL TRAINING

In the previous stage of training you should have become familiar with the use of fins, mask and snorkel which will have given you the basic facilities required for diving. You will also have become familiar in a practical, as well as in a theoretical manner, with the effects of pressure on the human body. You will have worn a lifejacket during the introductory stage but the purpose at that time was in the main to give you familiarity in wearing one. Advanced Snorkel Training provides the rest of the facilities you need for snorkelling in the sea and in continuing aqualung training. In particular this part of the training concentrates on lifesaving, giving special attention to the use of lifejackets and to artificial resuscitation methods. A lesser, but still important, feature of the training familiarises you in the procedures to be used if you lose your mask while snorkelling or diving or if it becomes useless through breakage, as of a strap or the glass of the face-plate itself.

In detail

The Advanced Snorkel Training is carried out with the trainee learning to wear and use an ABLJ (or SLJ) and weight belt with basic equipment. Though you, as a trainee, are wearing a lifejacket, you should not fill the lifejacket with air at the start of the training. Training should normally be done with the lifejacket empty and the trainee at neutral buoyancy. Thus the BTP may need to remove any bottle on the ABLJ and/or weights from the weight belt. You, as a trainee, should try finning with a fully inflated lifejacket; you may be surprised how slow and ungainly you become.

1. *100 metre fin with weight belt.* The point of this part of the training is to ensure that you are happy with and can cope with the situation in which you are slightly negatively buoyant. This simulates the condition that might occur with a misjudged weighting while on the surface at the start of a dive, or the loss of buoyancy you would experience if you had to support someone at the surface before you inflated their or your own lifejacket. A 55 to 75 kg. person of normal build will probably need about 5 kg. on their weight belt, less buoyant people less weight.

2. *Adjust buoyancy to neutral, remove mask, placing it on the pool bottom and surface fin 200m using snorkel tube without mask.* You should adjust buoyancy to neutral, with the lifejacket. Remove mask and then fin 100m without mask. A very important test showing you can breathe through your snorkel (and later your demand valve) even if the mask is lost or broken. Some trainees have a lot of difficulty here and the reason is that they cannot seal their nose.

If you can't, try the following self-training. Stand in shallow water or on the pool side. Fit a snorkel but no mask. Take a deep breath. Block the end of the snorkel, say with your thumb, so that air cannot escape. Now try to breathe out through your nose but try and prevent the breath escaping by pressing your tongue forward against the palate with the tip of your tongue about 1 cm behind your teeth. Doing this will make your palate arch up at the back and seal off your nose from the rest of the respiration. If you can pull the front of your palate down at the same time the effect will be better still. Incidentally this method often clears ears as well. Don't spend too long not breathing while you're thinking about it, or breathe too hard. Five seconds at a time is enough, otherwise you may make yourself faint if you considerably over-exert yourself in this exercise. The tongue and palate part of the exercise can be done without using a snorkel. Use of the snorkel merely helps to emphasise that you must be able to seal off your nose while you've got a snorkel in your mouth.

Your BTP will ensure that you do as much as possible to prevent collision while finning without a mask. You should help yourself by keeping your eyes open underwater and stretch one hand forward to at least prevent a collision starting with your head. During testing the tester should make very sure you are not sneaking your head up briefly for a quick little breath and that you keep your eyes open.

3. *Complete at deep end, surface dive to recover mask, replace mask while treading water, give OK signal.* This part of the training shows that you are able to refit equipment even after quite a long time with your face underwater. Signals must be crisp and continued until acknowledged, even in training. See Fig. 3 for OK signal.

4. *Orally inflate and deflate lifejacket at surface.* The SSAC insists that you wear a lifejacket whether snorkellng or aqualung diving, because so many fatal accidents have happened to divers (not SSAC) who did not wear lifejackets. In addition, if you have to rescue someone else, you may need to inflate their lifejacket orally with speed. Whenever you use a lifejacket of a type with which you are unfamiliar, or whenever your dive partner wears a lifejacket unknown to you, always check, before the dive, that you know how to inflate and deflate the lifejacket. You, as a trainee, should realise that oral inflation may be very difficult if your lips are cold – you may need to use your hands to seal your lips. Mouthpieces with tooth grips are usually easier to use than any other when your lips are cold. Know how to use bottle or direct feed inflation on your own and your buddy's lifejacket.

5. *Carry out a simulated rescue, giving EAR in the water.* This part of the training should teach you all the techniques required in the rescue of a fellow snorkeller, or aqualung diver, who has surfaced, or even anyone else in distress on the surface of the water. The training starts with your recognition and response to a 'Distress' signal, see Fig. 3. You should respond immediately to such a signal by giving the OK signal. This will tell the victim that you are coming to his or her aid. When a diver surfaces, he should give the OK signal. If he or she does not, you should give an OK signal as a question, the reply being either an OK signal or a distress signal.

Since you may well have to fin some distance to the victim in a real emergency, we train you to fin 50m rapidly, though not so rapidly that you reach the victim gasping for breath. Then the training continues by inflating the victim's lifejacket, and possibly your own if you are low in the water so you should have checked beforehand how to do this. In real practice, it will not always be necessary to inflate the lifejacket, in which case, if your judgement is right, you can start EAR sooner. In actual rescues, the need to inflate a lifejacket will be determined by matters such as the buoyancies of the victim and the rescuer, the state of the sea, and on whether you intend to carry out EAR by the 'overhead' method, see Fig. 14, or from the side. In rough water you will probably need to inflate the lifejacket, so that the victim lies with his mouth and nose relatively clear of the water. If you choose to carry out EAR over his head, you can carry out EAR while continuing to fin, so that your motion and your finning will tend to lift you up and there will be less need to inflate the victim's lifejacket. The other method of EAR in the water places the rescuer to one side of the victim. He then raises himself over the victim either by finning or leaning on the victim's inflated lifejacket. This method of EAR is cumbersome since the rescuer has to change position from behind the victim (while towing) to a side position (while giving EAR). In addition it is probable that the 'overhead' method allows you to protect the victim from waves in rough water to a greater extent than with the 'side' method.

It is essential to start EAR as soon as you reach the victim. Remove any snorkel from the victim's mouth, and lift the mask off the face, pushing it perhaps down onto the hair. Delay in starting EAR reduces the chances of a victim of drowning recovering. Even one or two breaths may restart breathing in the victim. Mouth-to-nose EAR is recommended in the water since this minimises the risk of the victim taking in water through the mouth during the exhalation phase of the EAR cycle.

Your examiner will particularly check that you get yourself high enough in the water using your fins to really be able to get your face over the victim's. He or she will also check that you hold the victim so that his or her airway is straight (head well back). As soon as you reach waist-deep water stop finning, stand up and tow the victim to shore. In training use this method in any shallow part of the pool. Now it's easy to continue to do EAR though it would not be so if this were the breaker zone of a beach on a rough day (in that event you pull the victim through the breakers as fast as possible).

Support at pool side and lifting out. Your training officer should have demonstrated these items to you. EAR on pool side. Victim must be correctly positioned for efficient EAR, see Fig. 11. Coma position Fig. 15 should also be taught. The Silvester-Brosch method might well be taught with advantage for use on victims with damaged faces.

The BTP must make allowance for the relative weights of victim and rescuer and the height above water of the pool side. A poor performance should be excused so long as you can instruct persons on the side on how to help. An 8 stone person just cannot do a good lift on a 15 stone giant. But also note that you must at all times have the victim under your control and at least partially held by you. If you let the victim go at any time, you should fail the test.

OPEN WATER SNORKELLING

Though you may have been told that snorkelling is nothing more than an essential skill and a tiresome stage in your training there is every reason for becoming a good snorkeller. The reasons are as follows:

1. All aqualung dives begin and end with snorkelling, if only for a short period. You may need to spend some time at the surface, perhaps finding your dive site or waiting for others before you start your dive. At the end of the dive, even if you manage to surface at exactly the right spot, you'll still need to snorkel for a short time. If anything goes astray with your dive, you may need to snorkel for a considerable period or distance.

2. Snorkel diving can be very interesting if you have any interest at all in marine life. In Scottish waters, choose a site with the bottom within 6m of the surface. On the Scottish west coast, you can often see the bottom 6m below while finning at the surface. Rocky sites are the most interesting.

Snorkel diving in Scottish waters requires the use of protective clothing, see below, but in Mediterranean or sub-tropical waters, you'll probably not need any clothing to protect you against the cold, though you may benefit from the protection from any nasty beasties that some sort of clothing will give you.

Snorkel diving teaches you respect for and understanding of the sea. A competent snorkel diver can cope with surprisingly rough seas and is thus, if backed up by a suitable boat, an excellent agent for rescue of others in the sea. It is impossible to provide advice on all the problems the sea may make but the following main points should be noted:

A. Adapt yourself to the rhythm of the sea, so that you know when the next crest and the next trough will come and what you'll be doing.

B. If near the shore, take rough transits on objects on the shore so that you can judge how wind and current may be drifting you.

C. The rougher the sea, and, in particular, the shorter the sea, i.e. the more frequent the wave crests, the greater the need to stay clear of rocks. Probably the most dangerous event for a snorkeller is to be thrown by a wave against a rock.

D. If you are going to end the dive by going ashore rather than by being picked up by a boat, take care about your landing places. If you start the snorkel dive from shore, pick possible landing places and, while on the way out from shore, look back to see what they look like from the sea. A good exit point should be sheltered from the wave action and

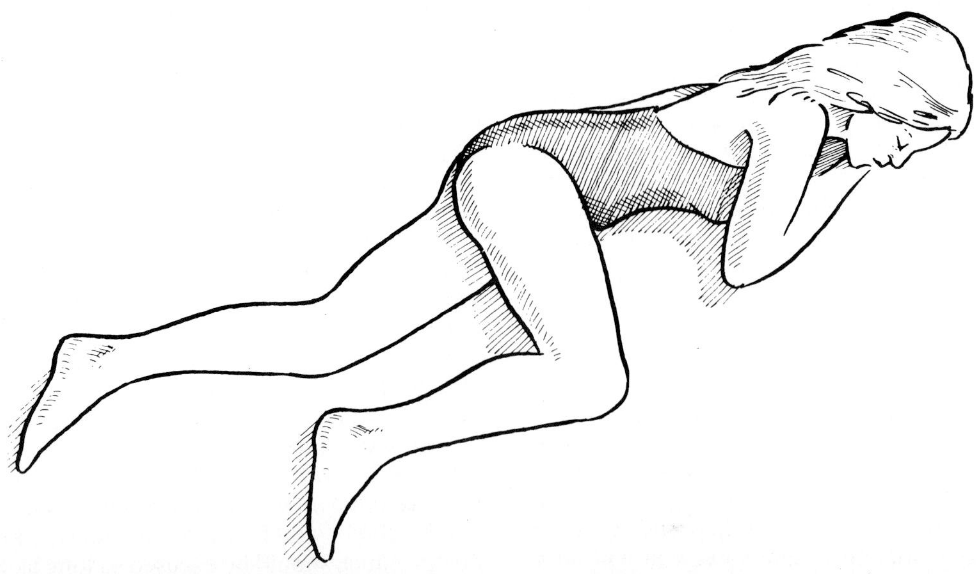

Figure 15. The Coma or Recovery Position. To be used when a victim treated with EAR has restarted breathing but has to be left while help is sought. This position prevents the victim falling over so that her or his face is flat on the ground and ensures that any vomit runs clear of the face.

allow an easy route out. If you have to go ashore without any previous knowledge of the shore, and the sea is rough, spend time observing the shore to find your best point and moment of exit.

Before you start snorkel diving, you will need, except in the warmest tropical waters, to know about hypothermia and protective clothing.

Open water training

Before you set out on the great day of your first snorkel dive in the sea you should have read the lectures on hypothermia, life-saving, protective clothing and lifejackets. If you have not received these lectures re-read the preceding pages. Check signals with your BTP. Check with the BTP how to establish neutral buoyancy: snorkel diving is impossible if you are say 2 kg. positively buoyant and dangerous if 2 kg. negatively buoyant (because you will be about 4 kg. negative at 10m depth and might never regain the surface, without weight belt release). Dry-suited snorkellers should try to arrange that they are neutrally buoyant with the minimum of air in their suit. If they fail to do this they may become negatively buoyant to a marked degree even in a 6m snorkel dive.

Fin Swim. Easy if you are fit so long as you start quietly and calmly. Can and should be done in sea states up to 4. Experienced snorkellers or/and boat with surface cover aboard must accompany you.

Snorkel Dive. Aqualung diver should be positioned at 6m (his depth gauge at this depth) (a) to check that you actually did reach 6m (b) for safety and (c) to provide a guide signal, i.e. a stream of bubbles if water is murky. Don't use lines to guide snorkeller because there is a slight risk of an inexperienced snorkeller getting caught and panicking and thus failing to free her or himself.

Do not forget to blow a little air into your mask through your nose as you dive. If you fail to do this you will get mask-squeeze in which the mask presses very firmly indeed on the face and causes pain. Do remember to clear your ears frequently in your descent. You should have practised ear clearing in the pool with the BTP previously.

Above all do not hyperventilate before snorkel diving. As explained on pp. 21-23 hyperventilation is potentially very dangerous.

Rescue Tow with EAR. Putting pool training into a still more real context. Trainee should give distress signal at start of tow because of course in reality he needs all the help he can get, but in this case he does not, unless situation really turns into a real rescue.

Snorkel Cover. One of the most important functions of snorkellers, also gives them experience of how divers work and should include work from a boat if possible, good use of signals should be made. BTP should never fail a cover who loses contact with divers (which can easily happen in deep water) so long as he stays in area and spots them on surfacing.

Completion of Snorkel Training. Do not forget that you are tested on your knowledge of the theory of snorkel diving before you receive the Snorkel Award. The theory sections in this chapter cover most of the knowledge you need to pass the test. See also the *Advanced Dive Training Manual* for the syllabus.

LECTURE 6

(*This lecture is appropriate for all types of trainee.*)

HYPOTHERMIA

Hypothermia is the depression of some part or all of the body below its normal temperature range. Hyperthermia is therefore the opposite i.e. overheating. Fairly low skin temperatures are acceptable on the skin of the feet and calves but an appreciable drop in the temperature of tissues which are not immediately adjacent to the skin is not. If the skin temperature of the fingers or toes drops below 10°C for a duration longer than one or two hours numbness and tingling sensations arise which may persist for a considerable time. The diver so exposed will find it very difficult to manipulate his equipment. Similar chilling around the mouth may make it difficult to grip a mouthpiece. The initial reaction of the body is to reduce the circulation of blood to the skin so that loss of heat through the skin is reduced. Eventually the 'core' temperature of the body, that is the temperature of the deeper tissues, will be reduced to levels at which pathological changes set in.

It is very important for the diver to realise that he or she or their companions may suffer from hypothermia without being really aware of it. The subjective impressions that you will probably experience as your core temperature drops are as follows, arranged in order of increasing severity:

Complaint of cold – feeling cold

Shivering (controllable, i.e. can be suppressed by willpower)
Uncontrollable shivering
Neurological symptoms, e.g. behavioural changes, lethargy
Cessation of shivering
Visual disturbance
Collapse and unconsciousness – leading to death

Neurological symptoms, cessation of shivering, visual disturbance and, obviously, collapse and unconsciousness are very serious symptoms indeed. Usually the victim will be only vaguely aware of symptoms beyond the first three so that his or her companions must always be on the lookout for the development of hypothermia in others when conditions are chilling. If controllable shivering develops early in a dive cut short the dive. If shivering becomes uncontrollable leave the water as soon as possible and move to conditions in which heat loss can be cut. If you observe someone pass from the uncontrollable shivering to the non-shivering state you have an emergency on your hands because the victim may move very rapidly into a state of helpless collapse. Bear in mind that you yourself may have negligible symptoms of hypothermia in conditions where someone else, perhaps similarly dressed and of similar fitness is suffering severely. If you are the sufferer never pretend that you are not being affected for fear that you will spoil other's enjoyment or be thought 'chicken'. If you are hypothermic you must take measures, see below, to stop further chilling and to regain your normal temperature.

Objectively speaking it can be stated that as the 'core' temperature drops the following symptoms can be expected:

37°C – normal body core temperature
36°-35°C – rise in metabolic rate and respiration
35°C – metabolism rate begins to decrease
34°C – respiration, heart rate and blood pressure fall
33°C and below – collapse of most body functions
28°C – repiration ceases
25°C – death

Hypothermia is, as stated above, a depression of the body temperature. It arises because the rate of heat loss is greater than the consequence of heat production, due to metabolism, and heat retention due to insulation.

The rate of heat production can be altered to some extent by increasing muscular activity, e.g. fast finning, but if the diver is naked or poorly clothed the movement may lead to faster cooling. The rate of heat production is also under fairly complex hormonal control so that different people react differently and the same person reacts differently at different times.

The rate of cooling is determined primarily, for the diver, by water temperature. Nevertheless you should bear in mind that wind-chilling may be a significant cause of heat loss in a suited diver standing on the shore or in a boat, especially after a dive, in a cold wind. In waters colder than 25°C cooling of a naked diver will occur sufficiently rapidly to make the wearing of protective clothing essential. At 20°C the naked body of a thin person may cool at rates as fast as 3°C per hour. Below 10°C dangerous hypothermia will probably develop very rapidly in the unclothed diver. However, if you wear suitable protective clothing, usually a wet suit or a dry suit (with thermal underwear in the latter case), cooling is almost stopped. For instance the wearing of a 6mm wet suit at 10m depth may reduce the rate of heat loss of a diver eight-fold. Bear in mind that these examples should only be taken as approximate illustrations of the possibilities of hypothermia in various situations. Variations in metabolic rate, subcutaneous fat, muscular activity and the effectiveness of protective clothing can also operate to alter the rate of development of hypothermia. For an example of an opposite extreme a wet-suited diver (6mm) finning on the surface in 3°C water in a fin race developed a slightly elevated temperature (38°C).

The treatment of hypothermia is a controversial and uncertain subject. In any event it is unlikely that you will have the ideal equipment to hand if you have to treat a victim. Very mild hypothermia can be treated with provision of warm dry clothing, moving the victim out of wind-chill and supplying warm non-alcoholic drinks. In more severe cases, i.e. at or beyond the severe and uncontrollable shivering state, remove the diver from the water, wrap him or her in anything that will prevent wind-chill and move him or her to a large boat or to shore to a place where further treatment can be carried out. Further treatment should be, if possible, under medical supervision since the victim may collapse without warning before or during rewarming. However, do not delay rewarming while waiting for medical help to arrive. Immerse the trunk of the victim in warm water

(42°C) until the deep body temperature and condition of the victim improves. Do not, unless it is unavoidable, rewarm the limbs because they may allow, on being rewarmed, very cold peripheral blood to move into the core and cool it further. Other specialist aids, such as breathing of heated air by the victim, can be very effective but the appropriate equipment is not usually available. The simple answer to the problem is – don't become hypothermic.

PROTECTIVE CLOTHING

The remarks made in the preceding section should make it clear that the main way of avoiding hypothermia is to wear some form of protective clothing. The main types of clothing worn by divers are Wet Suits and Dry Suits (membrane dry suits and expanded neoprene dry suits).

Wet suits are made from 'closed cell' expanded foam neoprene, often with an inner and sometimes an outer nylon fabric lining. The insulating properties of the material arise from the gas bubbles in the material. As the name implies when you enter the water a gentle seepage occurs at the cuffs, ankles, neck and head, and perhaps to a lesser extent through the zips. Provided there is little space between the suit and your body you soon have a thin but warmed layer of water between you and the suit. If the suit fits loosely at any point you may end up with rather a large pond of rather cool water sloshing around as you move. On the other hand too tight a suit makes dressing difficult, may constrict movement and breathing and produce a feeling of claustrophobia. There are various styles and different types of construction of wet suit. We do not wish to offer precise advice at this point but it is worth suggesting that very thin (4mm) suits are likely to be insufficient for Scottish waters even in summer and that very thick suits tend to immobilise you and require large amounts of weight on your weight belt.

Dry suits are, as their name implies, meant to be dry, though they often are not. Since air is a much better insulator than water a suit with a thin layer of air between you and the sea is likely to be warmer than a wet suit. It is usual to wear thermal underclothing inside the suit, which adds, so long as it remains dry to the retention of warmth. Thus dry suits are almost invariably warmer than wet suits, even if some entry of water does occur. The disadvantages are that they are more expensive and perhaps slightly harder to learn to use than wet suits. The membrane type of dry suit has the additional slight disadvantage that it is harder to fin fast in one than when wearing a wet suit.

There are three types of dry suit:

1. The membrane type dry suit made of a thin strong proofed material.
2. The expanded (foam) neoprene dry suit made of an impermeable neoprene material with neck, wrist and, if bootees are not fitted, ankle seals. These suits are quite warm even if no thermal underwear is worn or even when flooded. They do have appreciable buoyancy changes with depth but are very comfortable for finning.
3. The crushed neoprene dry suit. Here the material has been compressed during manufacture and as a consequence it has little volume change with depth and is incredibly resistant to abrasion.

See Fig. 16a, b, c.

There are also wet-dry or semi-dry suits where the manufacture does not guarantee total dryness but relatively little water enters the suit while in use. Normally dry suits and semi-dry suits are worn with a neck seal and a wet hood but some fairly effective systems of keeping the head dry or semi-dry have been developed. These systems usually are fitted with a neck seal just for a further line of protection.

Nearly all dry suits are entered through a waterproof zipped opening in the back though a few have front or diagonal zips. These zips require good maintenance and lubrication with beeswax or paraffin wax on frequent occasions. Do not use silicone spray which may damage the surrounding materials. When the zip is closed make absolutely sure that the zip really is fully closed.

Leaks at the neck, wrist or ankles may occur but represent either the fact that you have bought a suit with too loose a seal or have dressed wrongly. The membrane type seals of thin latex rubber should not have diagonal wrinkles in them. If they do these represent real routes for rivers. Defects in dump valves, see below, or dirt in them can also cause flooding. Leaks in other regions represent poor manufacture or the fact that you have holed your suit!

Thermal undersuits of various types or even clothing such as sweaters and jeans are invariably worn under the membrane types of dry suit and usually under the two types of neoprene dry suit. If the suits are tightly tailored, for example at the ankles or calves, lycra running tights or thin nylon socks make dressing easier.

All modern dry suits have some type of suit inflation and suit deflation system. They are absolutely essential. The ability to inflate the suit or to dump air from it allows you to compensate for changes in buoyancy during the dive and insulation can be increased to some extent by adding air to the suit. You may well start the dive by dumping air so that you become neutrally buoyant and then add air to re-establish neutral buoyancy as you descend. Not only is it essential to add air to the suit to maintain neutral buoyancy but you also have to add air after a certain amount of uncompensated descent to prevent the suit pinching you even through the undersuit. Inflation is usually through a low pressure take off from the first stage of the regulator but separate bottle inflation or even oral inflation may be used. The deflation system must be capable of working easily and rapidly but it must in addition only operate when the diver wishes it. Spontaneous dumping of air is dangerous to the diver as it may lead to unexpected loss of buoyancy. The automatic dump valves for suit deflation fitted to some dry suits are excellent especially if you have to cope with an overfast ascent, as in a rescue situation, but can lead to loss of buoyancy, often on the surface, so both the wearer and the buddy, as potential rescuer, must know how to close them to maintain buoyancy.

When you buy a dry suit you should bear in mind the type of ABLJ or Stab Jacket you are using or going to use. The design of ABLJ or Stab Jacket affects where the inflation and deflation valves on the suit should be fitted. The type of dry suit you buy depends on many factors but it may be helpful if friends can let you try two or three different types before you embark on purchase. It also depends on whether your dives are going to be arduous, long and in abrasive environments or whether you merely need a suit for the warmer part of the year for short dives. On the latter case a membrane suit or even a wet suit may be best. If you dive in polluted conditions a dry suit is essential and a full face mask is advisable. Note that a membrane type dry suit becomes fairly abrasion resistant if you wear a boiler suit over the membrane suit.

If you buy a dry suit, train for and take the SSAC Dry Suit Endorsement, see p. 102*ff*.

Chapter 4

Aqualung Training

If you have already read Chapters 1, 2 and most or all of Chapter 3, and even better have begun to put the advice in those chapters into practice by passing the Swimming Assessment (see pp. 12-13) and developed Basic Snorkel Skills (pp. 15-16) you are ready for Aqualung Training. Indeed you may have already 'had a taste' of the aqualung under careful supervision. This chapter is devoted to explaining and discussing training with the aqualung in the pool and for your first dives in openwater.

Before starting aqualung training you should have attended lectures on : Basic Equipment, Signals and Surfacing skills (see pp. 6-8), Ears, sinuses and effects of pressure (pp. 10-12), Aqualung use and buoyancy control (pp. 16-21) and burst lung and emergency ascent (see *Advanced Dive Training Manual*). You should also read the sections on Hypothermia and Protective Clothing in Chapter 3 (pp. 33-36) see Fig. 16a, b, c for illustrations of the appearance of the three types of diving suit worn with full equipment.

Introductory remarks

Aqualung training starts for most trainees in a swimming pool. On rare occasions a pool is not available and then training can be carried out in the open water, provided that protective clothing is worn and the wearers are familiar with it in the water before attempting to learn to use the aqualung. The training progresses to the open water and we emphasise that training is not complete at the 3rd Class level until you have experienced a small variety of open water situations and shown that you can carry out the appropriate responses for emergency situations in the open water. The training is strongly oriented towards your being capable of handling the following situations without panic, though of course they are only simulated situations and not ones which really have taken place:

1. Loss or displacement of mask or of your regulator mouthpiece.
2. Failure of your air supply.
3. Disorientation.
4. Rescue of your partner (buddy) from underwater and then on the surface.
5. Buoyancy control and control of ascent rate.

All of these situations require that you let your companion or other persons (usually on the surface) know how you are and what the problems are, so you must have a good knowledge of diving signals.

Before you start the training you must have completed the Basic Snorkelling skills training and attended the four lectures outlined above. You must also have passed a Medical Examination for Sports Diving of the type laid down by the SSAC and you must have obtained a signed certificate from a Medical Practitioner that you are fit to dive. Medical Certificate forms are issued with other documents at the time of joining but extra copies can be obtained from Club Headquarters. Aqualung diving is dependent upon the use of compressed air. Thus an understanding of the physics of compressed air and of the related physiology is essential. We have already introduced you to the physics of compressed air but it is appropriate to provide further information at this point. In addition you need to understand the principles of operation of the aqualung.

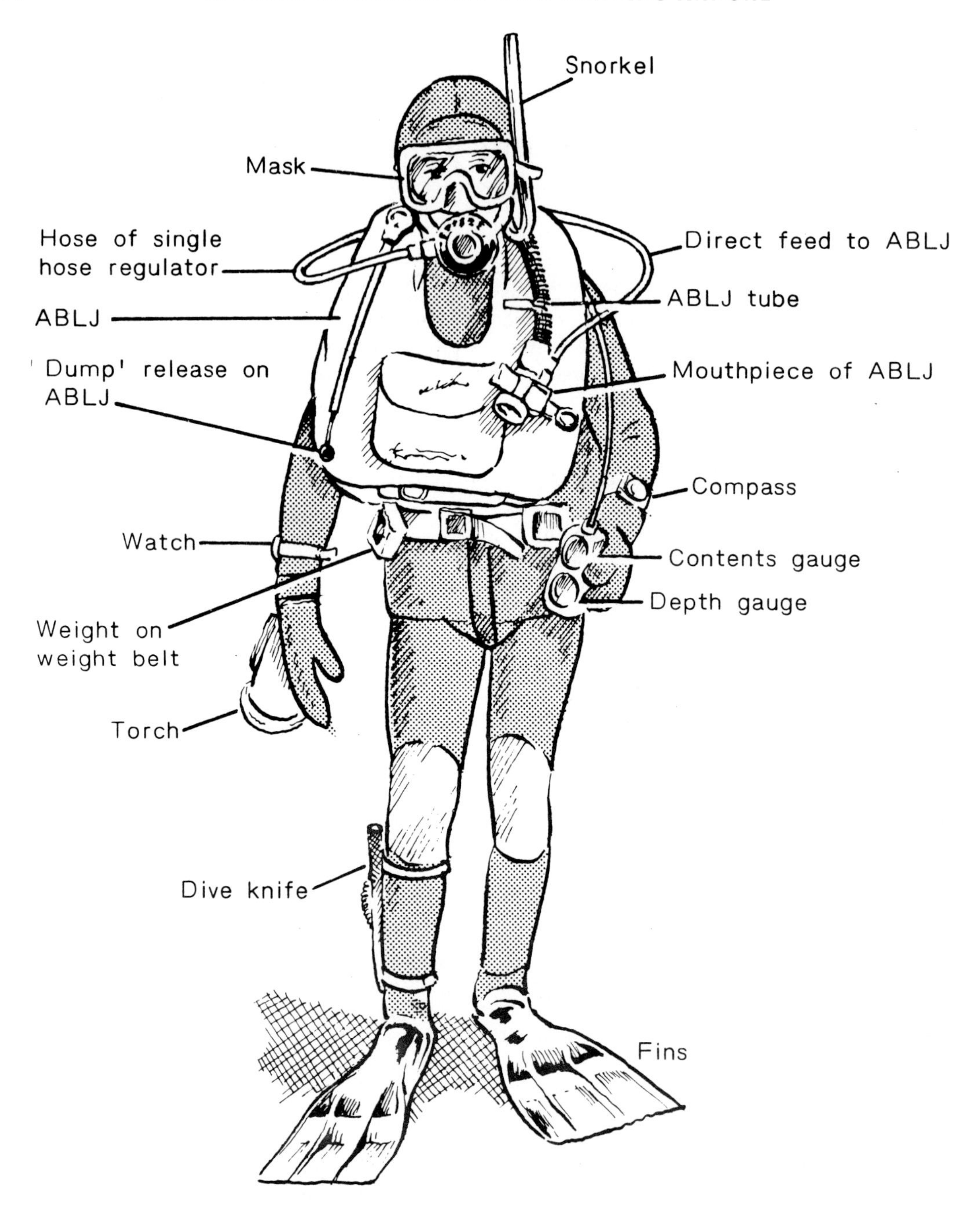

Fig. 16a. The wet-suited aqualung diver wearing full equipment. Note that this diver is using both a direct feed to his ABLJ (Adjustable Buoyancy Lifejacket) which comes from the first stage of the demand valve (behind his neck) as well as an independent bottle (just visible at the base of the lifejacket). His contents gauge and depth gauge are in a console which he is holding in his left hand. Other arrangements of depth gauges etc, are possible, see next figure. This diver carries a torch which should not be regarded as being essential equipment for all dives. Note that the weight belt and its buckle are clearly visible since they lie outside the waist-strap of the aqualung. The jock-strap of the ABLJ is not as clearly visible as in the next figure.

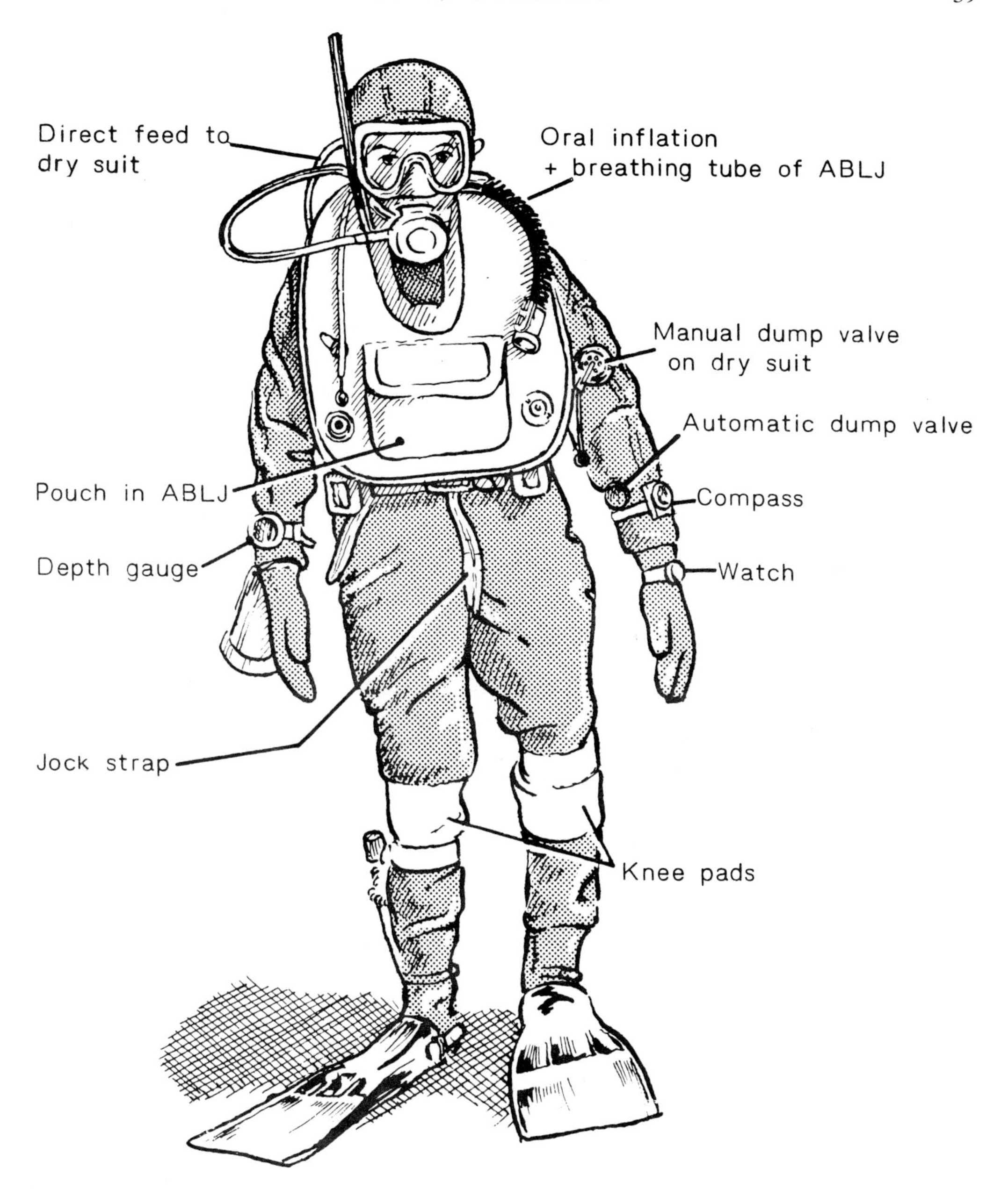

Fig. 16b. The dry-suited diver wearing full equipment. This diagram concentrates on features of the dry suit: the previous figure should be consulted for other items of equipment. The direct feed to the dry suit enters under the ABLJ. Note that the ABLJ does not have a direct feed. The contents gauge is not visible because the diver has tucked it through her ABLJ harness.

Note that wet and dry-suited divers have a considerable choice of having equipment which can be placed on the right-hand or left-hand side. The two divers shown have right-hand positioning of the demand valve hose and left-hand of the ABLJ hose. Some types of equipment would allow a reverse of this positioning. Divers should place their equipment on the side that suits them best but should note that it is unwise to place all the main items on one side. The positionings of the dump valves on the dry suit are considerably variable and the illustration carries no implication that the arrangement shown is the best one. The dry suit shown is a membrane-type dry suit, usually worn with heavy thermal-type underclothing. Foam neoprene dry suits are also available.

Fig. 16c. The stab-jacketed diver who wears a crushed neoprene dry-suit. Perhaps at the time of writing this represents the most 'avant-garde' type of diver in UK waters.

LECTURE 8

MORE ADVANCED PHYSICS

As we wrote on page 12, an appreciation of Boyle's Law will help you to understand the use of aqualung cylinders and the operation of the regulator, and the next section will deal with just that matter. However, there is a certain amount of slightly more advanced physics which will help you to an understanding of a wider range of phenomena associated with the aqualung diving.

The first aspect is the cooling of gases when they expand and the warming when they are compressed. The phenomenon is described by **Charles' Law** which states that the temperature of a gas falls by an amount proportional to the change in pressure when it is expanded, or alternatively that it rises by an amount proportional to the change in pressure when the gas is compressed. The law may be stated in other parallel ways. One of these is of practical importance in the filling of aqualung cylinders. This alternate statement says that the pressure of a gas is proportional to its temperature.

Examples of the application of **Charles' Law** in diving are manifold. For instance, the compression of air in a compressor leads to very marked heating which is largely counteracted by having cooling fins on the compressor cylinders and interstage piping. As your aqualung cylinder is charged with cool air, the temperature inside the cylinder will rise as the pressure rises. Later, when the cylinder cools, the pressure will drop and you may feel that you have less air than you had at the time of filling. On the other hand as the air in your cylinder has its pressure reduced in passing through the valves of a regulator it will be cooled and, occasionally, if the cooling is very marked and the regulator is damp internally, ice may form perhaps leading to the rare event of your regulator freezing-up.

The second aspect of importance is the concept of **Partial Pressures. Dalton's Law of Partial Pressures** states that the pressure exerted by one gas in a mixture of gases is identical with the pressure that the same amount of that gas would exert by itself in the same conditions of volume and temperature. In other words mixing gases does not cause interactions between the gases which might alter the pressure. Thus in a mixture the total pressure is the sum of the partial pressures of each gas present. The relevance of this law comes from the fact that all divers breathe gas mixtures. Sports divers breathe that gas mixture known as air, which is composed approximately of 21% Oxygen and 79% Nitrogen. At surface pressure, i.e. of 1 Bar, as you should remember from page 9, the pressure due to nitrogen will be 79% of 1 Bar and that due to oxygen 21% of 1 Bar. At 4 Bar total pressure the Oxygen will exert a pressure of 21% of 4 Bar, i.e. approximately 0.84 Bar and the Nitrogen 79% of 4 Bar, i.e. 3.16 Bar.

The relevance of **Dalton's Law** arises in particular in connection with physiological aspects of diving because the various effects of the various gases under pressure are of course related to their partial pressures, in particular Inert Gas Narcosis and Decompression Sickness, see later.

The third aspect of gas physics relates to the solubility of gases in fluids. The relevance is that the human body is in effect so largely fluid that it can be treated as a fluid or set of fluids by the diving physiologists. The phenomenon is covered by **Henry's Law** which states that the solubility of a gas in a fluid is proportional to the partial pressure of that gas in equilibrium with the fluid. Thus twice as much nitrogen will dissolve in the body fluids at 2 Bar pressure as at 1 Bar pressure. You should be aware that the solubility is defined as the total mass of gas that can be dissolved in a given fluid under defined conditions. It will always take some time for a fluid to take up the total mass defined by the partial pressure, temperature, nature of the gas and nature of the fluid, though the rate of solution will also be proportional to the difference in partial pressures of the gas in the gas phase and that in solution. When the total mass that can be dissolved has dissolved that fluid is termed to be **saturated** with that gas. The main gas acting through solution is nitrogen because oxygen is rapidly metabolised by the tissues so that the oxygen in solution never rises to levels of saturation. **Henry's Law** and **Dalton's Law** lie behind decompression sickness and decompression procedures.

THE AQUALUNG: CYLINDERS AND REGULATOR

A moment's thought will make you realise that there are two reasons for carrying the diver's air highly compressed in cylinders. First, the diver requires a large volume of breathing air if the dive is to last anything but a very short time. Obviously it would be ineffective to carry the air in a very large volume container at low pressure. Highly pressurised cylinders will contain a volume of air which when released to lower pressure will expand considerably. The second reason is that the aqualung diver will wish to operate in depths from the surface down to 30m and occasionally deeper to 50m. The pressure varies between 1 Bar (at the surface) and 6 Bar at 50m. He or she must breathe air at the same pressure (the ambient pressure) as the water around them. If the air supply was at lower pressure any attempt to breathe would make it impossible to inhale. If the air is at higher pressure inhalation would be involuntary and pulmonary barotrauma (see page 11) would result. Obviously a system for reducing the cylinder pressure to ambient pressure is needed – this is a regulator. In turn the pressure in the cylinder must be appreciably higher than the maximum ambient pressure the diver is likely to encounter.

Breathing air is compressed into cylinders using compressors specially designed for this purpose. Many cylinders now in use are designed to be filled to a maximum working pressure of 200 Bar (= 2940 p.s.i.) and somewhat higher pressures are in use for some cylinders.

Air cylinders: Contents, endurance and buoyancy

Diving cylinders are made either from steel or aluminium alloy. Cylinders used in the UK must conform to the requirements of British Standard 5045 if fabricated at the present time. Cylinders made to the earlier Home Office T and S and HOAI, 1, 2, 3 and 4 specifications may still be used provided that the cylinders concerned have passed the compulsory cylinder tests (see below). When they are filled with compressed air from a compressor, they should be filled to no more than the pressure stated on the outside as their working pressure (W.P.). The working pressure for many modern air cylinders is 200 Bar = 2940 p.s.i. = 20.25 MNm^{-2}. The internal capacity of a cylinder might be 10 litres = 0.34 cu.ft., but when it is filled with air at 200 Bar it contains a volume of air which would at surface pressure (1 Bar) occupy 200 × 10 litres or 200 × 0.343 cu.ft., i.e. 68.6 cu.ft.

In other words the **capacity of a cylinder** is the volume of air if brought to 1 Bar pressure that the cylinder would contain at its full working pressure. It is given by:

Working Pressure × Internal Volume of Cylinder = Capacity

It is usual to refer to cylinders by the volume of air that they could release at 1 Bar pressure, so that cylinders are known by such names as 72 cu.ft. or 45 cu.ft. sizes or by their capacity in litres. There is one very simple advantage in this because it gives a rough measure of the air duration that you would obtain from a full cylinder. Moderately active divers who are not experienced in air conservation tend to consume air at the surface at a rate of 1 cu.ft. (29 litres) per minute. Thus a 65 cu.ft. cylinder would contain enough air for 65 minutes breathing at the surface. Thus by simple use of **Boyle's Law** you can calculate that at 10m depth where the volume of a given mass of air is halved, but the size of each breath is just the same, you consume air at twice the rate at the surface. Similarly at 20m depth your air consumption will be three times that at the surface. Thus by **Boyle's Law** the **air consumption rate** (theoretical) is given by

$$\frac{\textbf{10 + Depth in metres}}{\textbf{10}} \times \textbf{Surface rate}$$

and consequently the **duration of a dive** on a given cylinder will be (in theory) given by

$$\frac{\textbf{Contents of cylinder at working pressure}}{\textbf{Air consumption rate}}$$

Note that air consumption rates are theoretical and only serve as a rough guide.

Air weighs 1.2 gm per litre at surface pressure. Thus a cylinder containing 2,000 litres (at 1 Bar pressure) contains

$$\frac{\mathbf{1.2 \times 2000}}{\mathbf{1000}} = \mathbf{2.4\ kg}$$

of air. As this is used by the diver the weight of air will diminish. The consequence of this is that his or her buoyancy will increase. Obviously the larger the cylinder(s) the more your buoyancy will change during a dive.

So we have considered the contents, endurance and buoyancy effects associated with air cylinders. The next aspect to examine is their construction.

Air cylinders – construction

As we said above air cylinders are made from steel or aluminium alloy. Cylinders bear marks, either on the shoulder or on the neck, which are most informative, see Fig. 17. The cylinder should be marked with the specification under which it is made, the initials of the maker, the batch number of the maker and the individual cylinder number as well as the Working pressure, the Test pressure, the water capacity (a measure of volume but often given as a weight of water) the date(s) of testing, expressed as month and year and the test station mark. On occasion one or more of these pieces of information is missing but if the cylinder lacks details of its working and test pressures, test date(s) and manufacturer, be suspicious. Note that there are a number of other cylinder specifications for cylinders intended for surface use or for use with other gases.

Cylinders for compressed breathing air are required by law to be tested hydraulically immediately after manufacture and then every four years. An internal visual inspection should be carried out every two years. Details of the tests are specified in BS 5430. If a cylinder has not been tested as recently as required by these rules it is described as being 'out of test' and its use in a charged state in the public domain or transport in a vehicle on the roads is illegal. Carriage of a charged 'out of test' cylinder in your car might even in the event of an accident in which the cylinder played no contributory part, invalidate your car insurance. Cylinders which have become 'out of test' often pass a BS 5430 test and then can be used in the public domain since they are now 'in test' again. Normally the testing body, often a dive shop, will issue a certificate of test but the vital evidence that others will look for is the stamped date on your cylinder. Cylinders will fail if they are internally corroded or pitted or if they are externally corroded, pitted or dented to more than a certain degree, specified in BS 5430. The main reason for test failure is that when exposed to the hydraulic test pressure the cylinder expands (stretches) and does not return to its original dimensions (or to within some close value specified in the test regulations) on removing the pressure. This distension of the cylinder is described as permanent set, permanent since depressurisation is not followed by return to the original dimensions.

Cylinders can remain in good condition for many years provided that care is taken to ensure that water never enters the cylinders and that mechanical damage never occurs. Water can enter the cylinder from condensation from improperly dried air used to fill the cylinder from poorly operated compressors. Water may also enter if the cylinder is completely emptied and then allowed to lie in a wet place, say a boat, with the pillar valve open.

If water is known to have entered a cylinder seek professional help to devalve the cylinder,

IWKA 2657 EA 3784
BS 5045/I/CM/S TGV 6 83
TARE WT 14·78KG
VO 12L
WP 207 BAR TP 363 BAR

Fig. 17. Cylinder markings. The top line gives the initials of the manufacturer and their design and batch numbers. The tone in line two emphasises that the cylinder bearing this set of marks is made to BS 5045, Part 1, and the second piece of tone gives the month and year of initial test. Line three tells us that the cylinder has a tare weight, i.e. empty, of 14.78 kg., while line four tells us that the interior volume is 12 litres. The final line tells us that the working pressure (WP) is 207 Bar and the Test Pressure 363 Bar. The four patches of tone emphasise the pieces of information that you and a filler of your cylinder will be particularly interested in. Note that it is unusual to find all this information laid out in one block like this – usually it is spread over the neck of the cylinder.

empty the water out, wash the inside with clean water and dry the cylinder. Then an internal inspection should be carried out by a professional tester and if necessary a hydraulic pressure test as well.

On occasion the inside of cylinders may become oily due to the use of poorly operated compressors. If this happens the removal of the oil should be left to experts.

Pillar valves are fitted to the neck of the cylinder so that the flow of air into or out of the cylinder can be controlled. Pillar valves, see Fig. 18 are of three types. The type usually fitted nowadays is the 'balanced' type but on occasion the 'unbalanced' and the 'glandless' types of valve may be found. The 'balancing' is against the air pressure inside the cylinder. The 'unbalanced' valve has the pressure of air inside the cylinder thrusting the inner part of the valve against the valve body. The result is that when the contents are at high pressure it is exceedingly difficult to open or to close the valve, in addition, wear of the valve parts is rapid. The 'glandless' valve is unbalanced but is designed in such a way that there is less wear on the valve parts. A small diaphragm on the spindle of the valve prevents air escaping to the low pressure end of the spindle. The 'balanced' pillar valve has no direct metallic connection between the valve head and the spindle which is turned when the valve is opened or closed. The valve head has high pressure on both sides when the valve head is in the open position so that there is no thrust from high pressure air on it. The valve spindle keys into the valve head but does not receive any thrust from it. It does of course receive a much smaller thrust (because of its small cross-sectional area) from the high pressure air.

The pillar valve is extended into the cylinder with an 'anti-debris' tube which prevents dust, rust, etc. from entering the valve when the cylinder is in an inverted position, as will happen when the diver is descending head first.

The pillar valve is attached to the regulator by a clamp or threaded screw. The former system is used in the UK and USA, though the threaded connection is becoming commoner in these countries. The clamp, see Fig. 19, is usually referred to as an 'A' clamp. If the diver uses two or even three cylinders simultaneously these are joined together by a manifold, which is simply a tube connecting the cylinders together and to a single point for connecting a

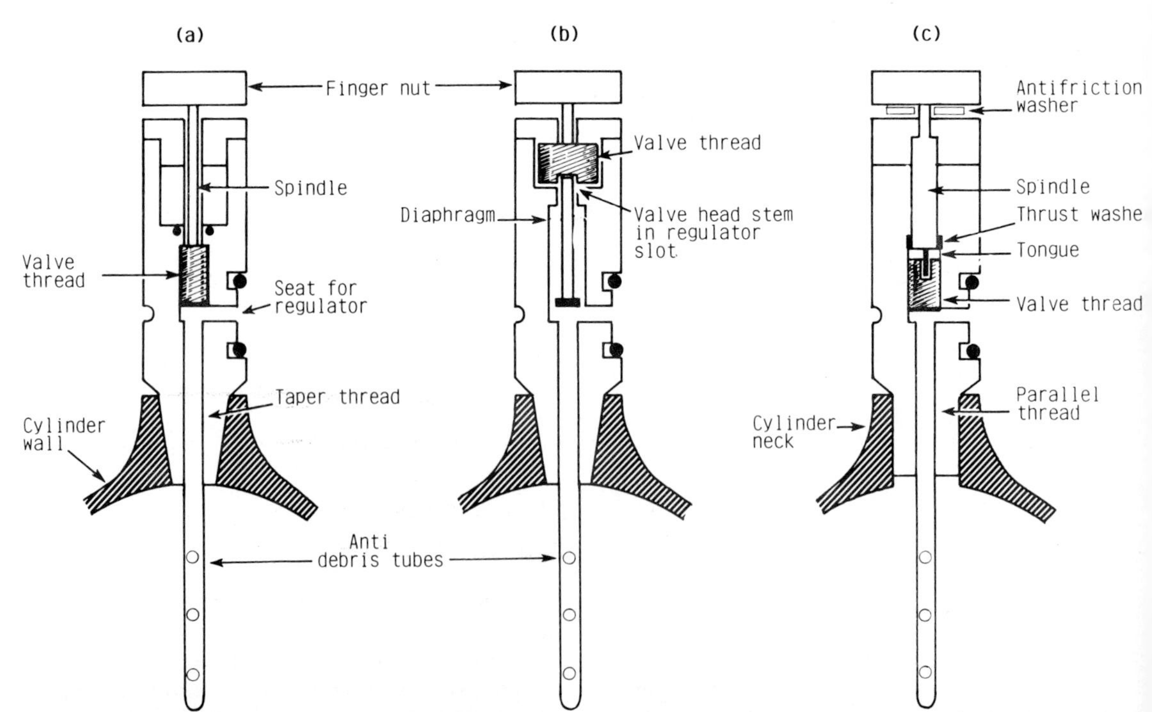

Fig. 18. Pillar valves. (a) Unbalanced, (b) Glandless and (c) Balanced types shown in section. Constructional details have been simplified and spaces between various components enlarged to aid clarity. Rubber or neoprene washers etc. in heavy black. The locating pit ('nipple') for the screw of the A-clamp is shown on the left-hand side of each valve.

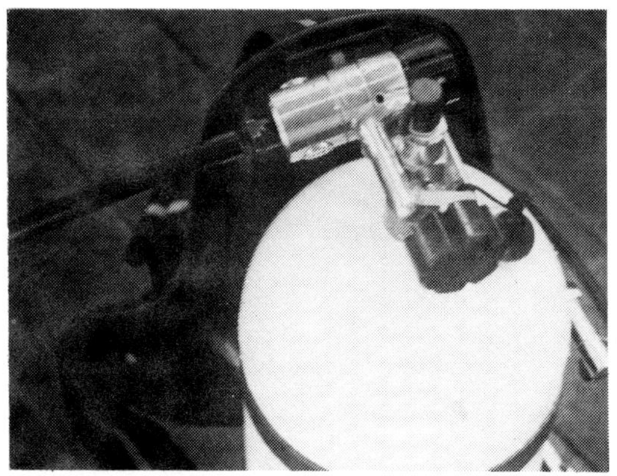

Fig. 19. A view of a first stage in place on top of a single cylinder. The hand wheel for the A-clamp faces the camera and the valve dust cap for use when the regulator has been removed from the cylinder is seen on its right. Note the A-clamp whose frame passes on either side of the pillar valve. The intermediate pressure hose of the regulator runs out of the first stage to the left. The cylinder has a fibreglass backpack.

regulator. Manifolds are of two types. In one type the cylinders retain their pillar valves. In the other, the pillar valve is fitted onto the manifold which is attached to each cylinder by a threaded connection.

In the USA and Continental Europe it is usual for the pillar valve to be fitted with a reserve valve which starts to close as the air pressure in the cylinder falls to about 30 Bar. This is carried out by using a spring-loaded valve. The advantage of a reserve valve is that it gives you warning of air supply exhaustion by ensuring that breathing becomes more difficult. Pulling a lever on the reserve valve lifts the restriction so that you can then breathe easily but are aware that you should finish the dive soon. However, since reserve valves can be pulled by accident without the diver being aware, it is better practice to monitor your air consumption with a contents gauge.

Regulators (Demand Valves)

Cylinders carry a large amount of air for the diver at far higher pressure than the ambient pressure even on the deepest dives. In order to provide the diver with air at ambient pressure it is necessary to use a valve or regulator which reduces the pressure of the air from cylinder pressure to ambient pressure. Furthermore the regulator should only operate on demand, that is, when you want to inhale. If the valve supplied air constantly it would be both unpleasant and wasteful. Hence the diver uses a 'demand valve' known also and perhaps more widely by the slightly less precise term 'regulator'.

All modern regulators reduce the air from cylinder pressure to ambient pressure in two stages and are thus known as two-stage regulators. The first stage reduces the pressure to about 5 to 12 Bar above the ambient pressure and the second stage then reduces this interstage pressure of 5 to 12 Bar above ambient pressure.

The basic principle of the valves in each stage is that they operate in relation to the outside water pressure, and the air pressure downstream of the valve. The air pressure downstream, i.e. nearer the diver's mouth, falls when he inhales and this allows the valve to open. However as the air pressure in the downstream side of the valve rises, the valve closes.

The second stage operates exactly in terms of the statement in the last paragraph. When the diver inhales the air pressure in the mouthpiece drops slightly below ambient pressure and air flows through the valve but as he stops inhaling the air pressure rises to ambient pressure and the valve sensing this closes.

The first stage operates in basically the same manner but it opens when the pressure in the interstage hose drops slightly and closes when the pressure in the interstage hose rises to its present maximum value of 5 to 12 Bar above ambient. Of course consumption of air through the second stage causes the interstage pressure to fall.

There are two main methods of valve construction used in the first stage to relate air pressure to ambient pressure. These are the Diaphragm and the Piston types of construction. In the second stage Piston or Tilt-valve constructions are used, see Figs. 20 and 21. All these valves, except the Tilt-valve, relate the position of the valve (open or closed) to the pressure of the water, the pressure of air on the downstream side of the valve and the tension in a spring. The spring can be set at a tension such that the valve does not close until a pressure appreciably above ambient has built up (say in the intermediate pressure hose). Let's consider these valves in some detail.

First stages

The early type of first stage valve was the diaphragm type valve shown in the diagram in

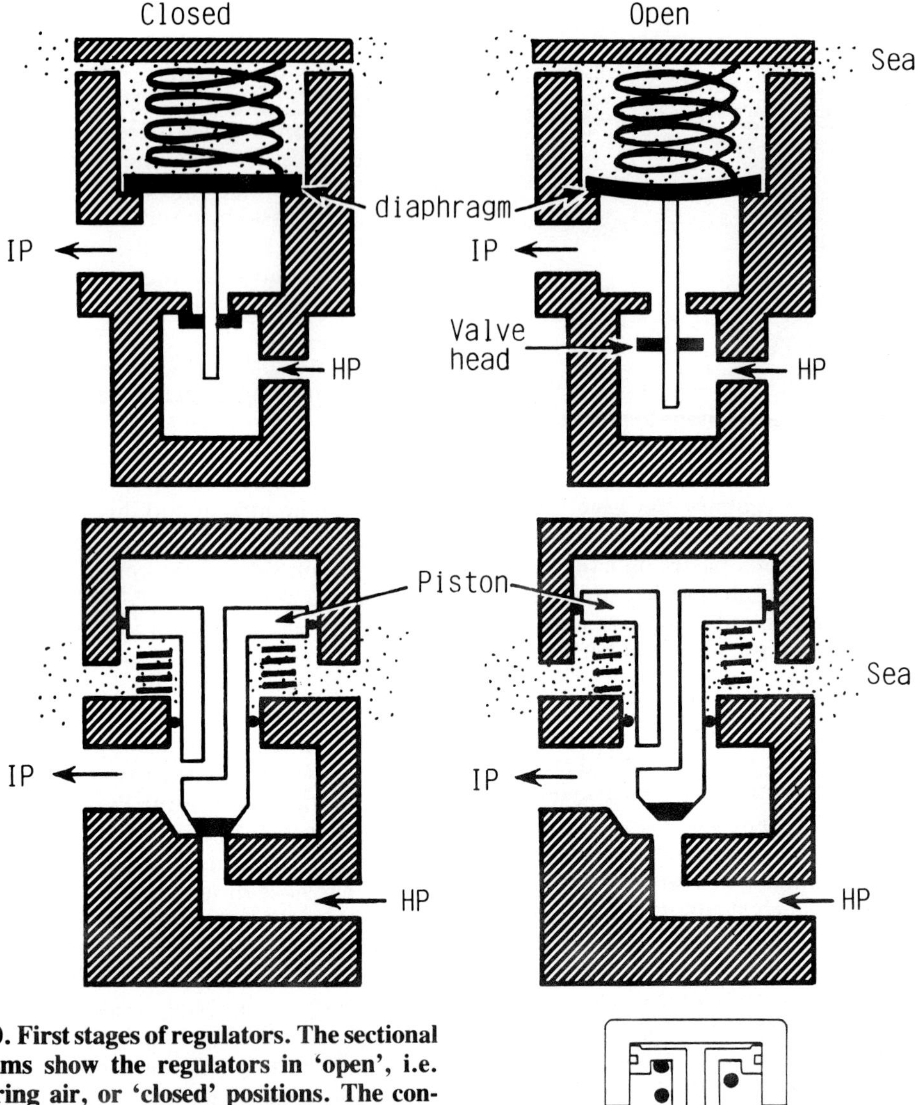

Fig. 20. First stages of regulators. The sectional diagrams show the regulators in 'open', i.e. delivering air, or 'closed' positions. The constructional details and proportions of the regulators have been omitted or altered slightly to aid comprehension. The top two diagrams show the diaphragm type first stage Water ('Sea') is shown by fine dots to indicate where it enters the valve. HP indicates high pressure, air at cylinder pressure, IP indicates air at intermediate pressure, i.e. about 5-9 Bar above ambient. Details of the A-clamps have been omitted. The lower pair of diagrams show a piston type first stage with 'balanced' action; the balance is achieved by allowing IP air to flow up the centre of the piston stem to its 'top' side. In some versions the IP air flows out through the piston into the hose to the second stage. Right – First stage of a typical regulator to show the details of construction is shown in section.

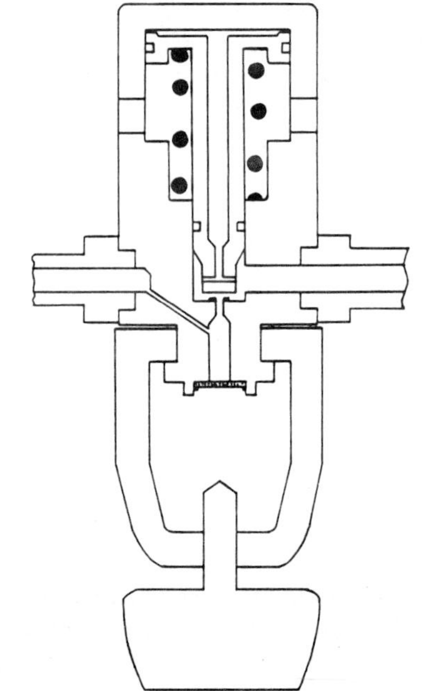

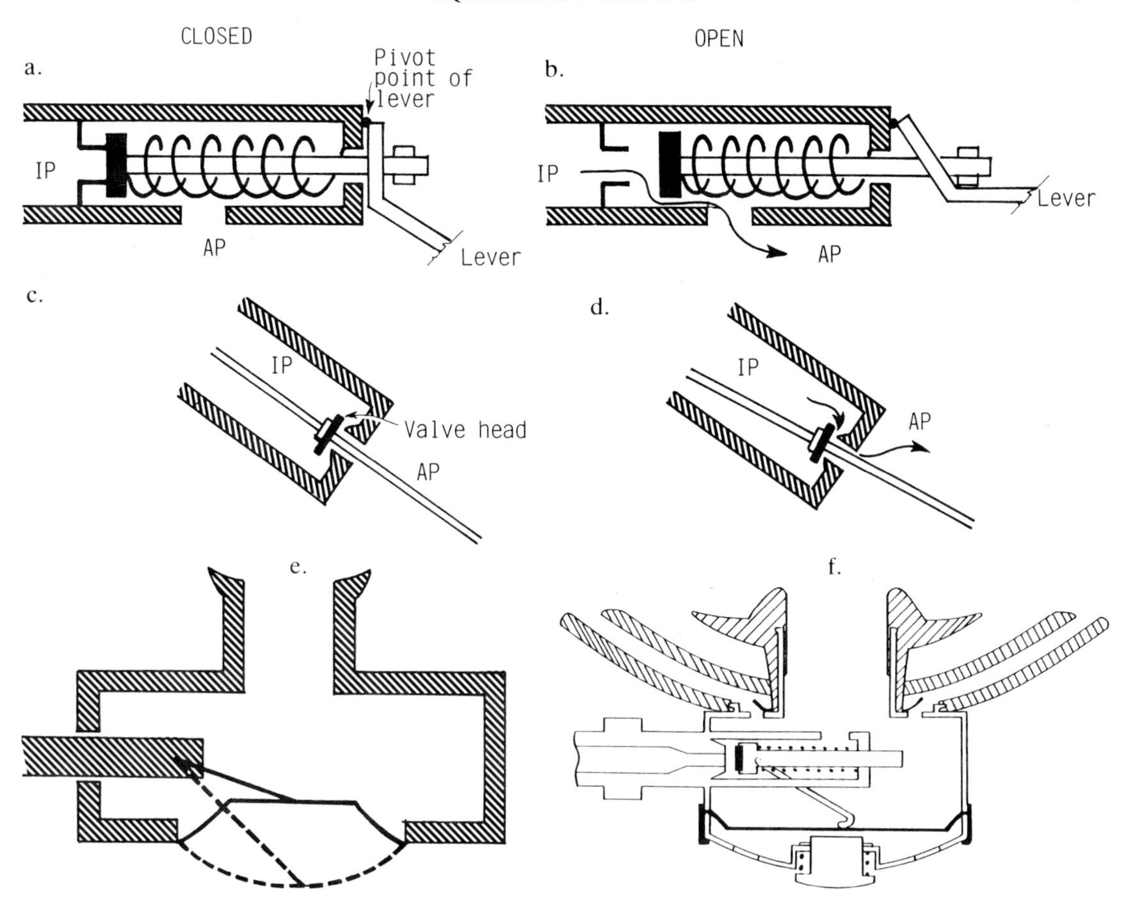

Fig. 21. Second stages of regulators. (a) and (b) show sections of a piston type second stage. The lever rests on the diaphragm shown in the lowest part of the diagram (e) where it can be seen that the diaphragm can lie in the 'inhalation' position (heavy black line) or in the exhalation position (heavy dotted line). Inhalation alters the position of the lever and this is translated in various mechanical ways to move the valve spindle against the spring so that the valve head lifts off the valve seat. The valve head has a synthetic rubber head. (a) and (b) show one of the many ways in which the mechanical movement of the lever outside the piston barrel is connected to components within (c) and (d) which show a tilt valve in the closed and open positions respectively. The change in angle of the lever is somewhat exaggerated. Details of the exhalation parts of the valve have been omitted but these are in effect fairly simple flap valves. (f) the second stage of a typical regulator shown in section.

Fig. 20. When air is breathed from the second stage the pressure in the intermediate pressure hose is reduced and the diaphragm bows in pushed by the pressure of the surrounding water. This pushes the stem of the valve so that the valve seat lifts off its seating and air flows from the high pressure side of the valve into the intermediate pressure side. However, as the intermediate pressure rises, the diaphragm is pushed away and the valve closes. The valve is of the 'upstream' type, that is the valve seat lies upstream of the orifice into the lower pressure side.

In the more modern first stage diaphragm valves a 'balanced' design is used. In this both ends of the valve stem are exposed to the downstream (intermediate) pressure. As a result the valve stem is not pushed with considerable force against the valve seat by the high pressure air.

The piston design used in many modern first stages has the moving part of the valve in the form of a piston pushing against a spring and water pressure, see Fig. 20. Details of the spring are shown in Fig. 20; it serves to ensure that the valve delivers air at the intermediate pressure (IP) about 5 to 12 Bar above ambient. The spring fits into the compartment open to the water under the piston. The valve shown is a balanced one with air at intermediate pressure acting on the back of the piston as well as on the front face of the valve seat. Note that many modern first stages are of the flow-through type in which the IP hose is fed through the piston.

Note that if the first stage valve jams open the pressure in the intermediate hose will rise. If the second stage is of the downstream type there is no problem though the valve will free-flow as air emerges through the second stage whether you are inhaling or not. This is a little unpleasant but it is still possible to breathe. If the second stage is an 'upstream' valve, i.e. one which tends to close as the higher pressure forces on it, but the first stage jams open or leaks, you have a potential problem because pressure will rise in the intermediate hose. In order to cope with this problem a pressure relief valve is fitted to the first stage so that should the pressure in the hose between the two stages begin to rise the excess pressure is relieved by the valve opening and releasing air into the water. Never adjust the setting of the pressure relief valve. If you tighten it up you may increase the interstage pressure to a point where the hose between the two stages bursts. If you slacken the relief valve you may set the interstage pressure to too low a value. Adjustment of the pressure relief valve needs expertise and access to a suitable gas pressure gauge. If the pressure relief valve leaks there may well be a small fault in the first stage.

Second stages

These are illustrated in Fig. 21. There are two main types of second stage. The more modern type of second stage is a piston-type of valve. The earlier second stages are of the 'tilt' valve type which is in effect an 'upstream' valve. In both types of second stage the pressure differences between the external (ambient) water pressure and inhalation or exhalation are sensed by a large thin diaphragm. In front of these valves the diaphragm may also serve as an exhaust valve, but it is more usual to fit a separate exhaust valve so that exhaled air passes into the surrounding water. The diaphragm moves in towards the mouthpiece on inhalation and outwards on exhalation. This movement is used to open and to close the valve. In the 'tilt' valve the diaphragm position acts directly on the valve stem, see Fig. 21. The 'tilt' valve is rocked by movement of the valve stem so that it lifts off one side of the valve seat, thus allowing air to pass through to the mouthpiece.

The piston-type second stage operates when a lever or series of levers attached to the diaphragm are moved by the movement of the diaphragm. The lever(s) pull the valve stem against the spring so that the valve opens, see Fig. 21. When the diver exhales the diaphragm moves outwards and the lever then moves so that the spring closes the valve.

Additional features of regulators

The first stage will normally be fitted with a port 'take-off' which allows a hose to a high pressure gauge to be fitted. This gauge reads the cylinder pressure and allows you to estimate the 'contents' of air you have left in the cylinder. Thus it is known as a 'Contents' gauge. It is usual in the better makes of demand valve to fit several ports on the intermediate pressure side of the first stage so that air at intermediate pressure is available for suit or/and ABLJ direct feeds and for the fitting of an extra second stage, usually known, rather quaintly, as an Octopus rig.

Care and maintenance

Regulators, though robustly made, are precision pieces of equipment so dirt, salt and sand may clog, impede or wear the valve. So the prime aspect of maintenance is to keep the regulator clean and well washed. Don't let your regulator trail in the sand on the beach or the dirty water in a boat. Wash your valve well by allowing it to soak for an hour or so in freshwater after a dive. Check that the filter on the part of the first stage that fits to the cylinder is clean and unclogged, replace it if it appears to be dirty. Bear in mind that the various 'O' rings in the regulator wear as time passes and that they will need renewal from time to time. It is a very good idea to have your regulator serviced once a year so that worn 'O' rings and other parts can be replaced and the moving parts cleaned professionally.

Other types of regulator

The original regulator used by sports divers was the single stage valve with twin hoses coming round from the valve body, behind the head, to the mouthpiece. Such regulators are almost museum pieces nowadays, even though non-divers usually imagine that they are still in use. A later variant of this valve was the twin-stage, twin-hose regulator with both valves in a single body. On occasion air may be fed to the diver from a surface supply through the intermediate pressure stage of a twin stage regulator but if this is done the diver must carry an independent reserve supply in cylinders.

(*End of Lecture 8.*)

STARTING AQUALUNG DIVING

3rd Class Diver Training

As you can see by reading the Training Schedule the 3rd Class Diver Training starts familiarising you with all the equipment you are likely to use in straightforward sports diving. You have already used mask, fins and snorkel and an ABLJ or Stab Jacket in your Snorkel Assessment. Now you add Scuba (Self contained underwater breathing apparatus) otherwise known as the Aqualung, with the weight belt you will almost certainly need to keep your buoyancy low enough for you to be able to submerge, and at least a hood and gloves. Why wear a hood and gloves? The hood gets you used to the slight isolation from noise typical of diving and using the gloves as you normally would when diving in Scottish waters means that signals have to be given very clearly and you also find that it is a little harder to use equipment when your hands are gloved. Of course you don't have to start the training wearing a hood and gloves and it is probably a good idea to work up to more and more complete equipment as your training progresses before you take any test.

You should be introduced to the equipment in a gradual and progressive manner. The first five tests must be trained for in the pool and passed before you may proceed to confined open-water. What do we mean by 'confined open-water'?

Confined openwater is water 3 to 6 metres deep with reasonable clarity and having a sand, gravel or smoothish rock bottom which slopes gently. It should be free from adverse currents or waves when it is used for training. It should be impossible to wander away from the area or to be swept out into deeper water. Long weeds or silt must be absent so that your instructor(s) can see you at all times.

After you have completed the first five tests you may at the discretion of your Instructor(s) or BDO and at your own wish move the training and testing into safe confined openwater. You will find the training slightly more difficult because you will almost certainly be using a diving suit and will have to learn buoyancy control with the suit. On the other hand you will be doing your training in almost the same conditions as you will practice diving. Obviously inland branches and anyone in winter will be less happy to move to the sea for training but in summer, and if your branch is on the coast, you may find it better to do so.

Bear in mind that you must be 15 or over and have passed a Medical Examination using the Club's Standard Form before you start using the aqualung.

During training the trainee must start with a depth of water of 2 metres or less. Your BI or BDO must have explained the dangers of pulmonary barotrauma and the methods of ear clearing and the rest of the contents of Lectures 1 to 4 before you start using the aqualung. You must always breathe regularly when using the aqualung and ensure that you surface slowly breathing in and out. Your BI must be certain that you will breathe out during ascent. If your ascent is very fast – it should not be – breathe out almost continuously but otherwise keep a steady continuous rhythm.

If you find you are getting cold during aqualung training consider using a wet or dry suit. It may be a trifle harder learning to use it but you will be more comfortable and readier for the sea when your training is complete.

THE TRAINING AND TESTING

1. *Assemble, test and put on equipment.*

The correct sequence of dressing is:

1. To don suit if used.
2. Fit hood if separate from suit.
3. Fill emergency bottle for ABLJ or Stab Jacket from the main cylinder and then refit the emergency cylinder to the jacket.
4. If an ABLJ is being used put it on now.
5. Attach the Regulator to the cylinder and test its function.
6. If an ABLJ is being worn put on the aqualung and do up its harness, *or* if a Stab Jacket is being used attach the aqualung to the Stab Jacket and then put on the stabjacket plus aqualung. Do up harness.
7. Fit the weight belt. (If using certain types of stab jacket this will have to be done before stage 6.)
8. Have the BI check out your equipment. Obtain his or her permission to enter the water having received a briefing on the training testing you are about to undertake.

In detail the stages you need to work through are covered by the following paragraphs.

The Emergency cylinder is filled by mating its filling port under the A-clamp to the orifice of the pillar valve on the main cylinder. Make sure that the O-ring of the pillar valve is correctly seated under the filling port. Open the valve on the emergency cylinder. As you do this keep your head well clear since in the remote event of the O-ring bursting out under pressure you do not want to catch the ring in your eye or ear. There is also a remote possibility of the circlip fitted to stop the 'bleed' valve, a short cylinder, breaking or being missing. If either of these events happen then when you turn on the cylinder with air pressure in it the valve body will fly out like a projectile. So that is another reason for standing clear. Then open the main cylinder valve and allow the emergency cylinder to fill so continue to keep your head clear. Provided both valves are properly open the emergency cylinder will fill rapidly. Turn off both valves and then use the bleed valve to remove pressure from the small space between the two valves. Then you can remove the emergency cylinder and refit it to the ABLJ or Stab Jacket, making sure that it is properly in place. And then put on the ABLJ if you are using that type of equipment. Note that the long strap from neck through the crotch to the front of the jacket should be fitted before any waist strap so that the waist strap holds the other one in place and stops it drifting into other bits of equipment.

The Regulator is fitted to the pillar valve by the same type of A-clamp as is used on the Emergency cylinder (in UK, US and most of Europe), though screw threads are used in some countries often on a reverse (left-hand) thread. Once again make sure that your head is well clear when you turn the pillar valve on just in case an O-ring escapes. After a moment or two the various correct air pressures will be established in the various sections of the regulator though some modern regulators will produce a two to three second blast of air through the regulator mouthpiece at this moment. The pressure on the contents gauge should now show the correct cylinder pressure and thus indicate how much air you have for your dive. If there is any appreciable sound of escaping air turn off the pillar valve. If there are small leaks ask your BI for help and advice.

The next stage of testing that your equipment is working is to try breathing from the regulator. If it breathes in and out without undue resistance, especially on exhaling, your equipment is probably working correctly.

But there could be a problem still. Turn off the air supply at the pillar valve and then continue breathing from the regulator. Very soon you should empty the regulator of any high pressure air and there will be total resistance to breathing. Or at least there should be. But if you can still draw air in then there must be a leak, probably in the second stage of the regulator. In that case the equipment is faulty and you would breathe water as soon as you submerged. Always carry out this test.

If the equipment passed this test turn the pillar valve on again. Read the contents gauge if fitted and be prepared to tell your BI what that pressure was.

Incidentally, you should note that all modern contents gauges are made with a bursting disc in the back or side of the gauge so that if air escapes from the Bourdon tube or other sensor inside the gauge it must have an escape route. Consequently it is exceedingly improbable that the contents gauge face glass (or plastic) will break if the gauge is faulty.

If you are using an ABLJ you already have it on you but if you are using a Stab Jacket you fit the cylinder into the Stab Jacket (most of which are fitted with a cam-action lever to snap the binding band around the cylinder tight). Make sure that the cylinder is at the correct position in relation to the rest of the jacket. If it is too high the pillar valve will tower over or even bump into your head. If it is too low the cylinder will bump into your bottom, make it difficult to put on a weight belt and make use of the regulator difficult.

Then put on the cylinder plus regulator over your ABLJ or with Stab Jackets put on the whole assembly. Connect up the Stab Jacket harness. Connect any direct feeds ports that may be fitted to suit or/and Stab Jackets to their hoses from the regulator. It should be noted that during initial training it may be confusing to use these direct feeds during the first few pool sessions.

Some people will find lifting the equipment onto their back difficult and help should certainly be sought if needed. However, if you do have difficulty work out a way to get it on efficiently and easily by yourself. You might find that you have to put it on by yourself in an emergency where your help is really needed! Putting the equipment on a ledge is often a help. Make sure that the shoulder straps are sufficiently loose for you to be able to get into the equipment easily.

Finally, fit the weight belt. Make sure that it lies over all other equipment so that if released in emergency it will fall clear away from you. Make sure that the belt is reasonably tight so that it does not slip off or turn round on your body during the dive so that the quick release is behind you. Also make sure that the weights on the belt are placed equally on either side of your midline, otherwise you may find yourself 'listing'.

Check-out.

This is an essential practice for real diving so start getting used to the practice as early in your training as possible. First, you should check everything yourself. It is a good idea to work out a system for this so that it is easy to remember all the items that should be checked.

The check-out makes sure that (i) that you have all the equipment you need for the dive, (ii) that it is correctly and securely fitted, (iii) that you have sufficient air in your main cylinder and any emergency cylinder and (iv) that the regulator and all other items are actually working. It is also essential that your BI or an experienced buddy checks everything, not only because two pairs of eyes are better than one pair, but also because your BI must be assured that you are properly equipped for training. Since you may be working in confined openwater in full equipment from quite an early stage in training this check out is for real right from the start. You should also check out your buddy, not only because once again two pairs of eyes are better than one pair, but so you learn that others rely on you to, which is your correct role as a buddy diver.

2. *Snorkelling in full equipment.*

Once you move to the openwater you will need to snorkel out to the dive site and back inshore at the end of the dive. (Or usually at least a little way on the surface if you dive from a boat.) Using your regulator while you are doing this is wasteful of air. So in this piece of training you get used to snorkelling in full diving equipment. You start by adjusting your buoyancy so that you are neutral in the water. If you are very over-weighted or underweighted take off or add weight to your weight belt until you are approximately at neutral buoyancy. Then complete final adjustments by adding or dumping air from your ABLJ. Try and get the weighting so that you have very little air left in your jacket when you are neutral. This will (see page 18 keep your jacket from taking in a little water when you dive).

During training try to make sure that you use the same aqualung and ABLJ/Stab Jacket each time: otherwise you may have to readjust your weighting at the start of every session. It is in your interest as well as that of the BI to use the same set of equipment each time at this stage of training. Later on, when you are fairly experienced, it becomes a good idea to learn how different types of equipment change your buoyancy requirements as well as other matters.

How do you judge buoyancy neutrality? Well, on the surface you should float if you are upright in the water with the water level near the top of your mask. You'll have to be using your snorkel to check this buoyancy. Don't cheat yourself by finning during this buoyancy check.

Then fin 200 metres making a duck dive to the bottom (2m-3m) at least once every 20m. Show that you can clear your snorkel, either by exhaling strongly into it or by raising your head a little and getting your snorkel to drain. The first method is the usual method of clearing. You must of course learn to judge when you have regained the surface otherwise clearing your snorkel will not work.

3. *Submerge for 30 seconds underwater without mask, snorkel or regulator.*

Keep your ABLJ/Stabjacket and weight belt on so that you can (a) submerge and (b) regain the surface easily if you have to by using your jacket for emergency buoyancy. But you should not have to because the preceding exercise should have got your buoyancy exactly right. Now all you have to do is show that you can hold your breath for at least 30 seconds underwater. Why? Because various of the following pieces of training need some ability at breath holding. Don't try to take in a large breath before submerging: this usually makes you want to breath again rather soon.

4. *Regulator clearing.*

If your regulator mouthpiece falls out, or gets pulled out (eg. by finning past an obstruction that catches a regulator hose), or if you have to share a regulator with a buddy or if you start to breathe from your ABLJ/Stab Jacket, or if you fill it orally and then return to the regulator you have to be able to clear the mouthpiece of water.

Methods.

1. Clear the mouthpiece by exhaling into the regulator. This assumes that you have some air

in your lungs when you need to clear the regulator.

2. Use the 'purge' button on the regulator housing to clear the mouthpiece.

3. Drink the water down. It sounds unpleasant but is not really so though if the water is polluted you might hesitate.

4. With some regulators you can get the regulator to purge itself, either by jerking on the intermediate pressure hose or by suddenly pulling the mouthpiece upwards in the water.

If you are using an old-fashioned twin hose valve you may find that rather a lot of water has to be cleared and, of course, you do not have method 2 available.

5. *Adjusting buoyancy to neutrality underwater orally and with a direct feed.*

When you are diving you need to develop a very good sense of whether you are neutrally buoyant or not and of adjusting buoyancy to achieve this. If you don't learn this you will either fail to get underwater or have to fin very hard to keep yourself in position or find yourself sinking. At least you will have to work much harder than you ought and run the risk of 'yo-yoing' up and down as you try to get your buoyancy right. Worse, you put yourself at more risk of accident if your buoyancy is wrong.

For this exercise, and only for this exercise, add 3kg of weight to your weight belt. Submerge using full equipment in 2 to 3 metres of water with your BI beside you. Learn to add air to the ABLJ/Stab Jacket orally (see pp. 17-19) till you float in midwater with little or no finning. Then repeat this practice using the direct feed to fill the Jacket. You must remember just where the dump valve pull or the ABLJ/Stab Jacket mouthpiece dump are so that you can release air if you become too buoyant.

6. *Mask clearing.*

An essential skill for the diver because you are almost certain to get water into your mask while diving and are nearly as certain to get your mask totally flooded. See p. 15 for methods.

You should have been following the training and testing in the sequence laid down here and in the Training Schedule. If you have, and both you and your BDO wish and agree, you may move to safe confined open water for the succeeding stages of training. (Tests 7 to 12.) If you do you will have to use a wet or dry suit in UK (and many other) waters which requires some experience in itself. You do not have to move to open water if conditions or your wishes are so until after Test 12.

7. *Refitting equipment underwater.*

This perhaps is the central part of Third Class training. Several of the tests you should have passed by the time you come to the training for this exercise are designed to help you with this part of the training. Basically this training ensures that:

(i) You have a familiarity with your equipment and are utterly happy with it.
(ii) You can work with equipment and adjust it when you can only feel it, and solve problems with its adjustment underwater.
(iii) You can do all this with water in contact with your face and with a certain period of breath holding.
(iv) You have good buoyancy control.

The good diver – you do plan to be one, don't you – knows the feel of his or her equipment all the time and senses if anything is getting misplaced, slipping off or starting to work erratically or wrongly. When things go wrong your reaction should be one of calmly thinking what to do and of not rushing into some reflex reaction. Since an accident may knock your mask off or leave you in black water without a working torch you must be able to do things by touch and without panic. For instance if your mouthpiece comes out and your first mouthful is water.

This training examines the skill and potential of the diver more thoroughly than any other. It's true that it is unlikely, though not impossible, that you will really have to refit your complete equipment underwater during a real dive but you may well have to do some of it if bits of equipment fall off or start to come loose or displaced.

The test passing performance is one in which the equipment to be refitted lies in a difficult unknown position and which you refit onto yourself in a methodical manner. A very slick performance in which everything happens to be in just the right place might be no test at all. BIs should never take a single correct performance as proof that you can refit the equipment reliably. Reliably means every time.

Training

Since this is a searching piece of training work though the component parts – which are:

Buoyancy control
Working without a mask
Feeling equipment to find where it is and how it is to be fitted.
Mask clearing
Regulator clearing
and
Weight belt positioning

Methods

There are many acceptable methods of refitting equipment. The most important matters are summarised by the word 'style', ie. calm, methodical, reliable and sensible.

It may help you to know that there are several successful sensible methods, and that you should try several methods and find which suits you best.

Remove the equipment on the bottom and pass to a BI who will return it to you to be refitted without resurfacing. This means that you should take the set off and continue to breathe from it till the last possible moment. The BI should not deprive you of air for more than twenty seconds, and less during initial training. So dump buoyancy from your ABLJ or Stab Jacket, take off your fins, remove your weight belt and lay it on your lap. Loosen all straps and undo any waist buckles. If you are using a Stab Jacket with the cylinder and regulator take it off probably as you would a jacket : continue to breathe from the set which you would stand up or lay beside you. If you are using an ABLJ take off the aqualung but keep your ABLJ on. Take off your mask. Lay it beside you. Hand the set to the BI relinquishing the regulator, and put the weight belt on the pool bottom.

The BI may turn off the aqualung but should advise you if he or she is going to do this. Refitting is started by the BI putting the set on the bottom very close to you and tapping you with a pre-arranged signal. Take hold of the weight belt and establish breathing at this point, put the set on, do up its harness, refit the weight belt, refit your fins and lastly your mask. The BI might make you swim a very short distance by putting the set just beyond your reach. If you happen to be very buoyant you may need to wear a very light additional weight belt that keeps you from floating up while you are waiting for equipment. Good luck!

If you can reach the set and weight belt you might as well remain sitting on the pool bottom, making sure that you put the weight belt first on your lap if the set is buoyant. But if you have to swim even a small distance things become harder. Your approach to the sequence of events will depend on how buoyant the set is. Possibly the weight belt will have been put on the set, lying across it to stop it floating to the surface.

How do you solve the refitting problem now. Here are some alternatives:

1. Swim across the pool floor and lie with your head at the pillar valve end of the aqualung, see Figs 22-39. Try to lie prone on the pool floor. Do not let any part of your body float up because that is the start of floating up to the surface. If the weight belt is holding the set down hold onto the set and weight belt with one hand, say by grasping the back pack and weight belt together and use your other hand to turn the pillar valve on. Put the regulator mouthpiece in your mouth and begin breathing. Put your free hand onto the pillar valve and take hold of it. Make sure that the weight belt is not snagged in the harness and move it away from the set, meanwhile still holding the set with your other hand. Roll back into a sitting position with the aqualung cylinder between your legs and simultaneously putting the weight belt across your lap or thigh.

Ensure that the set lies in the way shown in Fig. 28 so that the arm straps are nice and clear. Alternatively if you plan to put the equipment on like a jacket stand the set up beside you as in Fig. 36. It is important to get the set into a known position with the harness clear of tangles because if you do not you are going to get into an incredible tangle when you come to put the set on. You could end up with the cylinder upside down, or back to front etc!

When you are sure that everything is right, slip your arms through the shoulder straps and either put the set on over your head or like a jacket. When the set is in place on your back do up the harness, refit the weight belt, fins and then mask in that order.

Some important points.

Perhaps the most critical point is keeping yourself on the pool bottom. If the set or the set plus the Stab-Jacket are positively buoyant you must have the weight belt holding you down before you take hold of the set. If the set is negatively buoyant you will not need to take hold of the weight belt first. When you do take that first breath don't go for broke on the air, otherwise you'll become too buoyant with big breaths.

When you turn the pillar valve on do realise that you'll get a reasonable amount of air with

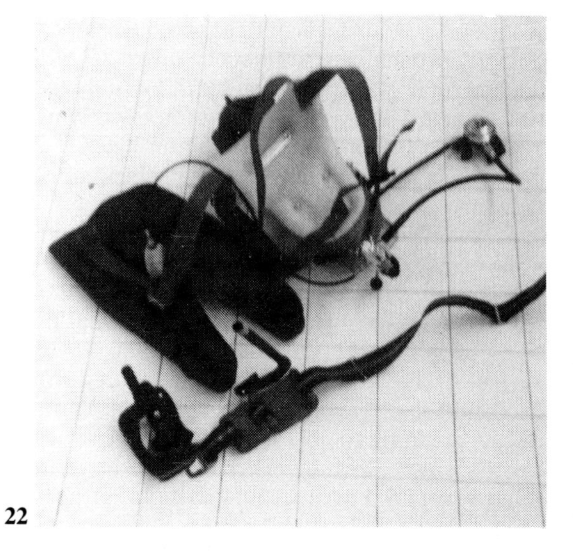
22

2

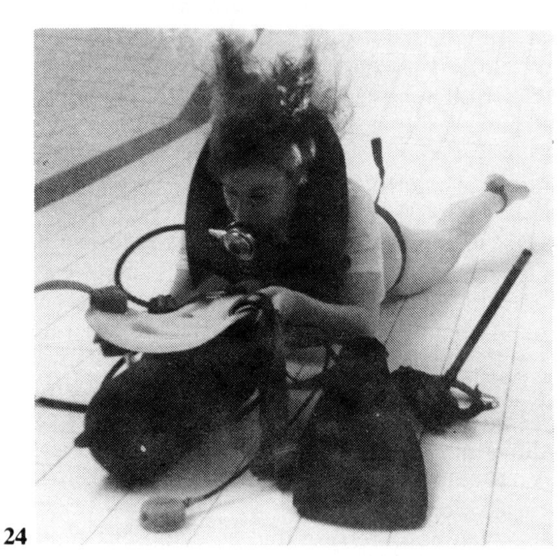
24

2

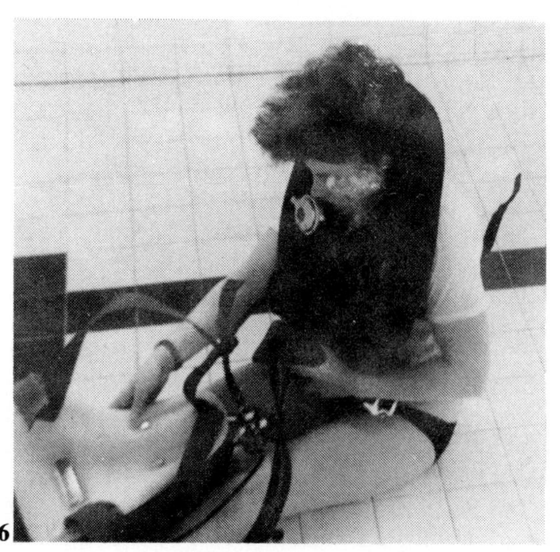
26

2

Figs. 22-35. Refitting an aqualung. Method A as described in the text.

28

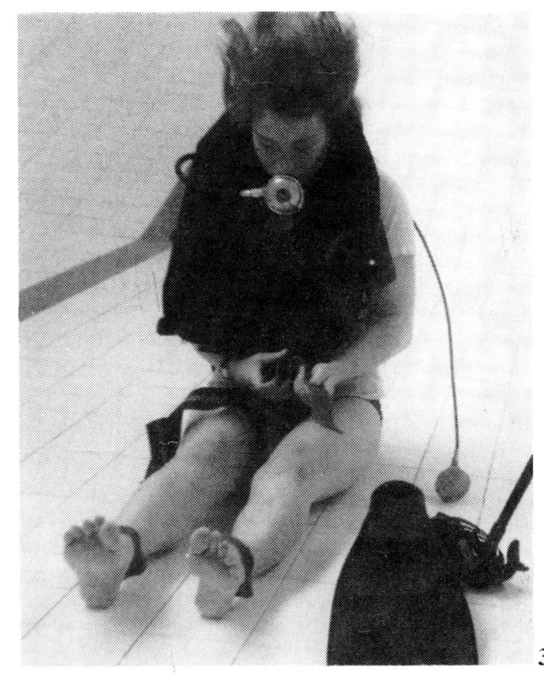

31

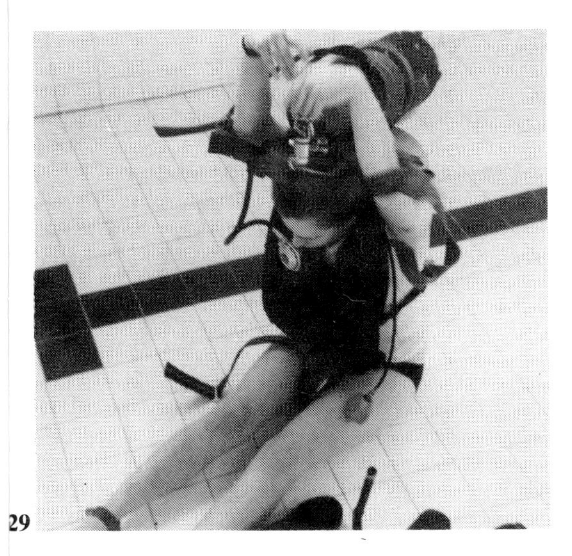

29

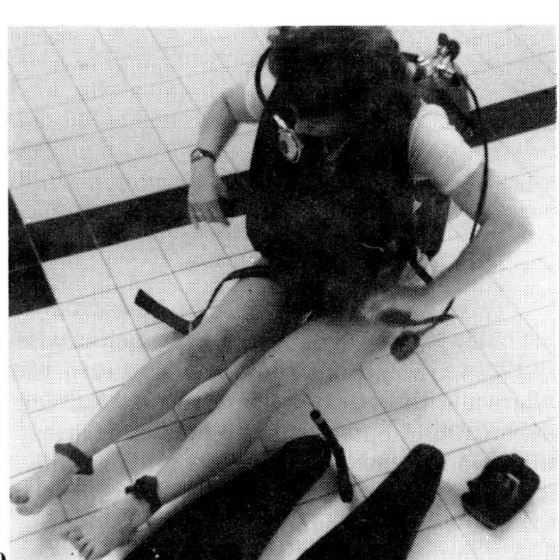

30

Fig. 22. The equipment laid on the pool bottom for refitting. Note the neat arrangement with each item separate but nearby. The aqualung lies with its back-pack uppermost which will help refitting, see later.

Fig. 23. First contact with the aqualung. Note that the diver is right down on the pool bottom. She is using her left hand to turn on the pillar valve while her right hand holds the aqualung itself. Note that she has not disturbed her fins and mask.

Fig. 24. The regulator mouthpiece is now in the diver's mouth and she has just taken the first breath from it and exhaled once. Note her prone position and that she has taken hold of the back-pack of the aqualung just before.

Fig. 25. Turning over to lift the aqualung onto her lap, Fig. 26. Note that she holds one fin in place to avoid displacing it while turning. In Fig. 26 she moves the weight belt to her lap.

Fig. 27. She finds the shoulder straps of the aqualung and places her arms through these straps using the system shown in Fig. 28.

Fig. 29. She now lifts the aqualung over her head, working the straps down to her armpits. If the cylinder is positively buoyant she may need to reach behind her and pull the cylinder down by its waist strap.

Figs. 30-31. The waist strap of the cylinder is now buckled up.

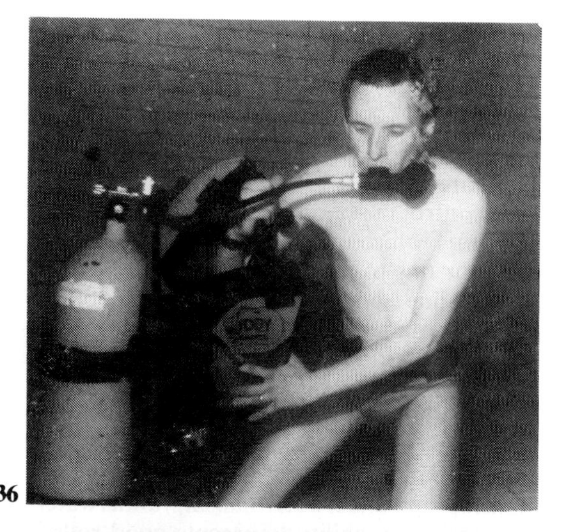

36

37

38

39

Figs. 36-39. Refitting a set mounted on a stab jacket. Fig. 36 shows the diver breathing from the set which is standing up on his right-hand side. Fig. 37 shows him putting his right-hand and arm through the shoulder strap of the jacket and starting to swing the equipment onto his back. In Fig. 38 he pulls the right-hand shoulder strap tight and works his left arm through the other strap. Note that he has already put the weight belt on because he finds it easiest to put the set on in a kneeling position. Later he will refit the belt over the stab jacket waist strap. Fig. 39 he does up the breast strap of the jacket.

No regulator or snorkel should be in use because you need to talk to the victim and maybe go on to EAR.

If the water was very rough you and the victim might be happier with masks in place and a firm grip from behind but this would not be effective for EAR.

10. *Simulating entry into a dive boat – refitting set etc. in water.*

We expect that very soon you will be diving and that some of that diving will be done from an inflatable or other small boat. Getting into such boats, and sometimes into larger boats, normally means, unless you are abnormally strong, that you must take off your weight belt and set and hand them to someone in the boat before getting yourself out of the water.

Occasionally you may need to refit a set on the surface while in the water so the training also experiences you in this aspect of diving.

First make sure that you are reasonably buoyant so inflate your ABLJ or Stabjacket slightly. In reality you'll probably come to do this almost naturally at the end of a dive-to make the end of the dive nice and relaxing. Loosen the weight belt, make sure that you have a good grip of it and take it off. Some weight belts are arranged so that the weights can slide off from the end opposite the buckle. In such a case make sure that you hold onto that end. Hand the weight belt to a person leaning over the pool side – or the boat if you are in openwater.

Then disconnect any direct feeds in use if you are wearing an ABLJ. Then undo the waist strap of your aqualung and loosen or open any shoulder straps that you need to to take the set off. Most people take the set off like a jacket but it is permissible to duck down and lift the set off over your head. If you are taking it off like a jacket you can turn your back to the boat or pool side and give the person on the boat or poolside the opportunity to lift the set by its harness from the water, see Fig. 40b. Otherwise you are going to have to push the cylinder up in front of you to your poolside or boat-based helper.

If you are using a Stab jacket you may be able to release the cylinder (plus regulator) if you can open the cam action binding band that may be fitted. Make sure that the cylinder does not drop away into the depths. To ensure this ask the poolside or boat-based helper to take hold of the cylinder before you release it. Otherwise undo the Stab Jacket waist belt, chest strap (if fitted) or unzip the front if that is the sort of Jacket you have and if necessary loosen or even undo a shoulder strap. Take the jacket plus set off and hand to the helper.

The final stage of this exercise is to refit the set or set plus Stab Jacket and then the weight belt while in the water. Basically fairly easy but you don't want to crash into the poolside or boat while you do this, so stand off a little. Leaning a little forward in the water will make it easier to get these items onto your body. Don't forget to reconnect any direct feeds which should be in use.

Fig. 40a. Using a diving ladder on a largish hard boat. Normally the diver takes off his or her fins before climbing the ladder. Note the way the ladder hooks over the bulwark and the arm with pad holding the ladder out from the hull.

11. *Alternating between snorkel and aqualung etc.*

The training for this stage simulates the process of starting a dive by changing from snorkel to aqualung and also the process of finishing a dive by surfacing and returning to snorkel from using the aqualung. It is wasteful of air and reveals a lack of competence if you start and finish a dive by using your regulator on the surface as you fin out to and in from the dive site.

You must be able to dive down quickly and neatly at the start of a dive and not delay other divers while you get organised for the dive. If the dive leader has left the surface after exchanging 'Down' signals with you, you have not long before he or she will be out of sight in the depths though of course they ought to watch what you are doing. At times you may need to fit the regulator into your mouth while you are already underwater.

Surfacing procedures (see also p. 8) are also important. Many accidents have happened because the diver has surfaced in rough water taken out the mouthpiece and started to open his or her mouth, to breathe or talk, only to find that a wave jumps down his or her throat. This has been the start of a choking fit. So the normal practice is to approach the surface and change from regulator to snorkel just below the surface, clearing it as you break through the sur-

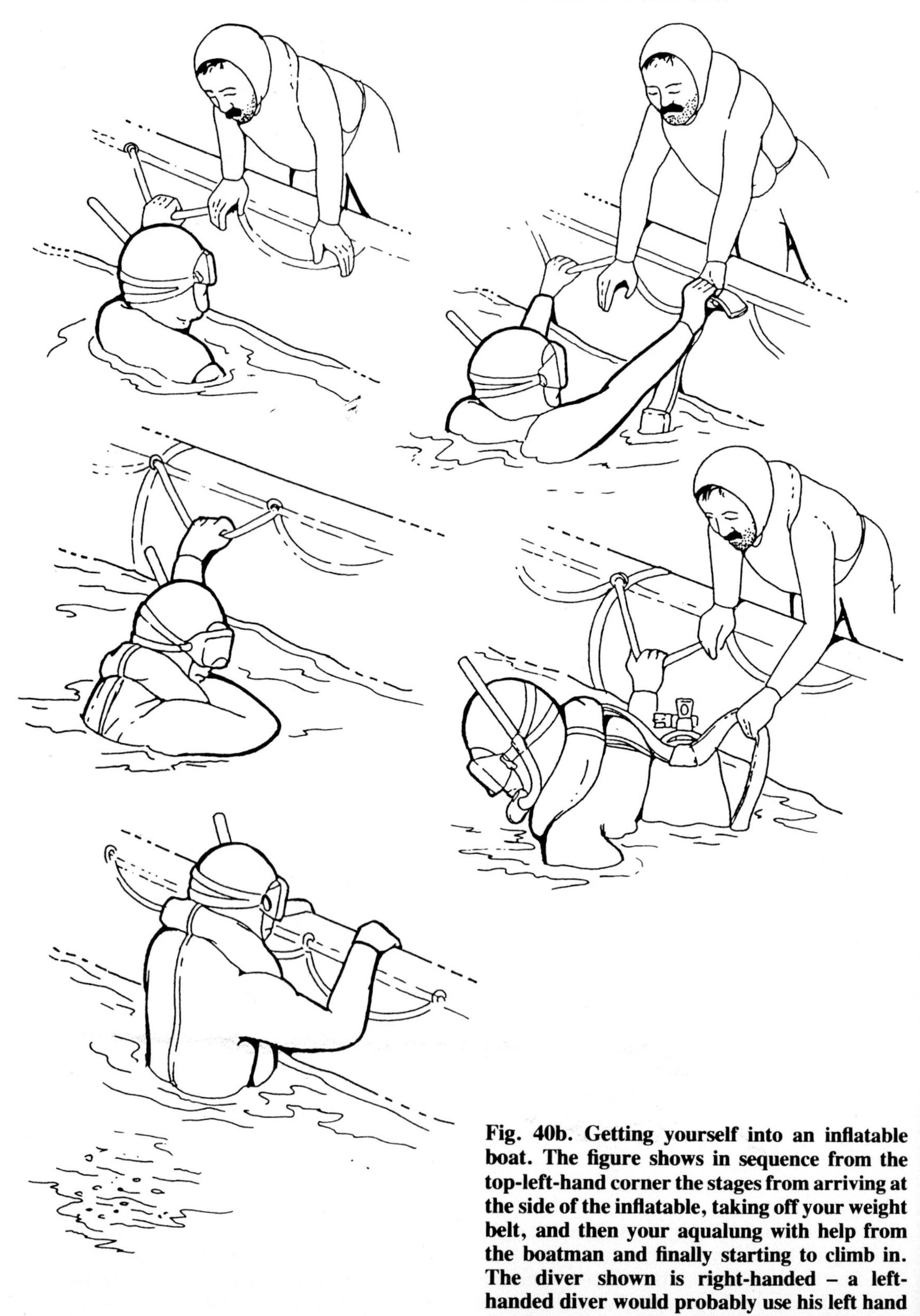

Fig. 40b. Getting yourself into an inflatable boat. The figure shows in sequence from the top-left-hand corner the stages from arriving at the side of the inflatable, taking off your weight belt, and then your aqualung with help from the boatman and finally starting to climb in. The diver shown is right-handed – a left-handed diver would probably use his left hand to release gear and would take the set off taking his right arm out of the shoulder strap first.

face. You can assess the surface situation while using a snorkel, give an OK signal to your buddy and then to shore and boat, and then if all seems well and the water is not too rough start that conversation. You can face away from the waves if you need to talk.

It is acceptable to fit the snorkel on the surface but it is much neater to fit in the last half-metre below the surface. This should also encourage you to make that last metre or two a slow ascent, a good practice in itself. This means that you must know just where to find the snorkel.

So in the first part of the exercise you alternate between snorkel on the surface and aqualung underwater. In the second part of the exercise you fin on the surface on your back breathing through your mouth (or nose) with your mask pushed back onto your forehead. This simulates the finning position of the slightly exhausted diver on the surface.

12. *Regulator sharing.*

Another essential diving skill! You may never have to do it in hot blood but you must always be prepared to do it. If your air supply, or that of your buddy, fails sharing is the preferred solution to the problem.

Basically, as you probably already know, you take two breaths from the regulator and then hand to your buddy who takes two breaths and returns the regulator to you. And so on with a nice controlled ascent as you do this.

So you must hold each other, not only for that friendly reassurance but to make sure that the regulator being used actually reaches to each diver's mouth. The type of regulator, the length of regulator hose and other matters determine how you will position yourself relative to the other diver. You must decide this in a predive checkout and perhaps even check on dry land just how each of you will position yourself. In most real situations you, if you are the person providing air, are effectively to some extent a rescuer and give, after agreement by signals, the lead in ascent. If the person whose air supply has failed is slightly worried or preoccupied the rescuer may need to do most of the finning and ascent rate checking.

How do you hold each other? Well it depends, as we said, partly on equipment but a firm one-handed hold under the armpit or possibly on the aqualung harness should be good. You need the other hand to pass the regulator over to your buddy and to fit it to your mouth when you are going to breathe. You need that hand to give signals, to make buoyancy adjustments etc. while your buddy is breathing. See Fig. 41 for a suggested hold. The sharing starts with its special signal, see Fig. 46 and if you are merely practicing a prearranged sharing drill combine this share signal with an OK signal to make sure everyone knows it is just a practice. In practice or reality spend a few exchanges just getting the rhythm of sharing before moving to the ascent and the donor should start moving after he or she has given an 'Up' signal to which the buddy has signalled 'OK'.

Fig. 41. The sharing position. The divers are shown well apart which is the best position if the regulator hose is long enough so that they have room to fin without colliding with each other. They hold each other by the arm-pits or by harness straps in the vicinity of the arm-pit. Note that the donor (on the right) does not hold the regulator while letting the victim breathe from it. The donor needs a spare hand for signals or adjustment to buoyancy etc. In a moment they will swop the regulator mouthpiece back to the donor and the victim will have a spare hand for signals etc. Note that the donor is breathing out while the victim has the regulator and is inhaling.

Do not ram the mouthpiece into your buddy's mouth. Try not to even hold the regulator hose while she or he fits it to their mouth. It gives a sense of near panic if you hang onto the regulator and if you have your hand anywhere near the mouthpiece while your buddy is trying to fit it to their mouth they are going to find it harder to do. Inexperienced instructors sometimes teach that the donor must always hold the regulator or its hose. In any event in reality you are going to need that spare hand for adjustments to your own equipment if nothing else. (We would agree that in the pool situation you might get away without having to use your hand for adjustment but not so in open water.) While you are giving the regulator to your buddy you must check that they do not drop it and be ready to pick it up and return it to the other diver.

Even in the pool situation, which is a simulation in which you are not making much of an ascent, bear in mind that there is a risk of pulmonary barotrauma and in a 'for real' situation or in open water sharing exercises this is much increased because you should be making a fairly rapid ascent, say 15m per minute. So while your buddy is using the regulator keep your mouth slack and let air trickle out as though it is expanding in your lungs.

There are several good training games to improve your abilities in this vital exercise see the *Advanced Training Manual.*

13. *Blacked out mask exercise.*

This is an exercise for which you cannot effectively train – the only one like this. If you are claustrophobic – fear of confinement and being in the dark – you should not dive. Wearing a blacked-out mask will stimulate claustrophobia in those who are susceptible. If you cannot manage this exercise you probably should not dive any more. Sorry! Forcing yourself through the test is not a good idea because if fifty metres in a clear warm pool is going to worry you what about the same distance in black, muddy water with all manner of obstructions around twenty to thirty metres below the surface!

In the test you will be required to fin 50 metres in mid water (ie. about 1 metre depth) using your aqualung and being led by your BI holding your hand. Extend an arm in front of you to warn you of worse collisions with others or the pool side. You will probably veer to one side or the other. Veering is not a reason for failing the test but it may be of value for you to know that you have right wing or left wing tendencies.

14. *Emergency Drill.*

This drill simulates a complete rescue from underwater. A fellow diver simulates unconsciousness and lies on the pool bottom or on the sea bed in shallow water. You fin 50 metres at speed to them. If the exercise is carried out in safe openwater, or in a pool without lane markings your BI may need to provide some indication of which way to fin, eg. a bottom line. The purpose of the 'speedy' approach is to simulate the fact that you will not be totally rested when you start your rescue and should already be closing in fast on your 'subject'.

Obviously if the diver is unconscious they are not going to give any hand signals but you should give an 'OK' signal on approach as the failure of a diver to respond to this signal is reason in itself for thinking something is wrong.

If necessary release the subject's weight belt, always before you release your own, so that the subject tends to float while you still have the ability to descend if necessary. Indeed do not release your own weight belt unless it is clear that you have got to in order to get the necessary extra buoyancy. If you think you can get the subject and yourself to the surface without any weight belt release all the better. Do not use any direct feed to add air to an ABLJ or Stabjacket underwater in this exercise. In reality you might add air this way to the victim's jacket. Oral inflation of the subject's jacket underwater is permitted in this exercise but will delay your reaching the surface if you could have reached it by sheer finning ability. And speed is of the essence!

Bring the subject up facing them so that in reality the condition of the subject could be watched. On the surface make the subject reasonably buoyant by jacket inflation and yourself as well but remember that achieving over-buoyancy can actually hinder a rescue and wastes time. Start giving EAR (see pp. 24-26 and Figs. 11, 13 and 14). When EAR is underway begin towing. A close in chin tow or an over the head tow may be good. Continue EAR while towing 50m.

Complete the exercise in water which is too deep to stand in (eg poolside at deep end or by a moored inflatable). Remove any remaining weight belts and hand to an assistant on the poolside or in the boat. Remove the aqualung sets. If either of you is wearing a Stab Jacket take off the cylinder separately if you can, see above, rather than taking off the whole device. Give the victim EAR from time to time at pauses in removing equipment.

Get yourself onto the poolside or into the boat. Lift the victim out by getting his or her chest onto the poolside or inflatable tube and then carefully lifting the rest of their body in. Hold their head carefully while doing this so that their neck is not suddenly strained. Carry out EAR and simulated external cardiac massage (ECC, see page 26). If you are landing the subject in a boat it may be necessary to transfer him or her to dry land or something else with a hard surface before attempting this part of the exercise. And while doing these last stages you are going to be asked questions about your knowledge of EAR, ECC and treatment of the drowning person!

15. *Dive practice.*

This is the practice either for your debut to the open water or if you have been training in 2 to 3 metres depth of open water to slightly greater depths (6 to 10m). You are using a suit, perhaps not for the first time, and of course, gloves, hood as well as all the essential equipment. In this dive your instructor is going to present to you all the problems that you have trained for. The exercise will certainly include a rescue and the adjusting of buoyancy to neutral. If you are wearing a wet suit the adjustment will be done with your ABLJ/Stab Jacket but if you use a dry suit you will need to adjust your dry suit. In addition the instructor should find a reason for including every signal so you are likely to have to share, adjust the instructor's equipment, show your contents gauge as well as deal with the loss of your mask and regulator.

DIVING HAND SIGNALS

It should be obvious that you must dive with one or two partners for reasons of your and their safety and thus that you and they should be able to communicate. The main cheap, simple and reliable method of signalling is the use of hand signals, though rope signals, either between divers by a 'buddy'line' or between a diver and a surface attendant, are easy to use. See *Advanced Dive Training Manual* for rope, torch and other signals. As a consequence there is an internationally recognised set of hand signals for use in diving and these must be learnt before your first dive. This hand signal system is the one adopted by CMAS (World Underwater Federation). Nevertheless if you dive with divers trained abroad you should check that they are using the same set of hand signals as you, because unification throughout the world is still far from complete.

Signals should always be given clearly and decisively. A vague slow movement of the hand might be mistaken by your partner for some meaningless accidental flapping of your hand. Face towards your partner as you signal and make sure that the signal is not concealed by you or his equipment or by disturbed mud. If you think that the signal might not be seen, tap your partner and then give the signal close to his face in his field of vision. If the water is dark and you have a torch illuminate the signal from the side: do not shine the torch into your partner's face. If your partner does not respond to a clearly given signal, which has been repeated twice, you should assume that he or she may be unwell or narcosed and consequently start lifting him or her to the surface or until a satisfactory OK signal is given.

Hand signals fall into four official groups and one optional group, the last being of useful signals used by SSAC but which have no official equivalent. These groups are:

(A) The OK signal.
(B) Normal dive signals.
(C) Adversity signals, requiring immediate action to help the diver giving the signal.
(D) Information signals.
and
(E) Additional information signals.

A. *The OK signal*

This signal, illustrated in Fig. 3 p. 8, has a unique status because it is used both to signal about your diving condition and as a response to other signals to indicate that you have received them. Thus your dive leader will give you the OK signal from time to time to check that everything is all right with you. Your response if OK is to give the signal back, if you're not OK you give the appropriate signal from one of the other groups. If your partner gives you any other signal you should respond with an OK signal if you agree to do it or a stop signal if you do not. Thus if your partner gives you the 'I'm out of air' signal and you are a few metres away, you give the OK signal to indicate that you've seen him and immediately fin towards him and offer him your mouthpiece when close up. In this particular instance the only permissible response is to offer air: anyone who refuses ought to be banned from diving forever. If your partner gave you a 'Distress' signal and you were a few metres away your OK signal in response would reassure him that help is coming. If he or she gave you for example a 'Down' signal you would normally give an OK signal but you might respond with a 'Stop' signal if for any reason you did not want to descend at that moment.

B. *Normal dive signals*

These are the signals which, together with the OK signal, will be given during a dive in which no untoward incident occurs. They are:

'DOWN' Fig. 42
'STOP' Fig. 43
'UP' Fig. 44
'I'M ON RESERVE' (CMAS)
or:
'MY CONTENTS GAUGE READS 30 BAR OR LESS' Fig. 45
'DIRECTION' Pointing extended arm and hand in direction to be followed (not illustrated).

These, together with OK signals exchanged with you by the dive leader, should form the set of signals used in a normal dive. The signal in the list above (**'My contents gauge reads 30 Bar or less'**) is the signal to terminate the dive and ascend to the surface at 0.3 metres per second or slower, turning around and looking up at about 3m depth to see if any surface hazards like boats (power boats can also be heard) or breakers are around. If these hazards are close wait at 3m till boats have moved away or move sideways if near big breakers. Then surface with arms outstretched upwards giving OK signal, unless in distress, to boat or shore dive marshal. Change over to snorkels as soon as possible and fin ashore or towards pick-up boat.

C. *Adversity signals*

These signals are given when something is seriously wrong and the dive partner *must* give help. The signals are:

'I HAVE NO MORE AIR' Fig. 46
'I AM IN DISTRESS'
For underwater see Fig. 3
For surface see Fig. 3
'I CANNOT PULL MY RESERVE'
or
'MY AIR SUPPLY IS GIVING TROUBLE' Fig. 47

'I have no more air' is given when the air supply fails, for whatever reason, and the partner must, on seeing it, respond by sharing or by providing the spare mouthpiece of an octopus rig (or if he or she is experienced, by handing over the mouthpiece and starting breathing from his or her ABLJ). The provision of air is followed by a controlled ascent to the surface.

'I'm in distress' may be given for a variety of reasons, such as feeling unwell or in a state of panic or being snagged by rocks or wreckage. The signal requires the partner to help the victim and usually means that the partner should assist or bring the victim to the surface though in some situations other solutions may be appropriate.

'My air supply is giving trouble.' This signal will be given when the air supply is constricted or erratic but while air is still available. It warns that sharing may become necessary (or some other type of air supply provision) and advises the partner to examine your supply for some obvious cause of lack of air, such as pillar valves being incompletely turned on or reserves not pulled or pullable. If the problem is not solved the dive should be terminated.

D. *Information signals*

These signals provide information which may be very valuable but which do not *necessarily* lead to any action by the partner other than giving an OK signal. The signals are:

'DANGER' Fig. 48
'I'M OUT OF BREATH' Fig. 49
'SOMETHING IS WRONG' Fig. 50 & 51
'YOU OR ME' Fig. 52

The **'Danger'** signal will be given whenever something is seen which might endanger you. For instance sighting a dangerous or unpleasant marine animal or the realisation that you are in or near a strong current might be reason for giving the **'Danger'** signal. The response would normally be to move away from the danger.

'I'm out of breath' is a signal which is given to persuade your partner to slow down so that you do not become exhausted. Normally he or she will give the OK signal and slow down or stop but there might be other occasions when safety demanded a rapid fin. However, the normal response is to slow down.

'Something is wrong' is a signal which is given by a diver when he or she knows or suspects that something is going wrong. For instance it might be given by you if you thought your backpack was breaking up but

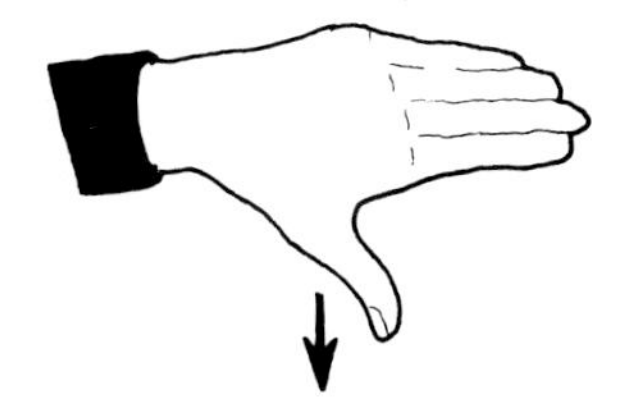

Fig. 42. 'Go down, I am going down.'

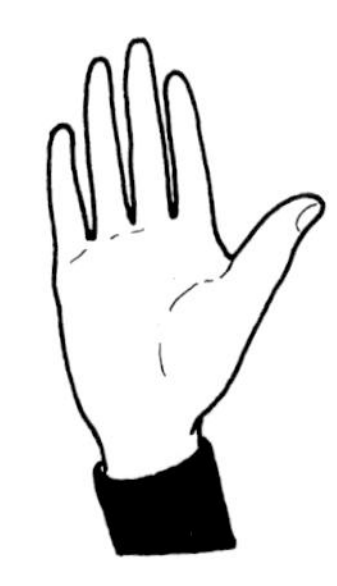

Fig. 43. 'Stop.'

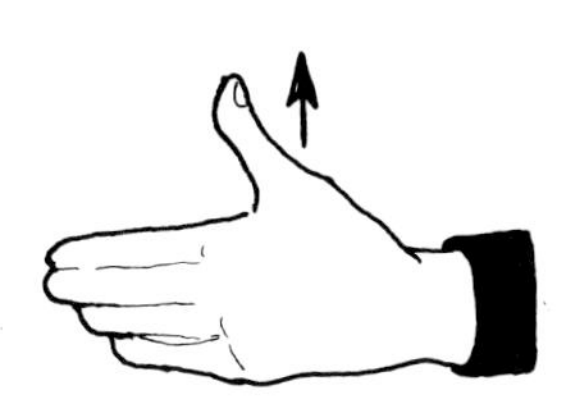

Fig. 44. 'Go up, I am going up.'

Fig. 45. 'My contents gauge reads 30 Bar or less.' Or for sets with reserves and no contents gauge: 'I am on Reserve'. Signal held by side of head.

Fig. 46. 'I have no more air.' Flat hand moved up and down from chest to mouth repetitively. Old signal was very similar but hand was cupped and turned towards mouth. An indication that fellow diver must share or provide breathing air by some other means.

Fig. 47. 'My air supply is giving trouble.' For sets with reserves only: 'I cannot pull my reserve'. Fellow diver must check pillar and regulator and be ready to provide air.

Fig. 48. 'Danger.' Diver draws forefinger across throat and then points to danger.

Fig. 49. 'I am out of breath.' Hands pat lower chest. Given when diver needs to stop or slow down to avoid exhaustion.

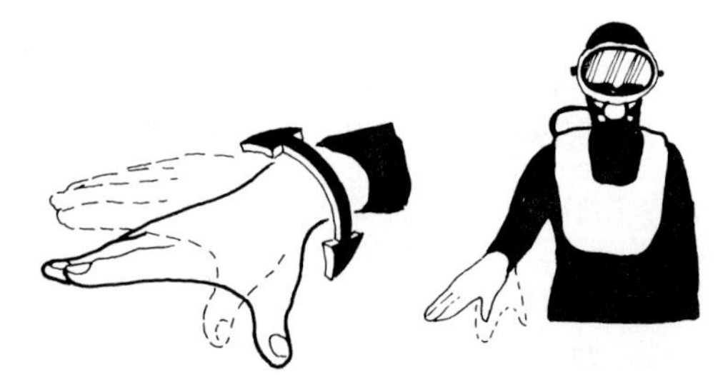

Figs. 50, 51. 'Something wrong.' Used either as a statement or a question to another diver. If used as a statement followed by an indication of source of trouble. If followed by signal 'You' a question as to whether other diver is in trouble.

Fig. 52. 'You or me.' Also direction signal if given with outstretched arm. For 'you', diver points to the other; for 'me' to himself.

Fig. 54. 'Show me your contents gauge.' Contents gauge held up at shoulder level, diver facing forwards; points with other hand and then gives 'You' signal. Other diver then shows his contents gauge.

Fig. 53. 'I'm cold.' Fluttering hands rapidly. This signal must not be confused with the 'I am out of breath' signal.

Fig. 55. 'I am narcosed or giddy.' Hand above head moving in spirals.

were not sure. After giving the signal you would point in the direction of the backpack and your partner would inspect the equipment, decide if you were right; if you were not, try and reassure you, if you were, try and do something to correct it.

'You or me' is simply a questioning signal to establish who should be doing something.

E. *Additional information signals*

These signals are not official CMAS ones but appear to be so useful that we standardised them in the Club. They are:

'I'M COLD' Fig. 53

'SHOW ME YOUR CONTENTS GAUGE' Fig. 54

'I'M NARCOSED OR GIDDY' Fig. 55

'Show me your contents gauge' is a signal the dive leader should give from time to time, especially with trainees to ensure that everyone on the dive has enough air. Even when the whole diving group led by one leader is of experienced divers the leader may still need to know about everyone's remaining air supply in order to plan the dive and in particular to avoid decompression problems.

Note that the apparent discrepancy between the SSAC titles of two signals and the CMAS titles is because the CMAS terminology presumes that you will be using equipment without contents gauges but with reserves; SSAC practice is always to use contents gauges and to regard reserves as optional extras. This practice is spreading world-wide but there are still divers abroad who do not use contents gauges. This change in practice means that the CMAS signal can better be used in the way we describe.

The illustrations show the signals both in close-up showing details of finger positions and in general view showing how they should be presented in relation to your body and head.

'I'm cold' and the **'I'm narcosed or giddy'** signals are ones in which the partner should ensure that the hazards of hypothermia or narcosis (etc.) should be removed. The normal way of dealing with both of these problems is to ascend to the surface or (in the case of narcosis) to a depth at which the symptoms disappear.

OPEN WATER DIVE ASSESSMENTS

If you are going to use a dry suit in your diving you should consider taking the training for the Dry Suit Endorsement, see p. 102*ff* if not the Endorsement Test itself.

Dives. These should be led by BIs. Your first dive should normally be a shore dive or if it has to be a boat dive this should be made in calm conditions. The site should be free of currents. Your first dive should be to depths of 6-10m. The BI should check beforehand that you are properly dressed and weighted. You should have already learned about positioning of equipment but if in any doubt check with BI. Contents gauges should be used and you should understand how to relate pressure to air still in your cylinder. Note position of lifejacket and weight belt in particular, and the need to carry a knife. Your BI should take you down gently, holding your hand if visibility is poor. He or she will frequently check that you are OK by the appropriate signal and you should respond appropriately.

Training schedule tests 1 and 2

These tests should be completed before you enter the water for your first dive, i.e. demonstration of buoyancy adjustment, and signals.

The reasons? It should be obvious already that you and your buddy must be able to communicate underwater, hence the need for signals. The buoyancy check must be done for if you are appreciably buoyant diving will be difficult or impossible while if you are negatively buoyant by more than a very slight extent you will become progressively and rapidly very negative indeed as you submerge, which will place you at risk. The test checks that you yourself know what neutral buoyancy is and can demonstrate it to another diver. Remember if you change your aqualung type for any dive you should recheck your buoyancy as you may need more or less weight on your weight belt. Buoyancy checks should be done in a depth less than your upright height so you can stand up for air if everything goes wrong.

These two tests should be taken before your first dive but the remainder should not be attempted until you have had experience of several dives. Dive procedure is detailed on pages 70-73. Read this before trying the other tests.

Remember not to carry out deep dives immediately. You are still inexperienced and have not met even a small variety of the very differing and sometimes dismaying problems and conditions that can occur underwater. Thus we ask you to limit your first three dives to the range 6-10m, and your next seven to the range 10-20m. Records from the past show that deep dives by inexperienced divers have led to a lot of incidents, a few of them of a very serious nature. This is the reason for the Club Diving rule about depth limitations on the first ten dives. The 'sharing test' should not be attempted as a test until after your third dive because it is to be carried out at 15m but you might wish to practice in shallower depths on your second or third dive.

3. *Jumping into the water*

A practice for (a) entering the water from a hard boat, where the deck may be up to ten feet above the water, and (b) for the sort of entry you might do in a rescue, for example jumping in off a quay. It is important that the BI should check that the water has a clear depth of at least 2m if your jump is from 1-2m height and 3m for a higher jump before you jump. You can jump from 7m into 3m safely. The only important points about the jump are (a) keep your fins together so that they don't splay out when you hit the water and forcibly split yourself, (b) hold on to your mask and (c) make sure that you fall feet first and don't roll over. If you have any doubts get your BI to give a demonstration first. If your harness is loose or the bottle poorly held it may be necessary to hold the cylinder.

4. *Taking off the mask and replacing*

An obvious test is checking one of the most important responses to an event, namely getting water in your mask.

5. *Regulator clearing*

Again an obviously necessary procedure. Try and combine this with some sharing. If you can clear your mask and regulator and share, you will give any accompanying diver a reasonable amount of confidence in your abilities.

6 and 9. *Sharing*

In view of the statement in the last paragraph you must be able to share with another diver in the sea. You've done this before in the pool. Before going onto an ascent (Test 9) you should carry out stationary sharing (Test 6). Five exchanges should show that you are sharing with ease. When you are the donor do not hang onto the regulator (or its hose) while your partner is breathing; you need one hand to hold your partner and one for signals or buoyancy adjustment while he or she is breathing: When you carry out the ascent follow the instructions set out on p. 61.

7. *Lifejacket inflation and deflation*

Just to keep you able to do these things even though you are heavily kitted, possibly in rough water and perhaps rather cold. Oral inflation must be used in this test. Note that you should face away from the waves during inflation. If your lips are cold it may be necessary to put your fingers round your mouth to seal it onto the inflation tube. It must also be done quickly for the reasons mentioned above and you must realise whether or not you are succeeding in inflation very quickly. If you are failing to inflate and spend ages trying to, a bad situation might develop just because you are pre-occupied with inflation.

8. *Snorkel swim in full equipment*

Checks that you can look after yourself on the surface. A dive may start with a long snorkel swim if (a) you enter from shore or (b) boat puts you in at the wrong place. The dive may end with a long snorkel swim if (a) you need to return to shore (b) you surface to find the boat in trouble or not spotting you immediately or (c) you have to surface unexpectedly early in the dive so that your position is unexpected by the cover boat. If you surface amongst rocks the boatman may very reasonably ask you to fin out to a position where he can safely pick you up without risk to the boat. Remember that there is always the remote possibility that when two or more parties are diving with a cover boat the other party will get into such trouble that the cover boat cannot come to you for a long time so that you've got to look after yourselves. If you start or end a dive with a long snorkel swim keep together with your fellow diver(s). Not only is it reassuring that you can tell each other what you plan and look after each other if any trouble starts on the surface. You'll also be spotted more easily by a cover boat if you're in a group.

9. *Shared ascent*

This is the basic rescue skill which develops out of all that sharing you have been doing in the pool or in very shallow openwater, but now you are closer to reality because you are sharing from 15m.

Before any practice or test, work out on dry land how you are going to arrange yourselves so that the mouthpieces can be shared and how you are going to hold each other. Also remind each other that sharing is to be started with the 'Share' signal, but one combined with an OK signal to show that it is not a real emergency.

So at 15m exchange OK signals and if all is well, the would be recipient of air gives the sharing signal. He or she has already taken out their regulator but has it readily to hand and arranged so that it is not free-flowing by making sure that the mouthpiece faces down. The donor hands over his regulator and sharing begins. When all seems well the donor gives the 'Up' signal and if the recipient agrees this the ascent begins. The donor leads the ascent and controls its rate. To do this each diver should grip the other, preferably under the armpit so that their faces are level. Both should fin but the donor should watch his depth gauge and the rate of ascent, stopping finning or/and dumping air if ascent looks as though it is becoming fast. The last few metres to the surface should be taken slowly and the donor should look around to check that nothing is on the way on the surface. The recipient should not rely on the donor to do everything for him or her. Shared ascents are meant to be ones in which both divers are in control though the donor is ultimately more responsible than the recipient for success.

In practice and in the test you should be both recipient and donor.

10. *Rescue by buoyant lift*

Like the last exercise this is also closely related to an important rescue situation. You raise the 'victim' from 10 metres to the surface by inflating the 'victim's' lifejacket, not your own. If you inflate your own and not the 'victim's' then you may lose your grip on the victim, shoot to the surface and leave the 'victim' without help. But if you inflate the 'victim's' lifejacket and not your own then if you lose control they at least should float to the surface. The inflation may be orally or by use of the cylinder or direct feed on the 'victim's' lifejacket.

So, exchange OK signals and if all is well take hold of the subject (victim) by one hand and use your other hand to inflate their lifejacket till they are neutrally buoyant. Then fin up very gently having one of your hands ready to dump air from their lifejacket (and dry suit if worn). The ascent should be steady and controlled. On the surface inflate their lifejacket further if necessary and carry out EAR and a tow.

Don't forget if either of you are using a drysuit to ensure that dump valves are closed at the surface for otherwise you or they may lose buoyancy rather embarrassingly. If the Draeger type automatic dump valve is used ensure that the arm carrying it is not held up clear of the rest of the body and that if possible it faces downwards so that it does not dump air automatically. If they are using the Viking etc. type of automatic dump valve which can be locked closed, do so.

11. *Compass course*

You should be learning to use a compass and here you fin on a bearing given to you by the dive leader or BI for two minutes slowly and then on the reciprocal bearing for the same time. Ideally you should end up where you started but failure to get back exactly is not a reason for failing the test. The performance which ensures that you pass this test is that you use the compass correctly. See pp. 89-90 for details on technique.

Dive experience and dive variety

You will have noticed that the Training Schedule requires that you gain experience of a variety of dive sites and dive types as part of your qualification for the 3rd Class Award. The reasons are to ensure that you have some knowledge of the different types of dive available and are not confined to, for example, experience of dives of good visibility in calm seas. Evidence from incident surveys shows that divers with a limited experience of dive types are much more at risk in unfamiliar conditions than those divers with a variety of experience.

The variety of dive types should include at least two dives from the following list:

Shore dive along a sloping seabed (a typical Scottish dive).

Dive in moving water, a current of 2 knots or less.

Low visibility dive with a visibility of 2m or less.

Dive in water of 10°C or less.

Note that a dive may combine two or more of these conditions. If by some strange chance you do not meet these conditions in your first ten dives you are asked to continue dives qualifying you for the 3rd Class Award until you meet these conditions. But this event is unlikely. Five of the dives must be in seawater. If you live inland you may replace one of these dives in the list of four above with a freshwater dive. If you live near the sea you may indeed wish to try a freshwater dive and this is quite acceptable (do not forget the need for less weight on the weight belt).

THE DIVE

Cardinal rules

This section is written as though the reader was about to go on his or her first dive but the information it contains applies to all dives so that readers should not feel inhibited from returning to read this section after they have started diving. The section is also written as though all dives were Club dives: we know that you may well on occasions dive outwith the Club but the basic safety rules remain the same and the procedures are essentially the same. More detailed explanation of dive procedures are given later.

As we said in Chapter 1, except in certain specified circumstances, you should never dive alone. Moreover as Leo Zanelli says, this rule should be enlarged to read 'Never dive without an adequate partner'. As a beginner on your first few dives you are necessarily inexperienced. As a result your partner, chosen for you by the Expedition Leader, in charge of each Branch or Club expedition, should be amongst the most experienced. This is a second cardinal rule, that the least experienced should be partnered with the most appropriately experienced in a dive.

Pre-dive equipment check list

Before the great day of the first dive arrives, and also before every subsequent dive, you will know who is running the dive, and where and when to meet. Since you need equipment for the dive and will need to be sure you get it to the dive site and home again, here is a check list. It is arranged into sections which may make it easier to memorise.

(A) PROTECTIVE CLOTHING
Dry Suit/Wet Suit. Bootees, Gloves. Swim trunks or suit.

(B) BASIC EQUIPMENT
Fins, Mask, Snorkel.

(C) SAFETY EQUIPMENT
Lifejacket, Knife, Weightbelt (with weights).

(D) BREATHING EQUIPMENT
Aqualung cylinders and harness, Regulator.

(E) ANCILLARY EQUIPMENT
(not essential for all dives)
Depth Gauge, Compass, Watch, Torch, Bag (for all these specimens you are going to find), etc.

(F) AFTER DIVE
(smartly termed après dive)
Food, Hot Drinks. Towel, Warm Clothing. Log Book.

At the dive site

Soon after arrival the Expedition Leader will have made plans for the dives and have made up a list showing with whom and roughly when you will be diving. This list will also name the:

DIVE MARSHAL (Beachmaster) to whom all divers must report before entering the water and at the end of the dive. He or she records the duration and maximum depth of each dive, primarily so that any need for decompression shall be recognised and acted upon and so that a check is kept on the whereabouts of all divers.

SAFETY OFFICER who is responsible for first aid or transport to hospital or decompression chamber in the unlikely event of an emergency.

DIVE LEADER(S) (1 per group of divers). Each pair (or at most triplet) of divers who dive together is led by a Dive Leader. Normally he or she will be the more experienced diver of the group. They are responsible for explaining to you what it is hoped to do during the dive (during their briefing), and for carrying out signals and actions that allow you to do this safely. The Dive Leader is responsible for checking the safety of his companion(s), in particular in being aware of how much air they start the dive with, the duration and depth of the dive (and ensuring that neither are arduous for beginners), and ensuring that the dive terminates at a convenient point on the surface with every member of the dive having a reasonable reserve of air at the end of the dive.

EQUIPMENT OFFICER. Responsible for providing, checking and recovering any Club or Branch equipment used on the dive. In addition, if the dive is a boat dive, one or more COXSWAINS (BOAT DRIVER) will be appointed.

(The duties of these officers are described more fully in the *Advanced Dive Training Manual*. Here the descriptions explain the things a diver on his or her first few dives must learn.)

The briefing

The Expedition Leader will brief you all with a general description of the site and any special problems it may present for the dive and will explain who is diving with whom. If you think that he has over-rated your capabilities don't hesitate to tell him. If you dive with a group who don't know you, talk to the Expedition Leader before he announces his plans and show your training schedule, so that he knows about your capabilities. If you are carrying out one of the first ten training dives necessary for qualification for the Third Class certificate and wish to have the dive signed as such in your training schedule, this dive must be led by your BDO or one of your BIs, unless previously agreed with your BDO.

Checking and fitting equipment

While you are waiting for the briefing you should be getting your equipment ready and checking the cylinder pressure and that the regulator is properly fixed. Remember to check the regulator and aqualung in the following ways:

1. Having fitted the regulator onto pillar valve making sure that the pillar valve O ring is in place and the regulator properly located on the O ring, turn the pillar valve on gently. **Do not look at the pillar valve while you do this** because the O ring, if misplaced, might shoot out at you. If there are any obvious leaks turn off and reseat the regulator.
2. Check that the regulator will give air.
3. Turn set off, breathe out air from regulator. After two to five breaths the valve should resist giving air, if it continues to do so there is a major leak in the regulator and it is unsafe to dive with it.
4. Turn set on again so that pressure in regulator is at set pressure. If the pressure is appreciably below the rated working pressure of the set, discuss this with your dive leader: it may be necessary to obtain another cylinder. If the pressure in the regulator drops rapidly once the pillar valve is turned off, there is a leak in the regulator which will need correcting.

(If your regulator lacks a contents gauge you will have to test the pressure with another regulator that has a gauge, or with a special separate gauge which your branch may have, and then fit your own regulator. In such a case leaks can only be detected by a hissing sound.)

Next check your lifejacket. If it is an ABLJ with an independent cylinder fitted you should have filled its air bottle from a cylinder. When you do this **do not listen to the filling of the bottle with your ear close to the pillar valve.** An escaping O ring could enter your ear or brain. Fit the bottle, making sure that it mates correctly onto the jacket. If it is a CO_2 surface type lifejacket check that the CO_2 cylinder is in place.

Changing time will depend of course upon the time of your dive but you should allow half-an-hour when you're inexperienced for changing and getting ready. However, if the weather is very sunny, don't get into your wet or dry suit too early or you'll boil.

The sequence of putting on most of your equipment is important for safety, so note that after you don your wet suit, fit the lifejacket (ABLJ, or with dry suit ABLJ or SLJ), and then the aqualung, with the weightbelt placed *last*. Thus your weightbelt will fall off easily if you or someone has to release it, and you will still be wearing a lifejacket if you have to take off your aqualung. The belt must have a quick release which is easily operated. When fitting a weightbelt make sure that it is fairly tight otherwise it may rotate so that the quick release is not immediately accessible. Other equipment such as mask, snorkel and fins are best fitted just before entering the water or on a shore dive while standing in shallow water. Ancillary equipment can be fitted after the aqualung. Note that if you're on a boat dive, the coxswain may wish you not to wear your aqualung until you are at the dive position. In such a case aqualungs and weightbelts are stowed on the boat floor.

Equipment check

Just before the dive your leader will brief you on the dive and check your equipment. The check, which he may ask you to give him in return, should cover the following main points:

1. Aqualung in place, cylinder binding bands tight, harness properly worn, cylinder turned on. Regulator mouthpiece accessible. Check contents gauge and that wearer can easily read the contents gauge.
2. Lifejacket in place. On SLJs inflation tube cap in place. On ABLJs drain valve closed, inflation bottle or direct feed properly fitted, operating and accessible for operation by hand.
3. Weightbelt correctly worn and note of type of quick release and colour of weightbelt. It is good practice to ensure that the weightbelt and aqualung harness belt are of different colour or have different types of release, or at least that they are fitted with the releases facing in different directions. All this helps you or a would-be rescuer to release the weightbelt and not the harness.
4. Knife worn and properly clipped into its holder.
5. All inflation hoses connected and tested.
6. All other necessary equipment present.
7. Test, by breathing, that the regulator gives air.

The dive

Then, if the Dive Marshal (Beachmaster) agrees that it is time to start your dive, you enter the water. Unless otherwise instructed, or when the water is immediately deep and there is to be no waiting on the surface, fit your mask, snorkel and fins immediately before you get in. If the water is immediately deep, fit your regulator mouthpiece in your mouth on entering the water instead of snorkel. Most dives start with a snorkel fin on the surface until the leader judges you are at the position to start the dive. When he or she is ready to start the dive the Dive Leader gives an OK signal to the Dive Marshal (so that timing of the start of the dive can be recorded) making sure that it is acknowledged. He then gives the down signal and you respond with an OK signal. You fit your regulator neatly, surface dive and you're on the way down.

As you descend remember to clear your ears, equalise pressure in your mask, and to respond to the OK signals that your Dive Leader gives you. Try to take up a position in relation to the Dive Leader where it will be easy to see his signals. Probably the best position is about 2m on either side of him, very slightly behind him and on the same level. It is very difficult for a Dive Leader to communicate with someone who is slightly behind and directly above him. Look around and enjoy yourself, if you want to know what something is, draw the attention of your Dive Leader to it and, hopefully, he will both know it and remember to tell you during the debriefing. If the Dive Leader is going too fast give the 'out of breath' signal. On your first few dives the dive should be quite shallow, certainly less than 10m. From time to time the Dive Leader will give the 'show me your contents gauge' signal, so respond but also note how fast you are using air. Try and get in the habit of looking at the contents gauge every five minutes. When your contents gauge reads 30 Bar give the appropriate signal and the dive group should start to surface slowly. As you approach the surface follow the surfacing drill (see above under Hand Signals) holding your hand outstretched in the OK signal as soon as you have checked your buddy.

If you lose your companions underwater

If you lose your fellow diver(s) underwater turn round slowly twice looking up and down. If you have a torch turn it on and wave it up and down as you turn. Frequently the column of bubbles is a better clue for the whereabouts of a diver than anything else. Then surface slowly and on the surface turn around looking out for your companions who should have gone through the same procedures as soon as they realise they have lost you. It may be very tempting to come to the conclusion that your companions are down near you, indeed you may see their bubbles on the surface but if you descend before they've re-established contact, there may ensue a mad, time-wasting and frequently stupid charade in which they surface while you're underneath and vice-versa. So wait on the surface. Give snorkel cover, boat or shore party a Distress Signal if your buddy does not surface within a few minutes.

The end of the dive

At the end of a dive once you are ashore or in a boat tell the Dive Marshal the main features of your dive and make sure that your name is checked off on the dive list. Unless you've other duties such as standby diver or snorkel diver you should change once ashore. Indeed at the earliest opportunity turn off your pillar valve and blow down your regulator – this will stop accidents wasteful of air. Take off your equipment carefully, check that it's all there and if anything is damaged remember to arrange repair (or if it's Branch equipment to tell the Equipment Officer). Change and if necessary, it usually is in Scotland, warm yourself with hot soup, and maybe with a fire if one has been made.

Après-dive

Largely a time of relaxation, yarn-telling and going over the pleasant points of the dive. If it's summer and the weather good, a picnic with the family, if it's winter a contented drink in the pub. However, there are a few duties (i) make sure that the dive site is clean and free from litter (ii) write-up and get your log book signed as soon as possible. Do try to make the write-up a reasonable report which would help you and others to go back to the site.

ELEMENTARY BOAT DIVING

Boat dives are essentially like shore dives but you must be able to get into and out of the water quickly because weather conditions may mean that the coxswain cannot hold the boat in position for more than a short time.

Techniques for entry into water from a boat

If you fitted your aqualung and weight belt before boarding the boat fit your fins, mask and snorkel when instructed to do so. If you did not fit them onshore, kit up onboard. This can be difficult if the boat is a small inflatable and the sea rough. In such cases it may be necessary for only a pair of divers to kit up at one time and for the others to help them.

Entry

From an inflatable the traditional method is to wait until the coxswain has put the engine in neutral and has told which divers are to go in what order. Fit your mask and snorkel. Hold on to your mask and wait for entry signal.

Entry can be by the following methods. See Fig. 56.

1. Rolling backwards into the water.
2. Standing and jumping in feet first.
3. Holding onto side rope (if fitted) of inflatable and putting first one, then the other leg over the side and sliding in (see Fig. 56).

Method 1 is traditional and easy in rough conditions. Method 2 can be fast. Method 3 is slow but advisable if in (or possibly in) a strong current because you hold onto the boat until your partner is ready beside you in the water for the dive.

If you're not sure about your buoyancy inflate your lifejacket slightly before entry and deflate in the water as necessary.

Head-first entry is recommended to those with quite a lot of show-off in their character. Unless you are absolutely sure that the water is deep enough and free from floating or submerged objects you could have a nasty accident using this technique. If you must enter this way, place not only your hand, but your elbow in front of your mask to prevent it being broken into your face.

Techniques for getting aboard

Inflatables

At the end of the dive you and your partner(s) should be in a close group on the surface. You've given the appropriate signal (OK or Distress) to the boat, they've acknowledged the signal, and they are coming to pick you up. As the boat approaches the group should split up so that one part is slightly more than a boat's width from the others. The boat will normally try and pick you up while heading up into the wind (and waves). As the boat slows and goes into neutral, fin towards it and grab the side lines. Hold onto the boat and take off your weight belt, hand it into the boat when requested, then take off your aqualung. To do this undo the waist strap, take off one shoulder strap and turn your back to the boat. The people in the boat can then lift the set in off your other shoulder. Then, when instructed by the boatman, get in by finning hard and pulling yourself over the sides. See Fig. 40b.

Larger boats with ladders

Fin to the side of the boat with the ladder, when she's in neutral, take off your fins and if possible climb in. If not, because you're too heavy, hand in weight belt and if necessary set, then climb in. On occasion lines may be thrown for you to hold onto or for you to fix equipment to for handing in. See Fig. 40a.

Fig. 56. Entry to water from an inflatable or moderate sized hard-boat. Above, ready to roll backwards but waiting for the signal from the boat-driver that it is safe to enter the water. Note that the snorkel and mask are in place and the regulator mouthpiece is being held. Below, rolling backwards holding the mask in place.

b. The jump 'feet-first' entry. Note that the mask and regulator are held and the feet are kept together. The cylinders should not need holding in place unless an inadequate harness is fitted. In both a. and b. the equipment on the divers has been simplified for reasons of clarity.

Small hard boats without ladders

Very difficult to enter but stern entry or carefully synchronised entry by two divers from opposite sides are the best ways.

LECTURE 11

DECOMPRESSION SICKNESS AND ITS AVOIDANCE

As soon as you start diving in the sea, if not earlier, you should become aware of the risks of decompression sickness, how to avoid it and the measures to be taken if you know that you or someone else may be suffering from the condition. This section of the Manual presents an introduction to the subject and provides that modicum of information the 3rd Class Diver must have about the problem. More detailed information is required by the 2nd Class Diver. The contents of this section represent the minimum content of the 3rd Class lecture on the subject.

The immediate causes and symptoms of decompression sickness

The immediate cause of the disease is due to the damage caused by nitrogen bubbles in and between the cells of the body damaging and pressing on the cells.

The bubbles may appear in any part of the body. Those in muscles and joint tissues give rise to pain, sometimes extreme pain, leading to unwillingness and weakness in using the affected muscles and joints. Bubbles in the nervous system may cause paralysis or loss of sensation in some part of the body. Bubbles in the brain or heart will cause serious, sometimes fatal, symptoms. Damage to tissues and cells may take a long period to repair and the damage caused by bubbles inside nerve cells is usually never repaired.

The basic cause of decompression sickness

The basic cause of the formation of bubbles which are sufficiently large to cause damage, is the absorption and solution of too much nitrogen in your body during a dive. As you dive the body picks up a load of dissolved nitrogen from the air you breathe under pressure. The amount of nitrogen that ultimately (i.e. in the long run) dissolves in your body is determined by Henry's law (page 34) which states that the amount of dissolved gas in equilibrium with the gas above it, is determined by the partial pressure of the gas. Thus ultimately (in about six hours) your body will contain twice as much dissolved nitrogen if you breathe air at 2 Bar pressure rather than at the surface (1 Bar). It takes time for your body to become saturated with nitrogen at a new pressure when you dive. However the greater the increased pressure (due to a deeper dive) the more rapidly does nitrogen dissolve in your body. Thus at 2 Bar pressure it takes about 6 hours to acquire the same loading of dissolved nitrogen that you obtain in 20 minutes at 4 Bar pressure. Ultimately at 4 Bar pressure you will have twice as much nitrogen dissolved in you as you would at 2 Bar pressure.

The dissolved nitrogen presents little problem, except as the cause of inert gas narcosis, see *Advanced Dive Training Manual*, so long as it remains dissolved. But once you ascend to a shallow depth, at which the partial pressure of nitrogen in your breathing air is less than that dissolved in your body the nitrogen starts to come out of solution. The excess nitrogen tends to form minute bubbles in the body fluids or inside the cells or is breathed out in the expired air. If there is a very large excess of nitrogen in your body as the result of the dive when you surface or approach the surface, the bubbles which are formed will be large enough to cause pain and tissue damage. These larger bubbles are the cause of decompression sickness.

The avoidance of decompression sickness

(a) Theory
The theory for the avoidance of decompression sickness is to ensure that the nitrogen bubbles formed in your body never grow to a size at which they can cause tissue damage. This is done either by ensuring that the maximum uptake of dissolved nitrogen in the dive is slight, by limiting depth and time; or by ascending at a sufficiently slow rate for most of the excess nitrogen to be breathed out before the bubbles grow too large.

(b) In practice
The simple way of avoiding the risk of decompression sickness is to follow the 'no-stop' dive times. i.e. dives whose duration is such that you can surface, at the recommended rate of 0.25 metre per second, from the greatest depth without carrying out a 'stop' i.e. a prolonged timed pause at some intermediate depth. 'No stop' dives ensure that the nitrogen load picked up during the dive is too small to give rise to dangerous or potentially dangerous bubbles on surfacing. Thus the various decompression tables always provide a series of dive times for various maximum depths, which if obeyed, reduce the risk of decompression sickness to a very low, almost negligible, value. For instance, current RNPL tables state that a dive with a maximum depth of 30 metres may be carried out with a dive duration of 20 minutes from leaving the surface to starting the ascent, without risk of decompression sickness, see Fig. 57. These tables presume a steady and known ascent rate after leaving the bottom, and for RNPL tables the rate of ascent is 15 metres per minute. It is important to adhere to this ascent rate. If your ascent is slower you may actually be absorbing quite a lot more nitrogen during the deeper part of the ascent, so that you have more nitrogen in your body than would be expected, if you had followed the standard rule – the consequences should be clear. Fig. 57 plots the 'no-stop' times graphically. The tables used by the SSAC, the RNPL 1975 tables, are listed in SSAC log books and on separate cards. Ensure that a copy is available on site every time you dive.

The more complex way of avoiding decompression sickness is to carry out 'stops', which are points in the ascent at which you wait for a certain time at a specified depth until you have lost a portion of the excess nitrogen from your body, before ascending further. The theory and detail of 'stop' decompression is given in pp. 92-100 of this volume. The simple rule for the inexperienced diver is always to dive on 'no-stop', or shorter times, so that 'stops' do not have to be carried out. The sensible rule for all divers is to follow this procedure but mishandling of a dive or certain operations may require diving with 'stops', see later. Note that the 'no-stop' time is timed from the start of the dive at the surface until the point at which you leave the greatest depth and ascend to the surface at 15 metres per minute. In practice most dives are not of this simple 'down to the bottom and up' type. The sports diver tends to make rather slow descents and then to work his way into shallower water. In such a case the safe rule is to regard the effective bottom time of the dive as being from the moment at which you leave the surface until the moment you ascend to a depth of 9 metres on your way to the surface. This rule may over-estimate your decompression requirement or give you shorter bottom times than you really need but it introduces a considerable margin of safety and removes any doubt that you may have run into a requirement for a 'stop' while slowly ascending. To illustrate these points, examine the following examples:

1. *A 'Square' Profile dive*

The divers on a dive wish to dive to a depth of 24 metres. What will be the maximum permissible Bottom Time if decompression is to be avoided?

Using the RNPL Tables the answer is 32 minutes.

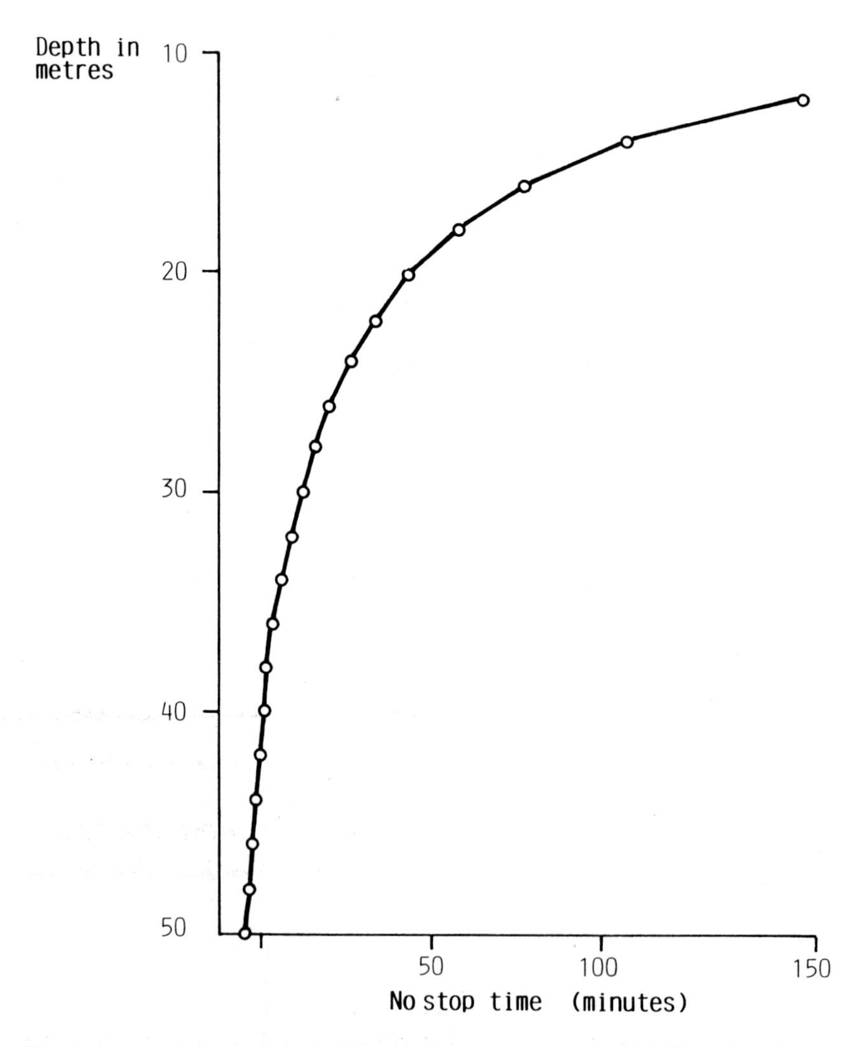

Fig. 57. The 'no-stop' times plotted for dive depths down to 50 metres. The values are from the RNPL 1975 tables. Note that points do not fall exactly on a smooth curve because of the practical need to express the no-stop times in multiples of a minute rather than in minutes and seconds, which would be impractical.

The Total Dive Duration is 34 minutes allowing ascent at 15 metres per minute. See Fig. 58.

2. *A second dive after Dive 1 above*

These divers plan to dive after an interval on the surface of 4 hours and 30 minutes to a depth of 22 metres using a 'square profile'.

How much bottom time will they have if they wish to avoid decompression stops?

If there is a four to six hour interval between the first and second dive use the RNPL rules which say that you should add quarter of the first dive time to the proposed second dive time to obtain the revised dive time on which decompression requirements (if any) are to be calculated.

So 34 minutes/4 = 9 minutes (rounded up to the next largest whole number of minutes). This is the PENALTY time for the second dive.

The tabled no-stop time for a single dive to 24 metres is 34 minutes. So 34 minutes − 9 minutes is the no-stop time for the second time. (24 metres depth is used because this is the depth of the deeper of the two dives, ie the first).

3. *Calculating decompression if a second dive goes over the revised no-stop time*

Using the same first dive conditions as in 1 and 2 above and the same surface interval what if any will be the decompression time if they plan to have a bottom time of 30 minutes on the second dive.

As above the Penalty is 9 minutes. So the total bottom time for the second dive is 30 minutes + 9 minutes.

Then the decompression time is calculated from the RNPL tables for 39 minutes at 24 metres. Use the tables and move down the depth column to 24 metres. Move along the table to 41 minutes. The tables tell you that stops are required at 10 metres for 5 minutes followed by a shallower stop at 5 metres for 10 minutes, see Fig. 59.

The 10m stop time start as you leave the bottom and ascend at the correct rate so a minute of the first stop is taken in the ascent from 22 metres to 10 metres. 20 seconds of the second stop time is taken in the ascent from 10 metres to 5 metres.

Square profile dives are done typically on a wreck, see Fig. 60. Just to re-iterate; in this type of dive you descend to a pre-determined depth and stay at that depth. Bottom time starts at the start of the dive and runs until you begin to ascend at the recommended rate. Total dive time is when you reach the surface.

Variable Profile Dives

These are dives with time/depth profiles such as those shown in Figs. 61a and b. They are typical of the 'exploratory' dive so many club members make. Fig. 61a shows a descent in very shallow water but they may be ones from a boat starting with a descent to ten to thirty metres followed by 'ups and downs' as the sea bed profile is followed.

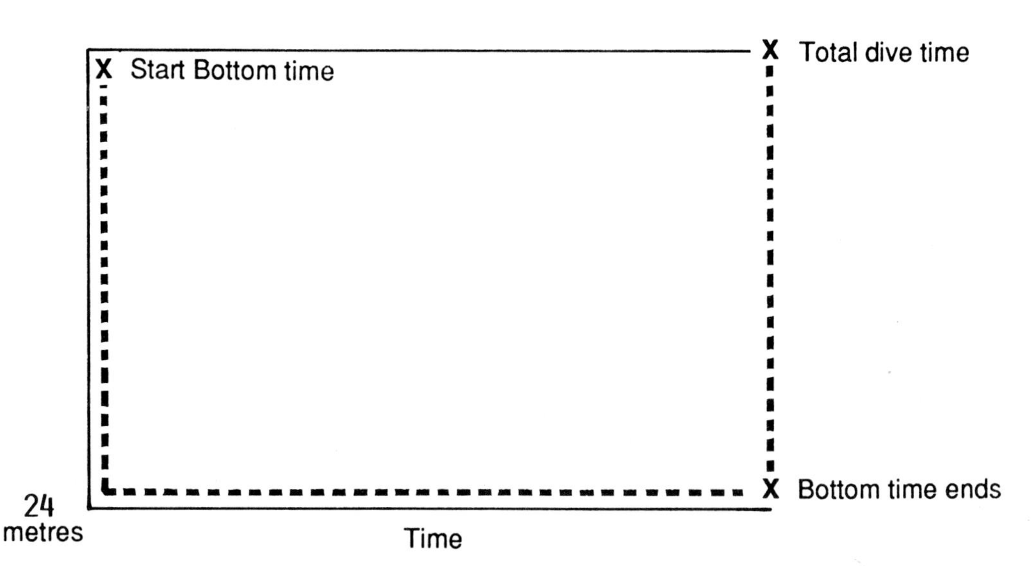

Fig. 58. A square profile dive showing definitions used in relation to dives and decompression tables.

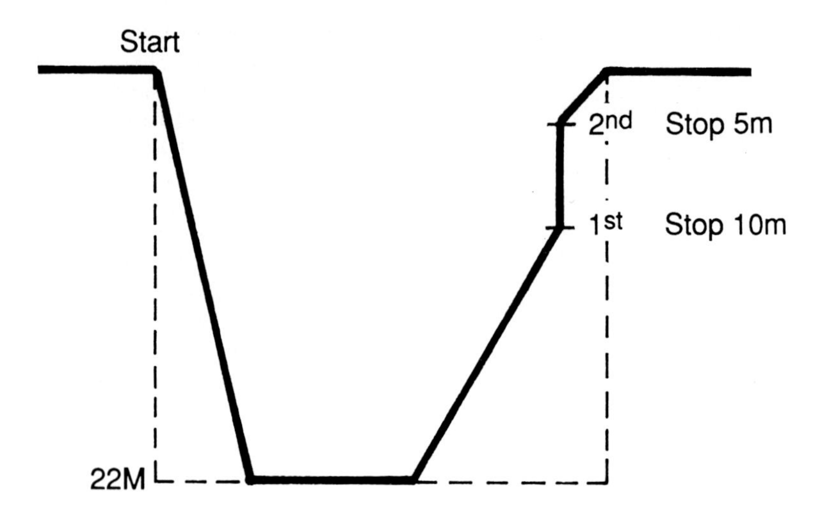

Fig. 59. A nearly square profile dive with two stops. (Stop times are not plotted.)

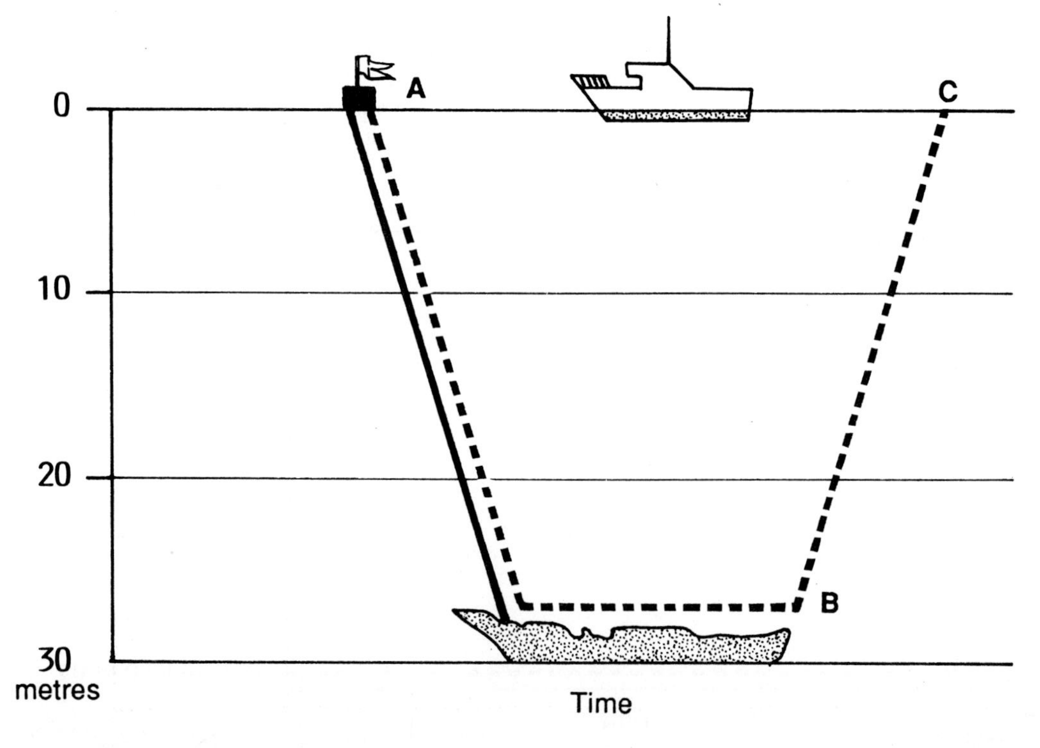

Fig. 60. The profile of a typical wreck dive.

In Fig. 61a you see that:
The descent starts at A. The final ascent begins at B. Bottom time will end at B if the correct rate of ascent is used but if dives are profiled as in Figs. 61 a and b Bottom Time ends when you pass the 9m depth level. Total dive time is as usual the time at which you reach the surface.

Fig. 61a shows you the profile of a dive to 32 metres on variable depth/time and Fig. 61b a dive to 20m.

What is the maximum permissible Bottom Time if decompression is to be avoided? When does the Bottom Time end? What should the total dive time be for the dive in 61b.

Answers: (For dive 61b.)

Using the tables you read the 'No-Stop' time as 47 minutes for 20 metres.

These 47 minutes will be completed when you reach 9 metres for the final time because you do not know what the equivalent 'Square profile' Bottom Time would be. The total dive time is 48 minutes. (47 minutes plus 1 minute to ascend from 9 metres : actually taking 36 seconds at the correct ascent rate.)

Treatment of known or suspected decompression sickness

The standard treatment of known or suspected decompression sickness is therapeutic recompression in a hyperbaric (recompression) chamber. This is undertaken by experts under medical supervision in the UK and most other countries. So if you have, or even are a known or suspected case of decompression sickness amongst your divers, the only effective treat-

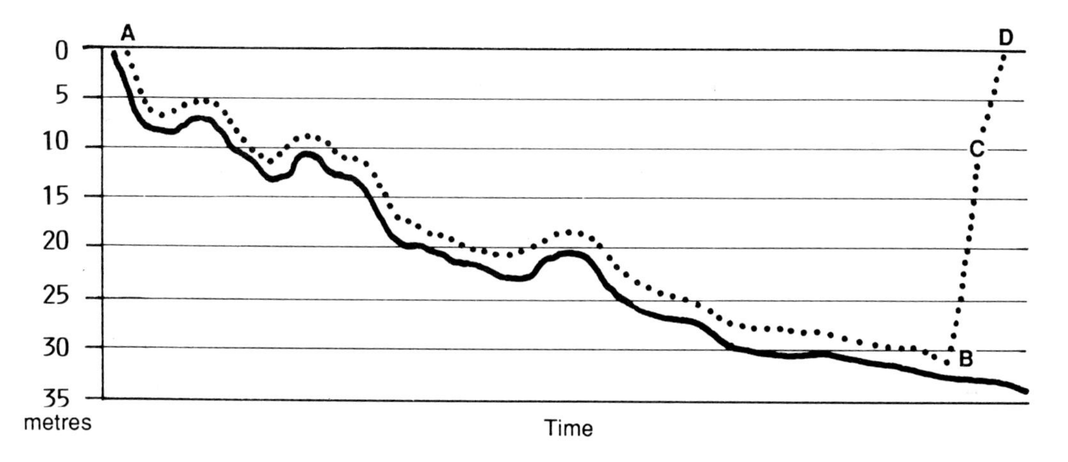

Fig. 61a. A dive with an irregular profile. See text for meanings of points A to D. 61b. A more typical dive with irregular profile, note the use of the time till ascending above 9m depth as the Bottom time of the dive.

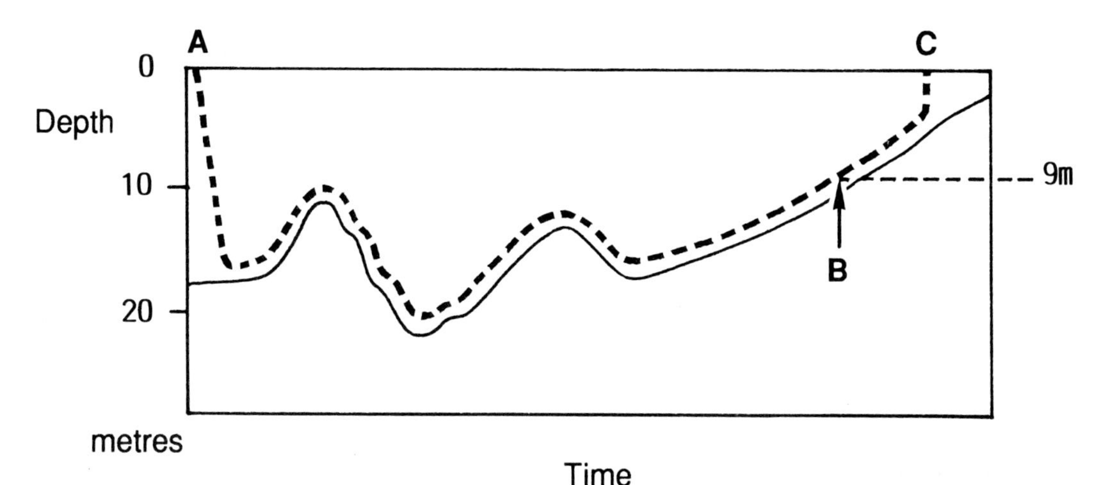

ment is to ensure that the potential victim is taken as rapidly as possible to the nearest operating hyperbaric chamber.

The symptoms of decompression sickness are very variable. They include pains in skin and joints, muscular weakness, and neurological symptoms (particularly loss of sensation, paralysis, speech and vision defects). They often have a superficial resemblance to other medical conditions. Nevertheless help from a doctor could be of value in the period before the victim reaches a chamber, provided that the doctor is told of the suspected cause – i.e. decompression sickness.

So how do you as a diver on-site handle a possible case of decompression sickness?

The handling will be carried out, normally, by the Expedition Leader, but all members of the party and especially those persons acting as Dive Marshals must play their part. The first question is: could the victim possibly have decompression sickness? The answer to this depends primarily on the depth and duration of the dive they have just had. The dive log-sheet should be studied and the general details of the dive and nature of the site considered to ascertain whether there is any possibility that the 'no-stop' dive times (or the dive depths and times plus stops) have been broken so that the victim has been at risk from decompression sickness. Bear in mind that depth gauges can be inaccurate, the victim's own recollections of the dive profile or maximum depth reached incorrect (e.g. misreading of gauge) and timing may, though it never should, be wrong. If it is absolutely clear that the dive site is too shallow or/and the dive times too short for decompression sickness, then, provided that the symptoms are slight, you may reasonably conclude that your victim is not suffering from the condition. But if there is any doubt on these points or if the dive clearly was one in which the victim was at risk or if the symptoms are neurological you should recognise that you have a probable case of decompression sickness on your hands.

Remember that the symptoms of decompression sickness are often progressive. i.e. starting with slight and relatively unserious signs and developing over quite long periods (up to 24 hours or so) into serious ones such as paralysis, so that a victim should be moved to a chamber at the earliest point before very serious and possibly irreversible damage has been done. The simple rule is, if there is any possibility that the case is one of decompression sickness, contact the nearest recompression chamber staff and take their advice. If contact is impossible, i.e. you are too far from a phone, suspend diving and move all directly concerned to the nearest phone.

Contact with and advice on recompression chambers should normally proceed through standard channels, details of which are published in the club magazine from time to time, and in the Training Schedule and in the Dive Log Books issued by the Club, but check that you have consulted the latest editions of these publications. In practice contact through the Coastguard is a reliable procedure but you or your Expedition leader should know the address and phone number of the nearest chamber for each dive site, before you start diving.

If symptoms, or possible symptoms, of decompression sickness have appeared in the victim do not attempt 'in water' decompression treatment.

If, however, you have a situation in which a person has, or apparently has, exceeded the 'no-stop' times or done insufficient stops, and has no symptoms, then they, plus an accompanying diver, should re-enter the water and carry out the omitted decompression stop or the remainder of it plus, we advise, a further precautionary stop of at least ten minutes. The provision of a 'stand-by' aqualung, i.e. an extra aqualung, on SSAC expeditions, ensures that air is available if such decompression procedure is required. If you have to use this procedure for completion of decompression ensure that surface time is kept to the absolute minimum. This is another reason for reporting to the Dive Marshal as soon as possible after surfacing. If you are in any doubt, for whatever reason, about any possible decompression requirement you may have as you approach the surface at the end of a dive, pause at 10 or 5 metres as appropriate and carry out as much decompression as might possibly be required plus a margin and then surface, pointing out your problem to the Dive Marshal as soon as possible.

Summary

In conclusion note the following main recommendations:

1. Plan and carry out your dives so that they are of a shorter bottom time than the 'no-stop' limit for the depth of dive. Set yourself a maximum depth limit before diving and obey it.

2. Ensure that decompression tables are available 'on-site' at a dive along with a spare charged aqualung cylinder and regulator. Ensure that the whereabouts of the nearest telephone, doctor and recompression chamber are known.

3. If there is any possibility that 'no-stop' times have been exceeded or if it is known that they have, carry out the appropriate decompression stop as soon as possible, provided that no symptoms which might be due to decompression sickness have appeared.

4. If slight symptoms of distress have appeared soon or up to 24 hours after a dive in which there was any possibility of 'no-stop' times being exceeded treat the case as one of possible decompression sickness and contact a hyperbaric chamber, usually through the Coastguard. Contact the nearest doctor for help and, if on land, contact the police for help with transport to the chamber. Ensure that any victim is accompanied at all times on his way to the chamber.

5. Do not carry out more than one dive per day until you understand the repetitive dive procedures.

The theory and practice of decompression stops, the theory of therapeutic recompression, repetitive dives and the problems of diving at high altitude or shortly before flying are dealt with in pp. 92-102.

DECOMPRESSION COMPUTERS

Also known slightly erroneously as Dive Computers or Decompression meters. These instruments basically integrate depth of the dive and the time at various depths to estimate whether there is any decompression requirement. Since these devices contain good pressure sensitive sensors and accurate timers together with electronic chips to make the appropriate calculations they estimate with fairly good accuracy the loading of nitrogen in your tissues that you are likely to accumulate during the dive as well as the rate at which you will lose that nitrogen as you surface, at a stop and on the surface. Thus a decompression computer will calculate

(*a*) the remaining no-stop time at the depth you are at, which remains available to you, or
(*b*) the duration of any stop if required, at a specified depth and the time at which you may ascend to a shallower depth or surface.
(*c*) your decompression requirements for a second or third or even fourth dive that day.

It will also display current depth, elapsed time from the start of the dive or time from surfacing,

These are minimum calculations and many will give you further information such as:

A look ahead to allow you to plan a later dive.
An indication of incorrect ascent rate.
Records of past dives.

The advantages of these instruments will vary according to your attitude to diving. Their predictions can be compared with the requirements of various tables and in most instances they will tend to indicate a lesser requirement for decompression than the tables. It is rather widely believed that they give shorter no-stop times on square-profile dives than the Tables when the dive is the first of the day and are therefore safer than Tables but neither of these statements appears to be invariably true. They tend to give longer no-stop times on variable profile dives than the Tables since most tables make you assume that you are at the maximum depth for the whole dive until the start of the final ascent. Certainly on some variable profile dives the Tables give you an excessively large safety margin but calculation of just how large this is or is going to be is really very difficult.

So the advantages are perceived to be that the computers give you longer dives with usually less requirement for decompression than the Tables would and that they calculate second and third dive decompression requirements for more realistic and varying surface intervals between dives than the Tables allow. Another important positive aspect of dive computers is that they should give you a very accurate reading of maximum depth or of the actual depth you are at at the time and that they remember the duration of the dive which you might have forgotten. Of course dive timers which are appreciably cheaper than dive computers also remember times and maximum depths as well as showing present depths.

If you purchase a dive computer bear in mind that it needs back-up from a watch and depth gauge or diver timer or another computer. If the decompression requirements indicated by one instrument differ very much from those shown by another system or if the requirements differ from table requirements adopt the conservative approach and take the safer route.

All the electronic decompression computers are based on a pressure sensitive sensor and a timing chip. Depth and time are integrated to model nitrogen uptake during descent and nitrogen unloading during ascent. Many of these models claim in their advertising that they are based on the Buhlmann tissue compartment hypothesis and parade their merits in terms of the number of tissue compartments modelled. In practice such claims matter little as the tissue compartment model is mostly a mathematical convenience and has little real biological meaning.

These computers either require to be switched on before the first dive and left on until all the diving of a certain period, usually 24 hours, sometimes longer, is completed with the computer coming into action once the diver has descended a very small way from the surface. Alternatively the meter switches on automatically once you have descended a very small depth. All models remain on for a predetermined time after surfacing, usually 8 to 12 hours. If they did not have this delayed switch-off the meter would switch on and off while you were moving about at just on the surface sometimes dipping your meter down to the critical depth. In addition if the meter did not remain on repetitive dives would not be accounted for effectively.

The diver usually wears the computer on the wrist. The computer displays depth, elapsed time, remaining no-stop time or stops required at the set depths programmed into the computer. It may indicate time remaining to the end of no-stop time at the depth you are at : obviously if it does this a slight change in depth, especially further descent, is likely to change that remaining time in a marked way. It may also indicate a safe ascent rate and nitrogen loading as a factor. After the dive the details of the last dive, the surface interval from the last dive and possibly desaturation data are displayed. Most experts hold that the computer should also give you a 'lookahead' to suggest to you the sort of repetitive dive you might be able to do some time after the dive just recorded. Most current computers do all these things and some do more : the only problems being perhaps that so much information can be available that the diver is confused by what is what!

Since most computers use LCD displays they may be difficult to read even with a torch, they are probably rather fragile though experience so far suggests that few have broken down for any reason and most of them do not indicate the total stop time ahead of you during decompression, unless of course you only need the shallowest stop. If they do break down they may do so catastrophically in which case you must fall back on depth, watch and dive tables, or by giving slightly curious readings which you may not realise are aberrant.

FINAL REMARKS

Once you have become a Third Class Diver

Soon after you have completed the number of dives laid down in the Training Schedule for the 3rd Class award you should have acquired a degree of experience about the running of and participation in dives which exceeds the very simple description of a dive given above. Soon you will be asked formally or informally to take an increasing part in the planning and organisation of dives, even if, perhaps particularly if, the number of divers involved is small. Consequently you will be imperceptibly acquiring the skills of a 2nd Class diver, so why not go on to complete the training and testing. The 2nd Class Diver is a person who can show a reasonable degree of competence in nearly everything to do with diving. Possession of the training by you is of course proven by passing the tests. A 2nd Class Diver will be welcomed in nearly all diving company as a person of competence and experience.

The only other remark we make as you finish your 3rd Class training is that the frequency with which you dive will play a big role in determining whether you progress as a diver or simply slip back into inexperience. Though it can be said simply that the more frequently you dive the better you will be, it may be of more use to give you the rough and ready rule that if you dive less frequently than once a month you will slip back, slowly losing the skills and watermanship that you have gained. Obviously work or colds etc. will keep you away from the water for several weeks at a time. Consequently when first diving after such an absence remember that you are probably not as fit as you were, and even if you are, you are not so experienced a diver as you were. So on such occasions make the dive one which is not too arduous or deep: confine yourself to calm conditions and depths of less than 30 metres. If on the other hand you are planning deep dives in excess of 30 metres, not only must you learn all about decompression and narcosis problems (see pp. 92-102) but also keep very water-fit by frequent diving and by working-up (or is it down?) to such depths.

Chapter 5

Increasing ability and experience: the 2nd Class Diver

INTRODUCTION

As we wrote earlier, the 3rd Class diver is a person who can look after him or herself but cannot be relied upon to care for others. Thus at the time when you've just qualified as a 3rd Class Diver nobody expects you to care for others, except of course if they require air from you or are in distress. But very soon your increasing experience and ability will teach you all manner of things that will increase your ability to improve your dives and help and please your fellow divers. In fact as you do this you are acquiring some of the abilities which are specifically taught and tested during 2nd Class training.

The description of a dive given at the end of Chapter 4 is pictured at a very elementary level; by the time you've done five or six dives you should know all that is listed there. There is much more to learn so why not go into 2nd Class training?

The chief problems that you will have to learn to cope with, in order to increase the safety of your diving and allow you to dive in a wider variety of dive sites, are:

1. Unexpected deterioration in wind and sea conditions, both above and below water.
2. Distress, panic, illness or other non-competence in your fellow diver.
3. The problems of deep diving, the risks of decompression sickness and its avoidance.
4. The ability to run dives for others in most conditions.

In part you learn about these matters by following the open water training programme set out in detail below, and by attending lectures or otherwise acquiring the information in them. You also learn by diving fairly regularly. Most divers find that to dive once a fortnight throughout the year maintains you at a fairly high level of ability which is likely to increase slowly simply through acquisition of experience. Diving more frequently keeps you fitter and allows you to learn from experience still faster. But if you dive once a month or less frequently you will probably find that you tend to slip backwards because you forget things if you are not being reminded by actual experience. It is for this reason, as well as for simple reasons of fitness, that you should choose an easy shallow dive for your first dive after a period of absence from diving whether because of illness or because of other cause.

You will also find that the chapters on deep diving, expedition organisation, boatwork for divers, elementary diving physiology and on the use of the ABLJ as well as that on diving in poor conditions will be of value in the process of training to be a 2nd Class Diver.

THE TRAINING

Second Class Divers should be experienced both as Dive Leaders and as Expedition Leaders. A person who holds this qualification should be well aware of the theoretical reasons for diving practices and the explanation of diving hazards as well as being practically experienced in how to dive. By the time the award is gained such a diver will have carried out at least forty dives so that a good deal of experience should have been acquired. Dives should have been made from boats and from shore, and boat cover should have been used.

Test 1. 3rd Class Diver qualification: obviously necessary.

Test 2. Qualifying Dives, forty in total. To build up experience.

3. *Acting as a Dive Leader*

Here the BI will be looking first to see that you brief your fellow divers properly so that they know how you plan how to run the dive, i.e. maximum depths and times, any particular hazards, surfacing drill to be used etc. and that you check their equipment and signals. A check list for Dive Leaders is set out later in this book. During the dive you need to keep your divers informed and checked by signals, and you need to keep your divers with you. The Dive Leader is still in charge of the dive until the whole party is safely back on shore or your base boat and the Dive Master (Beachmaster) informed of the completion of the dive. Finally, you as Dive Leader will debrief your group. If anyone feels unwell at any stage of the dive you abandon the dive, accompany or take them to the Dive Marshal who decides, mainly on your information, on what to do. It is suggested that no one should start dive leading on decompression dives or dives where decompression might be needed. Such dives require a fairly high degree of experience from their Dive Leader.

4. *Acting as an Expedition Leader*

The Expedition Leader has more responsibility than the Dive Leader for safe diving. Consequently this test should not be undertaken until you have (a) carried out several Dive Leader dives (b) carried out all the various jobs subordinate to an Expedition Leader, namely Equipment Officer, Dive Marshal, Safety Officer and (c) watched an Expedition Leader at work. On the first occasion the BI should take you by the hand and point out any errors immediately you've made them. On the second occasion you should know just how to do it and your examiner will only step in if he thinks that your actions or inactions have endangered people.

The Expedition Leader is usually responsible for choosing the dive site and finding out who will dive. You should thus get as much knowledge about the site as possible from other divers, charts, OS maps, pilot books etc. Establish when HW and LW occur and whether there will be any problem with currents. Check about access to site, i.e. is permission needed. Note how wind will affect the dive site. On the day before and the morning of the dive get an up-to-date forecast, decide what conditions will make you abandon the expedition. Very roughly, winds above Force 3 with a good fetch across the site will make diving impossible for inexperienced divers and those above Force 5 impossible for all divers. Check with divers before setting out if the site is far away. If you are going to use a boat inform the Coastguard, who will also often be able to give good advice on local conditions.

On arrival at the site, check that people have arrived and that all equipment needed is there. Have address of nearest doctor, decompression chamber and know location of nearest phone. Appoint and brief officers. Make up dives, remembering the following points:

(i) Normally the most experienced should dive with the least experienced. Never set up a dive that contains only inexperienced divers.

(ii) Tank capacities should be matched if possible, so that no dive is cut short by one person running low long before the others in that dive.

(iii) If the site is deep, check (a) that decompression will be avoided unless the majority of divers concerned are considerably experienced and that *Deep Diving Recommendations* (*Advanced Dive Training Manual*) are being followed, and (b) note that divers without experience or recent diving performance must not be taken on a deep dive.

(iv) Normally a dive should not contain more than two persons.

(v) No one should dive when they may be cold and tired after such matters as long periods of snorkel covering. Such people should have a rest period before their dive. The same may apply to boat divers and stand-by divers though they are usually at less risk of exposure.

(vi) Dive Marshals, Stand-by divers, Equipment and Safety Officers usually also want to dive. Give them their chance and make sure that someone takes over from them while they dive. Make sure that everyone then knows what they are doing and roughly when they are doing it. Don't run all your dives at once, that's obviously impossible for safety reasons. Don't run most of them at once, otherwise you may have difficulty in checking on all your divers both underwater and on the surface. With plenty of equipment and people you may be able to have two dives down at one time, but usually one dive at a time is enough. Make sure that all divers report to the Dive Marshal before and after a dive. Finally, do have an enjoyable dive yourself. At the end have a debrief if possible, check on tests (if any taken) and on any discoveries pleasant or unpleasant about the site. Complete a report form.

If all that sounds terrible, remember that it's not really so bad. Thousands of others have done it before! The check list (see later) will help you.

5. *Sweep Search (or other searches)*

It is of great value for a diver to be able to carry out effective searches underwater. Effective means that the whole search area is covered as rapidly as possible with the certainty that no area has been left out. It is important to be able to arrange a search because should two divers be overdue or a diver missing you will need to find them as soon as possible: an action to be co-ordinated by the Expedition Leader. In addition it is of great utility to be able to find and recover all manner of objects, large and small, that have sunk to the bottom. Finding is the first part of all such operations.

The simplest form of search to set up is the sweep search and since it gives you experience in a range of diving abilities it is ideal for the testing of training.

The sweep search should give you experience in:

(a) working with lines underwater,
(b) use of compass,
(c) control of movement and position in the water to produce minimum disturbance of the bottom,
(d) underwater rope signals.

All these practices are useful in safe and effective diving. Note that it may at times be inappropriate to carry out a sweep search. In such cases the laying and use of a jackstay search, a snag-line or swim-line search would be as effective a test. See Figs 62-64. BSAC Paper No. 2 by Commander Grattan details the swim-line search. A Jackstay is a bottom line layed on a definite bearing carrying marker floats at either end. In a snag-line search two divers fin with a taut non-floating line between them to catch on large irregular objects, see Fig. 64. This could be modified for smaller objects as follows: a small party linked

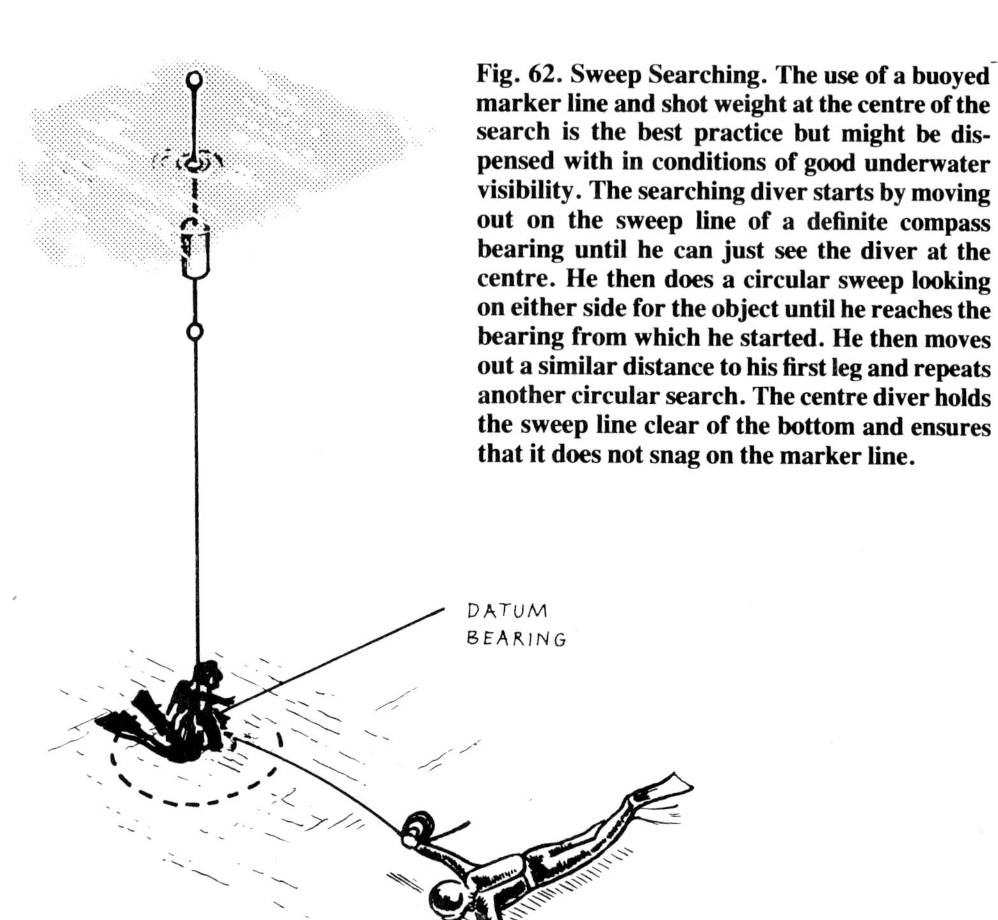

Fig. 62. Sweep Searching. The use of a buoyed marker line and shot weight at the centre of the search is the best practice but might be dispensed with in conditions of good underwater visibility. The searching diver starts by moving out on the sweep line of a definite compass bearing until he can just see the diver at the centre. He then does a circular sweep looking on either side for the object until he reaches the bearing from which he started. He then moves out a similar distance to his first leg and repeats another circular search. The centre diver holds the sweep line clear of the bottom and ensures that it does not snag on the marker line.

by buddy lines might fin with their centre diver over the line thus sweeping a rectangular area.

With the sweep search you should first work out a way to carry up to 15m of light non-floating line neatly with you while you dive. A reel is best but a bag may be a useful way of stowing the line. The dive should have at least three persons on it; one to be the centre anchor man around whom the circular search rotates, one to carry the line around the circle and to carry out the search; and of course the diver testing you. You should pay out the line, fin round the circle and carry out the search. Work out rope signals with the anchor diver so that he or she can signal you and be signalled to check that you are OK, or if in distress, or to move in on the line towards you or them. Instruct the anchor diver to hold the line above their head so that he or she is not slowly wrapped up during the sweep. When the anchor diver is in place and happy, work out to the limit of visibility for the sort of object being sought (the limiting distance is from the anchor diver), do this on a definite bearing. Try and stay clear of the bottom. Note how much line you have paid out. Check the reciprocal bearing on to the anchor diver and then swim around looking to right and left

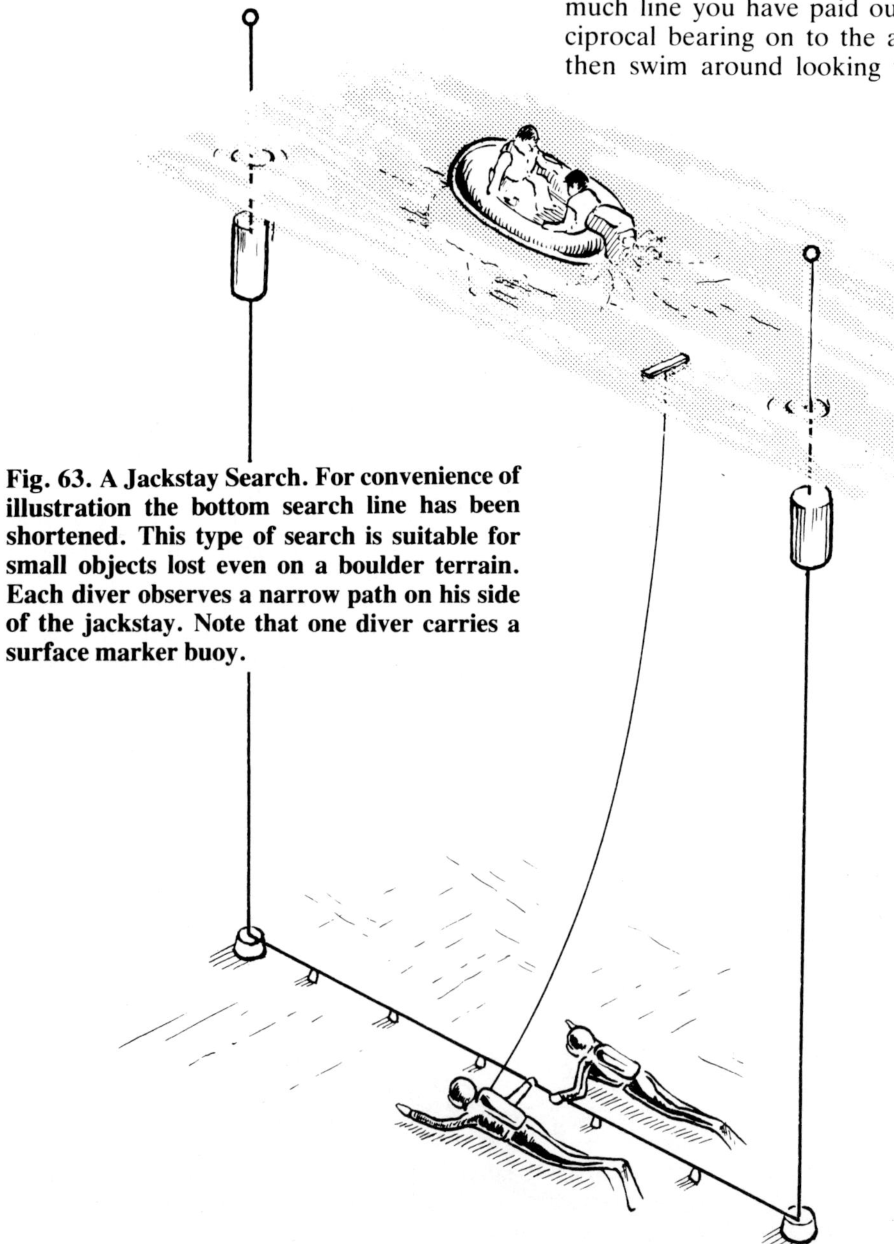

Fig. 63. A Jackstay Search. For convenience of illustration the bottom search line has been shortened. This type of search is suitable for small objects lost even on a boulder terrain. Each diver observes a narrow path on his side of the jackstay. Note that one diver carries a surface marker buoy.

until you find it or reach the bearing on to the anchor man from which you started. Then move out the same distance (or less if you've spoilt visibility). Repeat sweep and if necessary repeat once more for the test. Note that the sweep may take quite a long time and you should have checked other divers' air and your own carefully before and during sweep. Note that effective recovery of the line is also part of the test. During the sweep check that the anchor man is happy by OK signals by rope.

Note that other methods of search are often more appropriate than the circular sweep, and consequently it is just as acceptable to carry out one of these for the test so long as it involves the use of a line and a compass and rope signals. If the bottom is irregular or steeply sloping a sweep search is usually inappropriate. Jackstay, snag line and swim line searches are all acceptable for the test. See Figs. 62-4 for details.

6. *Successful use of a surface marker buoy*

There are various types of surface marker buoy, see Fig. 65, but they all serve the same set of functions, which are:

(a) The surface buoy, attached by a line to one of each pair of divers, shows surface

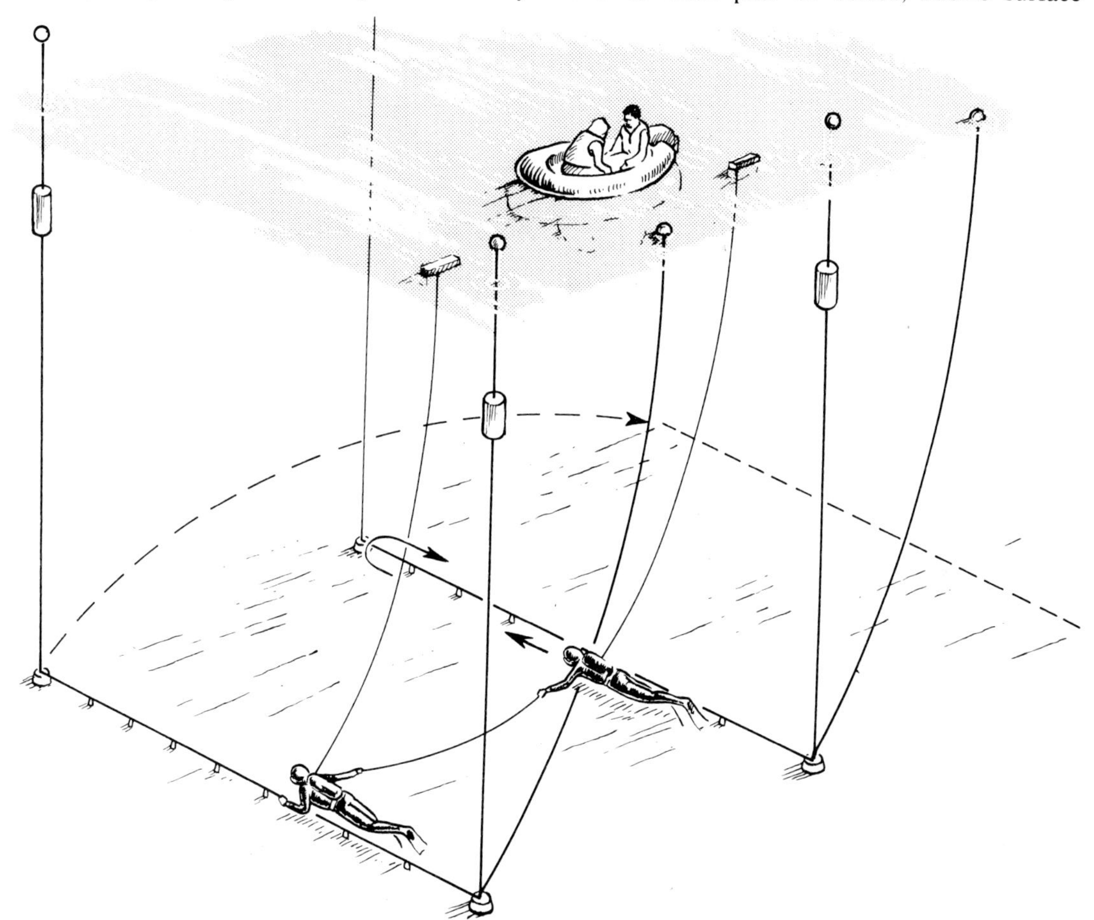

Fig. 64. A Snag Line Search. Suitable for searching large areas rapidly for large objects what would stand proud of the bottom. Not suitable on rough bottoms. The divers will probably be unable to see each other and must use rope signals. Their blob buoys are watched by the surface party who can use signals on these lines to speed up, slow-down, or bring up the divers. By this means the surface party know just where the divers are in a large area and which areas have been swept and can control the even-ness and rate of search. With more divers on the search line between the bottom boundary lines, smaller objects can be searched for using visual contact. Once again for artistic convenience the search area has been shown far smaller than it would probably be. After searching one area the whole party swings round to search an equivalent parallel area.

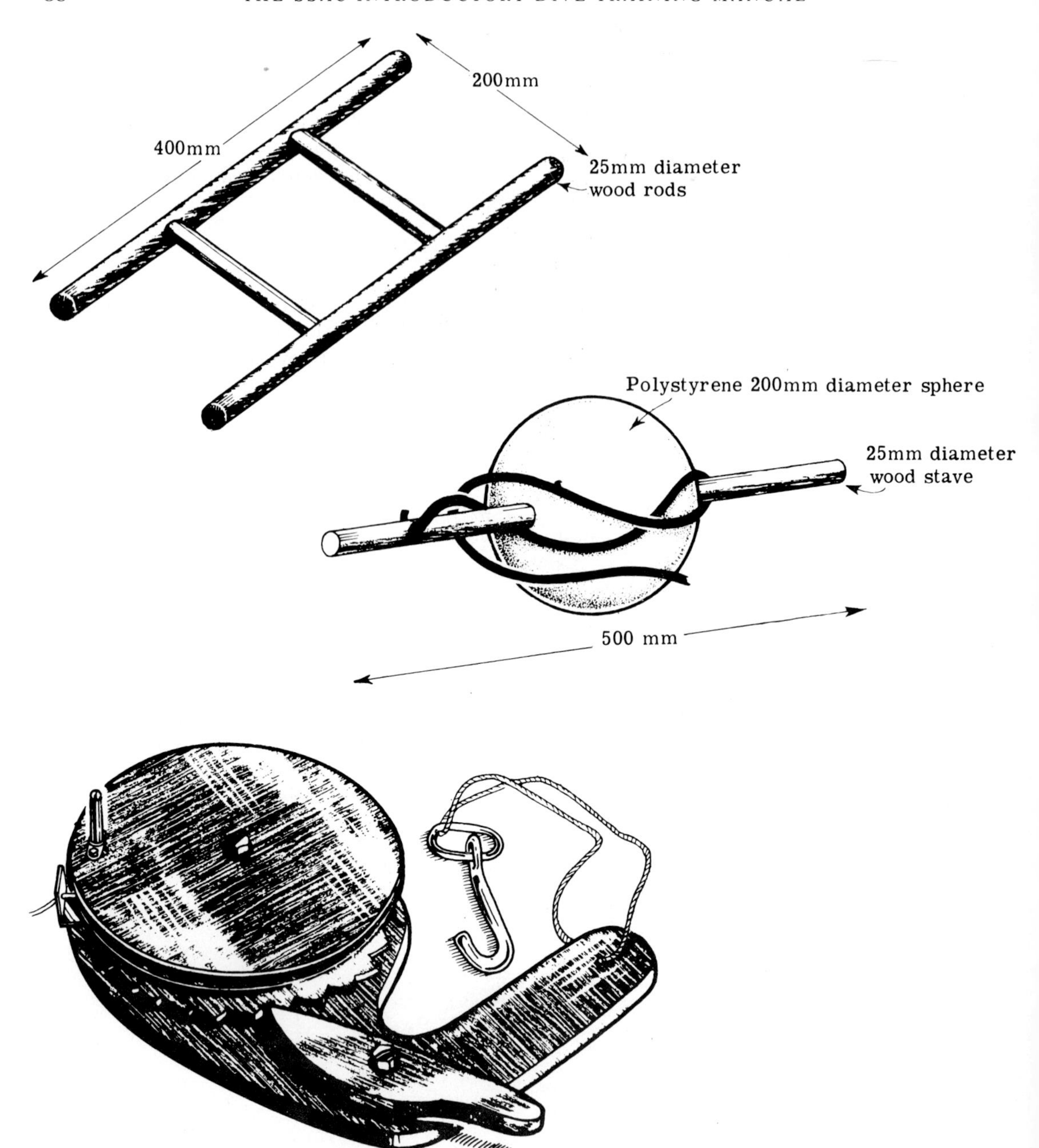

Fig. 65. Various types of holder for the line for a Surface Marker Buoy. The buoy itself should have at least ten pounds of positive buoyancy and should be of a conspicuous colour, perhaps bearing a small rigid diver's flag. The holders shown at top and bottom are carried by the diver and the line is unwound from or rewound onto the holder. The middle holder is a marker in itself and as it floats on the surface the diver unwinds line off it as he descends: of course he cannot reel up line on it as he ascends.

Fig. 65a. An 'H Frame' for winding up light cord. The diver would carry the frame plus cord. The other end of the cord is attached to a surface buoy. The diver winds cord out or in to keep the line to the surface marker taught. b. A 'blob' float which carries the line wound round it in a 'figure of eight'. As the diver descends the line unwinds automatically from the float. c. A winder which a diver can carry to wind line in and out as his depth varies. Note the pawl which the diver engages when he expects to be a constant depth so that current or wind do not pull the line out.

cover, and even unwanted intruders such as power-mad boat drivers, the whereabouts of the divers.

(b) The surface buoy and line can be used to give rope signals to the diver below. For instance, 'Come up' signals or 'OK?' signals might be given as occasion demanded.

(c) If the divers do not surface when they should, a stand-by diver can descend the line to see what is wrong. It may, in emergency, be possible to lift a diver by pulling on it, but do not do this unless the line comes steadily but easily. Otherwise send a diver down.

(d) Surface marker buoys can be used, with signals on their lines to direct a dive party's direction of movement if a prearranged series of rope signals have been arranged.

Obviously a knowledge of rope signals improves the skill with which you can use a surface marker buoy (SMB) but even without such knowledge use of SMBs improves dive safety especially in open waters. You will find it impossible to use SMBs on wrecks, amongst fixed buoys, or on a bottom littered with large irregular rocks but otherwise they are to be recommended for every dive except very deep dives, see *Advanced Dive Training Manual*, where shot lines should be used instead. It is very difficult to tend a SMB with a line longer than 30 metres.

The techniques in the basic use of SMBs are simple. During descent pay out the line at a rate commensurate with your rate of descent. If you have too small a surface float it may be possible to drag the float under the surface, thus rendering the SMB useless. Take care to keep the line gently taut so that it does not foul in your own or someone else's equipment. Current or wind effects on the marker will often tend to drag the line off the vertical so that you need quite a lot more line than your actual depth suggests. If you turn down-wind or down-current your line may suddenly go slack. During ascent reel in the line (or whatever method you have for collecting it) so that once again you do not have slack line.

8. *Compass course with at least four changes of direction*

The purpose of this test is simply to ensure that you can use a compass effectively underwater. The typical underwater compass (see Fig. 66) has a needle (north pointer) sealed in a viscous fluid and a fixed sighting pointer which the diver should align with the mid-line of his or her body. The most common error made in the use of the compass underwater is to fail to align the mid-line of your body with the compass fixed pointer – if you make this error you will deviate from the intended direction.

Two main types of compass are available. In one the graduated bezel bearing the degree markings is rotatable as with many land compasses – in the other the bezel is fixed (i.e. not rotatable) and the degree markings are marked off in reverse, i.e. counterclockwise direction. The reason for the counterclockwise graduation will be explained shortly.

Use of a compass with a rotatable bezel. See Fig. 66a.

To take a bearing align the fixed pointer with the object whose bearing you need. Rotate the bezel so that the 0° graduation lies on the line from the north end of the compass needle. Read off the value on the bezel to which the fixed pointer points. To use the compass to follow a fixed bearing set the bearing value required in line with the fixed pointer. Rotate the compass (and your body) so that the north end of the compass needle points to 0°. Then, making sure that the fixed pointer is aligned with the mid-line of your body fin in that direction.

Use of the compass with a fixed bezel. See Fig. 66b.

To take a bearing align the fixed pointer with the object. Read off the value to which the north end of the compass needle points. This is a simpler method than that used with the other type of compass. Note that the fixed pointer has to point to 0° because of the construction of the compass, so that the needle (in reality is still pointing to magnetic north) points to the difference in degrees between the bearing and magnetic north. The counterclockwise graduation of the fixed bezel is because of its fixed relationship to the fixed pointer, in other words as you (and the fixed bezel) turn clockwise to pick up a bearing the needle turns counterclockwise. (In the other type of compass as you turn clockwise to pick up a bearing you turn the bezel counterclockwise to hold the 0° marking in line with the north point of the needle.)

To use the compass to follow a given bearing, turn the compass and your body until the needle points to the desired value. (In most of the compasses of this type an additional rotatable plate with a fixed mark is provided so that you can set it over the needle in the bearing position required. This makes it easy to check that you are holding to a bearing.) Suppose you want to change (see Fig. 66b) from a heading of 000° to one of 120° you rotate yourself and the compass through 120° clockwise and the needle rotates anti-clockwise from 000° to 120°, thus you will incidentally see in another way why the bezel must be calibrated anti-clockwise.

Really accurate compass work underwater requires a lot of practice. It is very difficult to take account of any effect of current though if you are in sight of the bottom pick up objects ahead on the bearing you are following, fin to them and then repeat the process.

In the test you are asked to follow courses for four 50m legs. A 50m course (twice the length of the average swimming pool) will take a slow finner in calm water about 1½ to 2 minutes but is sufficient distance to end several metres off course if your compass angles are followed to within 5°. So obviously the test-passing performance is not the wholly accurate navigation of a course, but the correct use of the compass to find a bearing, the correct alignment of the body to the compass and the correct following of a heading as best you are able. The dive duration stated in the Training Schedule is not the duration for which you must follow a course, in this test it's the distance that counts.

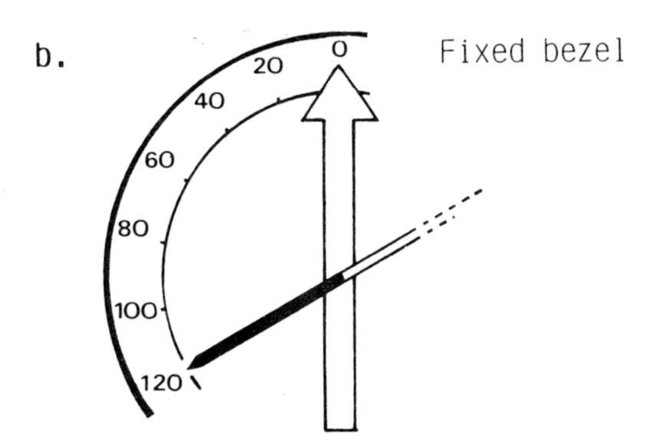

Fig. 66. A diagram to illustrate the two types of compass. See text for full details. In both cases the compass is set for a course of 120° (Magnetic). The needle is shown with its north pointing needle in black.

8. *Dive without mask*

Tests your ability to avoid panic if you really did lose your mask. Try and do this in summer, it's rather painful in February or March. Another diver should lead you by the hand as you do this. Stretch your other hand out in front to protect yourself from collision. Don't shut your eyes, you can still use them to some effect.

9. *Rescue Drill*

Putting together all that you've done before and adding the reality of a quick continuous descent to the victim and raising them from 15m. A BTP or Instructor should be beside the victim and light signals or a shot line provided for guidance. Victim gives distress signal (simulated) and you take hold of him or her facing them. Inflate victim's ABLJ but do not remove weight belt. Watch the victim's head position and that he or she is breathing in and out. If not pause and check head position. Maintain a slow steady ascent adjusting victim's and your buoyancy. On surface take victim's mouthpiece out and mask off. EAR and tow.

10. *Assisted (Shared) Ascents*

The purpose of this is to ensure that you can help a diver who has no air, or be helped if you get into this situation. You should have been trying this soon after you first started diving so that now the test should be little more than a formality. The procedure is of course nothing more than a development of what you were doing in the pool, paying of course very real attention to the fact that you are sharing. Make sure that:

(i) You have a good hold of your fellow diver. Not only does it make sharing easier but it also gives him or her some reassurance in the case of real emergency, and if they are rather weak you can haul them up.

(ii) You are really ascending (watch depth gauge fairly frequently).

(iii) But not too fast. Try and keep the rate to about a third of a metre (1 foot) per second and of course breathe out during the periods when you have not got the valve.

Do not hold onto the mouthpiece of the regulator when you're handing it to your companion. Not only does this decrease his confidence in your ability but worse, since you need one hand to hold him, your other hand is tied up with constant holding onto the mouthpiece. Yet you need your other hand free from time to time to give signals, to deflate your or his ABLJ etc.

If you are both really buoyant, say you'd both become rather positive as your air was used up, fin obliquely up to slow down the rate of ascent. If wearing a dry suit remember to dump air as you ascend, unless you have an automatic dump valve. Each diver should control his or her own buoyancy.

It's worth digressing for a moment to consider what you would do in the unlikely but difficult situation when your companion faints and drops his or her mouthpiece. Remember that an unconscious person relaxes their jaw so that putting the mouthpiece back is unlikely to be any help, though if you can put it back while doing the important matters mentioned below there is no harm in doing so. They'll probably have breathed water and hopefully had an epiglottal spasm which will have stopped further breathing. So take them to the surface as quickly as you safely can. Make sure that they have a clear airway so that expanding air can escape through the mouth or nose. Some experts advocate bringing them up head down so that the air blows out any water but this probably is very difficult. (The USN has advised this.) If the head is held back the airway should be clear in an upright ascent. On the surface immediate EAR is essential.

Note that there can be many advantages in using octopus rig regulators, i.e. two second stages on the same first stage. Such a system makes it easier for both divers to carry out an ascent in which one is being rescued after equipment failure. However, users of such regulators must get used to carrying the spare second stage in a convenient position where it is ready to hand but not likely to snag. It is appropriate at this moment to remind you that if you are using an ABLJ and a single hose regulator it may be a good idea to arrange them so that one hose comes from each side of the head. Two hoses on the same side can lead to confusion. In any event you must learn just how you arrange your own or borrowed equipment so that finding part of it by feel is done almost unconsciously and very rapidly.

11. *Remove set, disconnect hoses and replacement*

If you can take your set off, disconnecting the inflation and direct feeds that may be fitted to your dry suit and ABLJ, if necessary, fin a short distance holding the set in front of you while breathing from the regulator mouthpiece, and then replace all items, you are in possession of a skill which can be of value if you find your way impeded in a wreck or cave, or even if your equipment is fouled by items such as ropes etc, underwater. When you take your set off you will probably find that your centre of balance is entirely changed and you may discover yourself tending to fall forwards. Try practicing this procedure on a nice clean hard or sand bottom in 10m depth. First, unbuckle the waistband of your set. To do this you may need to undo your weight belt buckle for a moment but make sure that the buckle of the weight belt is securely refitted before you make any other move. Then disconnect the direct-feeds, if fitted. Take the set off and lay it on the ground in front of you. You'll find that if you are wearing the usual length of hose fitted to the second stage of your regulator you'll need to lie prone with the set in front of you. Then lift the set up and try finning a few metres, slowly. Then stop on the bottom and refit the set, finally reconnecting any direct feeds (check them) and if necessary ensuring that your weight belt lies outside your aqualung waiststrap. When finning with the set note that you will have to hold the set pointing upwards and away from you to get a good finning position. If you have any trouble refitting the set remember that you can fin to the surface while continuing to breathe from the set, though your instructor and/or buddy may need to help with buoyancy adjustment.

12. *Mask, demand valve and signals drill*

The first part of this test asks you to jump into water holding your mask in your hand and to fit it without surfacing. This stimulates the situation in which your mask comes off during an entry but you manage to retain hold of it and either a need for fast descent, as in a current or rough sea, or the start of a rescue leads you to fit it underwater. Misjudged buoyancy might also lead to a fast descent. In such situations all you should do is replace the mask and clear it without fuss as soon as possible.

The mask and demand valve clearing at 18 metres that form the next part of the test are simple repeats of these fundamental skills, already tested at shallower depth in the 3rd Class training. The substantial part of this test is the giving of signals and the responses to signals by the trainee. The signals test carried out in the 3rd Class tests were somewhat artificial. Now you are tested under more real conditions with the expectation that the BTP may ask you to do anything that you have been tested for in the 3rd and 2nd Class training. The BTP, who is testing you, may pretend to faint, give incoherent signals, or no answer to your 'OK?' signal. We hope that you'll remember to treat such behaviour as an indication of illness or distress and rescue and surface him. He might demand to share and then knock your mask off. Here you don't panic but replace the mask, clear it and carry on sharing as soon as possible. He may give signals suggesting something is slightly wrong with his air or other equipment. Do you remember to inspect, try and remedy the situation and check if things are 'OK?'

SECOND CLASS LECTURES

Safety and emergency procedure. See lecture syllabus in *Advanced Dive Training Manual*.

Oxygen poisoning and carbon dioxide poisoning. See *Advanced Dive Training Manual*. Note that carbon dioxide poisoning is also known as Hypercapnia.

Underwater navigation and search methods. This has already been described in part, under use of the compass, pp. 89-90 and in the section of search methods, pp. 85-87.

Basic seamanship. See *Advanced Dive Training Manual*.

Expedition organisation. See *Advanced Dive Training Manual*.

The 2nd Class Decompression lectures and the Compressor Operation lectures are covered by the material in the next two sections respectively.

ADVANCED DECOMPRESSION

At the end of Chapter 4 on Third Class Training we introduced you to the elements of the problems raised by decompression phenomena and suggested the simple solution of confining your dives to 'no-stop' times. In the present chapter we examine the subject in greater depth. The Club recommends that even the most experienced divers should try to ensure that all their dives are 'no-stop' dives but they should be well aware of the theory behind and the practice of decompression stops and of repetitive diving.

Introduction

Gases are soluble in fluids. One has only to think of the fact that fish breathe oxygen dissolved in the water to be reminded of this solubility. Thus there is a certain amount of nitrogen dissolved in your body fluids because you live in an atmosphere which contains nitrogen. The amount of gas that can be dissolved in a fluid – in other words the *solubility* of gas in that fluid – depends upon:

1. The partial pressure of the gas in question in the gas phase in contact with the fluid. It is important to appreciate that there must be some contact between gas and fluid. In the human body this contact lies mainly in the lung, because the skin permits only a very slow gas exchange between the body fluids and the surrounding air. This rule is termed *Henry's Law,* see also page 41.
2. The nature of the gas. Thus nitrogen is more soluble in water than helium.
3. The nature of the fluid. Thus nitrogen is more soluble in fat than in water.
4. The temperature of the fluid.

If we treat the human body as a unit, factors 3 and 4 should always be the same. This assumption is not strictly true because the fats in the body are in fact fluids and gases dissolve more extensively in them than in watery body fluids, and different parts of the body contain differing amounts of fats. Some parts of the body, particularly the cornea, tend to have a lower temperature than the rest of the body which would make gases more soluble there than in other parts of the body.

The uptake of Gases by the Body

When a dive is made on air to a certain depth the partial pressures of oxygen and nitrogen

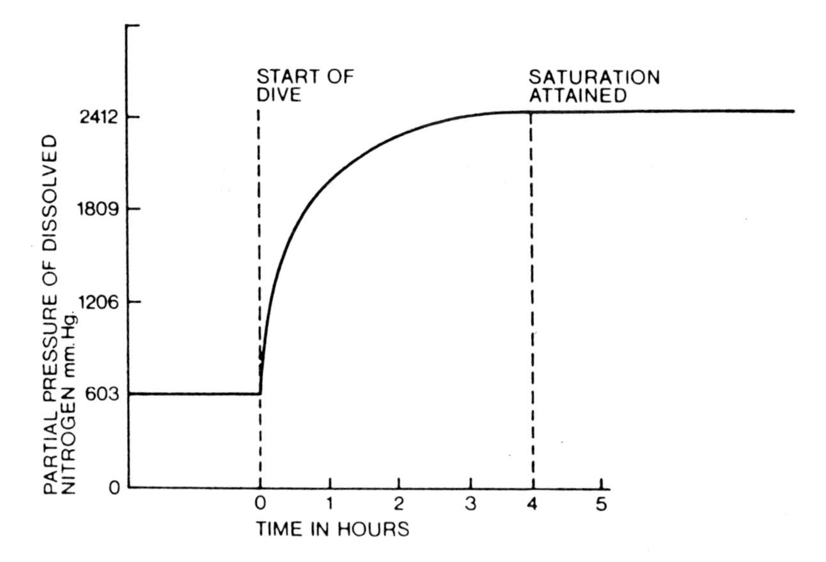

Fig. 67. To illustrate the course of nitrogen absorption in a dive to 30 metres depth. Before the dive the body is saturated with nitrogen at a partial pressure of 603 mm Hg. When the dive starts at 0 hours (the diver is assumed to reach 30 metres immediately and remain at that depth) the diver's body becomes unsaturated because of the increase in partial pressure in the breathing mixture to 2412mm Hg but as time passes he absorbs more and more nitrogen (in the manner shown by the curve) until the partial pressure of nitrogen in his body reaches 2412mm and he is again saturated with nitrogen (for that partial pressure in the breathing mixture). Note that the final approach to saturation is slow, and that it takes about 4 hours to reach saturation under these conditions.

(and other gases) in the breathing air increase. Thus both gases have become more soluble in the body fluids. The body takes up these gases into solution through the lungs. This, however, takes some time. It continues until the body has taken up as much nitrogen and oxygen into solution as will satisfy the solubilities of the gases in the body under the partial pressures acting at the depth of the dive. When as much nitrogen has dissolved in the body fluid as can under the partial pressure of nitrogen the body is said to be saturated with nitrogen for that particular partial pressure of the gas. Thus anyone who has lived at sea-level for some time is saturated with nitrogen for that partial pressure of nitrogen (79% of 760 mm = 603 mm for breathing air). If they then dive to say 30 metres depth the partial pressure of nitrogen and its solubility will have risen four fold. Since the additional nitrogen takes time to dissolve in their bodies they will be at first unsaturated but as they spend more time at 30 metres the nitrogen concentration in their tissues will approach saturation.

Figure 67 shows the rate at which saturation with nitrogen is approached in a dive to 30 metres depth. The rate of solution of a gas in the blood in the lungs is determined by the difference in the partial pressure of nitrogen in the breathing gas and the concentration of nitrogen in solution in the blood, and by the diffusibility of the gas across the lung lining. (Strictly speaking the first factor is expressed as the difference in partial pressure of nitrogen in the breathing gas and the partial pressure of nitrogen in that gas that would be in equilibrium with the nitrogen dissolved in the blood.)

Thus we can talk about the partial pressure of a gas which is in solution, in terms of the pressure that it would exert in a gas phase in equilibrium with the solution. This difference in partial pressures provides a driving force that determines the rate at which gas dissolves in the blood. Similarly, the nitrogen passes in solution from the blood to the surrounding tissues and the blood returns to the lungs with a lower concentration of nitrogen than it has when it left the lungs. Then it picks up more nitrogen to transfer to the tissues and so on. Initially the difference in partial pressures is very great so nitrogen starts to dissolve rapidly in the blood. As the amount of nitrogen in the

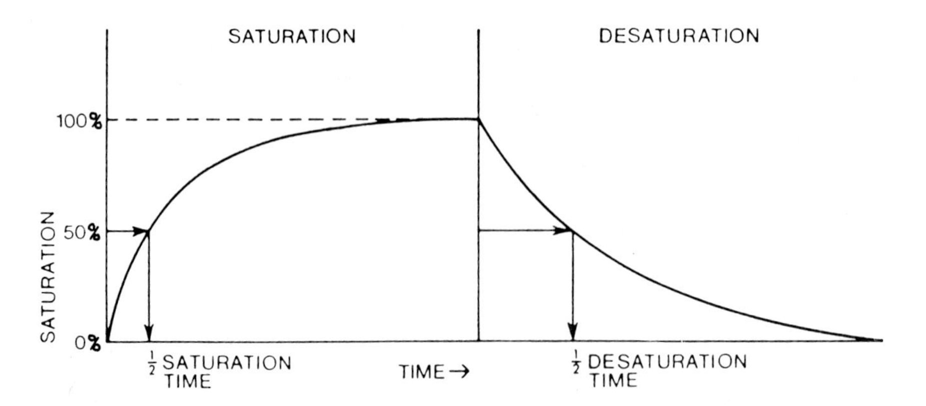

Fig. 68. Curves to illustrate the half-time for saturation and desaturation. The heavy curve gives the uptake of say nitrogen as a dive (at a constant depth) progresses. Eventually saturation is reached for the partial pressure of nitrogen in the breathing mixture at that depth. The arrow on the left from 50% saturation leads down to give the time for half-saturation. Similarly the right hand side of the graph outlines the loss of nitrogen if the diver returns to the surface. A similar time for half-desaturation is defined in a similar way by the arrows. Half saturation time has been depicted as being shorter than half-desaturation; this is normally so but the difference is accentuated in the graph.

blood and body rises the difference in partial pressures lessens, so that the driving force diminishes and nitrogen dissolves more slowly in the blood etc. The other factor that determines the rate at which the nitrogen or any gas dissolves in the body is the **diffusibility** of the gas in the various tissues. Diffusibility is the rate of transport under standard conditions and is determined by the chemical natures of the soluble material and the environment.

Diffusibility and partial pressure differences determine the rate of solution, solubility determines the amount that can dissolve. Diffusibility and solubility of these gases differs in fatty materials from the values in water. For example, nitrogen is about 1.3 times as soluble as helium in water but more than four times as soluble as helium in body fats. Nitrogen is however less diffusible in fats than in water. This means that the rate of saturation of fats in the body is much slower than for the watery parts of the body while the rate of release of nitrogen while and after surfacing is correspondingly slower from the fats than from the watery parts of the body.

Let us return to the saturation curve shown in Fig. 67. Because it is very hard to measure the full saturation time accurately (because the curve has flattened off so much that it is hard to say just when it stops rising), it is usual to use a simpler measure, the **half-saturation time**, i.e. that time at which the gas in a particular tissue has reached half saturation. See Fig. 68. Why do we state 'particular tissue'? The reason for this arises from the differing diffusibilities of a given gas in the different types of tissue, the differing solubilities and the fact that different parts of the body have differing blood supply so that blood reaches them both at differing rates and with differing concentrations of the gas in solution.

For example, the blood in the lungs is in direct contact, save for a thin layer of cells, with the breathing mixture so that the distance for diffusion is very small and the diffusibility of most gases fairly high while the solubility of most gases in the blood is fairly low. If the blood which circulates through the lungs very rapidly did not in turn hand on gases, that have dissolved in it, to tissues with a lower partial pressure of the gases, the blood would saturate very rapidly. Adipose tissue, which is very fatty and has a poor blood supply, will saturate very slowly having a half saturation time for nitrogen of perhaps four hours. Thus on a relatively short dive only the more accessible tissues will saturate while on a long dive all tissues will eventually saturate.

The release of dissolved gas from the body

In essence this is simply the reverse of nitrogen absorption. During an ascent the partial pressure of the gases in the breathing mixture falls. At some point the partial pressures drop below those in the blood. (This hardly applies to oxygen because it is used up by the body so rapidly.) At that point gases in solution start diffusing back from the blood into the lungs and are breathed out. In turn this transport of excess nitrogen etc. starts in the less and less accessible tissues (whose partial pressures of nitrogen etc. may be lower than that in the blood at the start of the ascent). Diffusibility, blood circulation and the partial pressure difference between the tissues and the breathing mixture determine the rate of release of dissolved gases into the expired air. This sounds very simple but it ignores the possibility that bubbles of gas can form in the tissues if the partial pressure difference becomes too great. This is the condition that produces the **bends**, or decompression sickness.

Everyone (unless they have just been at the top of a mountain or in a situation of reduced pressure, and had recently moved to a higher partial pressure of nitrogen or has just dived) is saturated with nitrogen. When they dive they are at first undersaturated with nitrogen because the gas has not had time to dissolve in their bodies to reach saturation (now that the saturation level has increased because gases are more soluble at higher pressure). Once they return towards the surface they will at some point have more nitrogen in their tissues than the solubility for the partial pressure of nitrogen in their breathing air at that depth allows. Thus they are *supersaturated* with nitrogen and this supersaturation is exactly the same as the partial pressure difference which drives gas out of the body into expired air. The greater the partial pressure difference, the greater the degree of supersaturation. At some point, determined by factors outlined below, supersaturation can become sufficient that the gases in the tissues come out of solution as bubbles in the tissues. This is the cause of the bends.

It now seems almost certain that once the supersaturation has exceeded a very small degree that part of the excess gas comes out of solution in the form of bubbles in equilibrium with a small excess of dissolved supersaturated gas. The excess nitrogen is lost from the lungs from the supersaturated dissolved gas. As the excess nitrogen load is lost, gas moves from the bubbles into the supersaturated phase and then into the lungs. With a slight degree of potential supersaturation part of the excess gas appears as tiny bubbles, which are too small to be harmful, the so-called *Silent Bubbles*, which cause no symptoms. If these bubbles grow in size by addition of more gas they may become large enough to cause tissue damage, i.e. they are *Overt bubbles*. With a very slight degree of supersaturation there is no risk of the bubbles ever becoming large enough to form overt ones. This is the reason why you do not need to carry out decompression stops on dives shallower than 9 metres.

The conditions under which overt bubbles just appear are defined by the Haldane rule and more accurately by its later modifications. This rule states that the amount of nitrogen dissolved in the tissues can reach twice saturation level before bubbles appear. In other words this should mean that the absolute pressure at which an infinitely long dive has been conducted (so that saturation has been reached) can always be halved without risk of bends. This rule would obviously not apply in the latter form if the breathing mixture were changed during the ascent because the partial pressure of, say, the nitrogen or helium in the breathing mixture might fall to less than half the partial pressure in the tissues even though the total pressure had been halved. In any case application of this rule has been found, as a result of observation, to lead to a small incidence of bends in shallow dives and a higher incidence in deep dives. This has led to modifications of the Haldane rule.

Bubble size from one moment to another will be determined by:

Change in (i) the total amount of gas that has come out of solution into the bubbles, (ii) the rate at which gas is coming out of solution into the bubble, determined in turn by (a) the extent of supersaturation, and (b) the local diffusibility of the gas, (iii) the change, if any, in the total (absolute) pressure on the body. If a bubble has formed at a certain depth, and even if no further gas is entering it, it will expand as the total pressure is reduced. Of course the change in total pressure during an ascent determines both (i) and (ii). Conversely, if a diver who has bubbles in his tissues is recompressed the bubbles (a) reduce in volume because of the increase in absolute pressure and (b) reduce in volume as the gas goes back into solution in the tissues, provided that the partial pressure of the gas in the bubbles exceeds that in the solution in the tissues.

Eventually all the excess nitrogen will leave the body and the bubbles and excess dissolved gas will have disappeared but by then, if the bubbles were sufficiently large at any time, tissue damage will have occurred, some of it is of an irreparable type.

The symptoms of decompression sickness

The following main types of bends symptoms have been recognised. These are arranged in order of increasing severity.

1. *Minor symptoms.* Itching of the skin or a mottled rash, or an inexplicable tiredness are the most minor symptoms of decompression sickness. These symptoms are not serious in themselves but since more serious symptoms can develop for up to 24 hours after a dive the appearance of such symptoms should be further proof of the need for recompression if the no-decompression limit has been exceeded.

2. *Pains in joints or muscles.* Due to the accumulation of bubbles in the synovial capsules of the joints or in the muscles. These symptoms are the classical 'bends', generally leading to difficulty in movement and sometimes to unusual posture. Pain may range from a dull ache to very severe pain. 'Niggles' is a colloquial name for slight muscle pain.

3. *The 'chokes'.* If the bubbles develop in the pulmonary capillaries or the mediastinum or perhaps the intercostal muscles there may be difficulty in drawing a deep breath. Attempting to do so may often lead to coughing fits. In more serious cases breathing may be difficult or even impossible. Hypoxemia, shock and syncope develop in serious cases. In such cases immediate artificial respiration and rapid removal to a recompression chamber are essential.

4. *Spinal 'bends'.* These occur if bubbles develop in the nerves of the spinal cord or if they appear in the myelin ('fatty') sheaths of the nerves. In the latter case there is perhaps rather more hope that any paralysis that develops will be temporary than in the former case where the nerve cells themselves are damaged. Paralysis and/or loss of sensation will appear in those parts of the body below the point of damage. Thus paralysis of the legs is the most common symptom but paralysis may develop at higher levels as well. Paralysis will of course incapacitate the diver. An initial symptom of the onset of paralysis can be 'pins and needles' in the region likely to be affected. Other symptoms are patches of numbness, burning sensations in the skin, and abdominal pain. Any of these symptoms should be regarded as demonstrating that the person affected is in a very serious condition which demands immediate recompression in a chamber. Bubbles in the main nerve roots from the spinal cord will produce similar symptoms.

5. *Brain involvement.* Damage to or pressure on nerve cells in the brain can produce a very wide range of symptoms including giddiness, visual or auditory disturbances, clumsiness, loss of or disturbance to speech, rapid change in body temperature, fainting etc. These symptoms are very similar to those that can appear with air embolism, where the circulation to specific parts of the brain is stopped by air bubbles.

6. *Major circulatory involvement.* In the rather remote event of a decompression accident in which a diver becomes massively supersaturated, as during a rapid ascent from a deep dive of very long duration, bubbles may form in the circulation. When they are trapped in fine capillaries there is an impairment of blood flow and a consequent local asphyxia of the surrounding tissues. If only a few cells are involved in a relatively unvital part of the body the symptoms will be mild. If parts of the brain or heart muscle are affected the effects will be very serious. The symptoms of circulatory blocking in the brain will be the same as those outlined in 5. If the heart muscle is involved effects ranging up to cardiac arrest may occur. For reasons that are not wholly clear blood pressure may fall, and the blood may become very thick and viscous with consequent appearance of shock in the victim. Again symptoms due to bubbles in the circulation are very similar to those resulting from air embolism.

Decompression Tables

In order to prevent decompression accidents *standard* tables have been prepared which give both the 'no-decompression' limits for dives at various depths and the 'stops' to be used on longer dives in order to prevent symptoms of decompression sickness appearing. In addition *Therapeutic* recompression and decompression tables of a very similar nature have been developed for the treatment of divers with bends symptoms. This section deals with the general principles and methods which

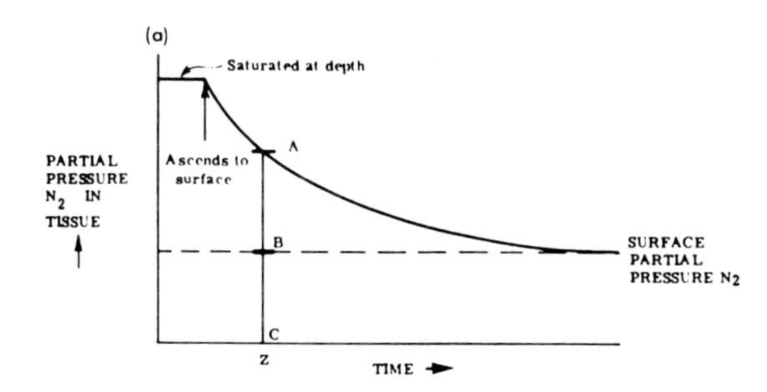

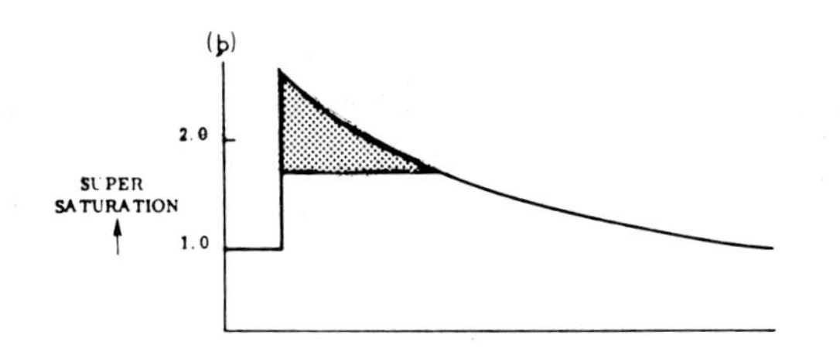

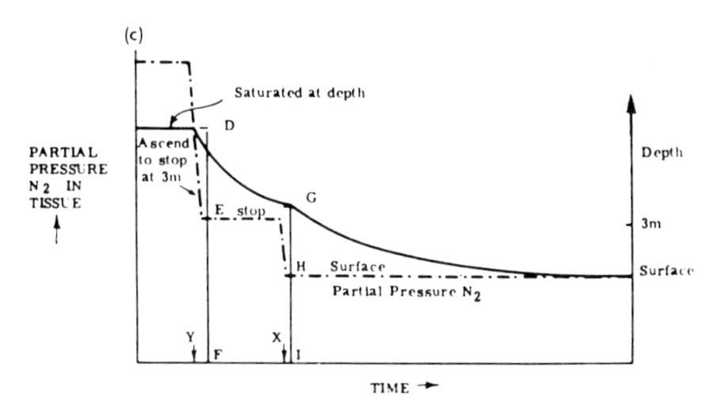

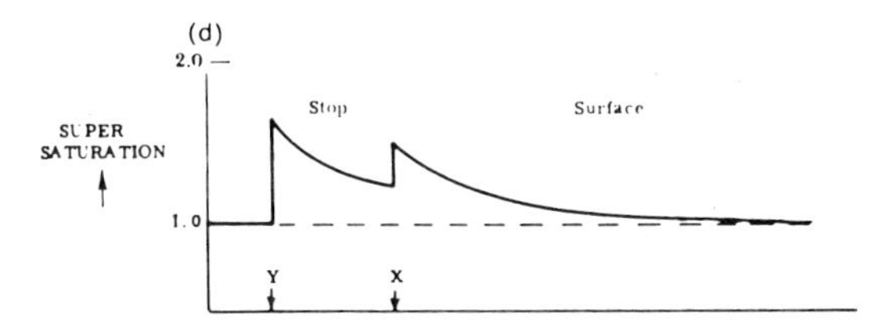

FIG. 69 TO ILLUSTRATE METHODS OF PREPARING DECOMPRESSION TABLES, AND SOME OF THE CONCEPTS USED IN THIS FIELD

(a) and (b) show the elimination of a dissolved gas, say nitrogen, from a diver who surfaces without any stop, after saturation at a depth greater than 10 metres (33 feet). (a) shows the fall of partial pressure of dissolved nitrogen in the tissues of the diver (in a simplified form as in fact each part of each tissue will follow a slightly different curve). (b) illustrates the supersaturation (relative to the partial pressure of nitrogen at the surface) in the divers tissue with time. On the modified Haldane theory the diver is at risk to decompression sickness while the supersaturation has a value greater than about 1.7, which is shown by the shaded area in (b). This can also be seen by considering the situation at time Z (see a). Here the supersaturation ratio is given by the proportion AC/BC, and at time Z this value exceeds 1.7. On the RN theory the risk of decompression sickness at time Z is determined by the magnitude of the value AB. Note that BC is not a necessarily constant value as it will be different for stops at depth or if the gas mixture is changed.

In (c) and (d) the use of a stop to avoid the risk of decompression sickness is shown. (c) shows the fall of the partial pressure of dissolved nitrogen in the tissues of a diver who ascends at time Y to a stop at 3 metres and at time X to the surface. The diver has been saturated at a depth greater than 10 metres before the ascent. When the diver reaches the stop the supersaturation ratio in his tissues (see d) is given by DF/EF, which is less than 1.7. According to the modified Haldane ratio theory this will prevent decompression sickness, while the fairly high value of DF/EF will ensure rapid elimination of nitrogen. Reference to (d) shows that the supersaturation ratio at no time reaches too high a value. On the RN approach DE is of insufficient magnitude to produce symptoms. When the diver surfaces a new set of ratios and values GI/HI or GH apply but so much nitrogen has been eliminated by now that they do not have dangerous values. Broken line in (c) shows the dive profile.

were used in producing such tables and their use in practice, though only brief consideration will be given to therapeutic tables since their use requires the presence of a medically qualified person and they are complex.

The basic aim of all decompression tables is to ensure that at no time does the supersaturation of the dissolved gas reach a point where overt bubbles are likely to form, while at the same time maintaining conditions for the most rapid elimination of the dissolved gas from the body. In view of what was said earlier it is clear that these two requirements are contradictory. The greater the difference between the partial pressure of the dissolved gas and that it has in the breathing mixture, the more rapid the elimination from the body, but if too great a partial pressure difference exists, i.e. if the supersaturation is too great, bubbles form. Decompression tables reconcile these differences. There are basically two types of decompression table, (1) the *continuous* decompression, in which the diver continually makes a very slow ascent following a time-depth profile laid down by the table, and (2) the *stage* decompression, in which the diver waits at a given depth after leaving the bottom until he has lost enough of the excess dissolved gas to be able to ascend to a shallower stop or to the surface. In practice stage decompressions are so much easier to follow than continuous ones that the latter should only be considered for situations such as hyperbaric chambers or SDCs (Submersible Decompression Chamber).

Use of decompression tables: a practical example

If you plan to dive to depths at which your air endurance time, i.e. the time your air will last at a given depth, could approach or exceed the 'no-stop' time for that depth you could end up with a decompression problem even though you plan to make your dive a 'no-stop' one. Mistimings, unavoidable delay, misreading of watch or depth gauge could all lead you into such a situation. Thus you should normally dive with an underwater watch and depth gauge and a slate bearing a copy of the RNPL tables and a means of writing notes of timings. Dives shallower than 9m present no problem and dives down to about 15m are unlikely to present a problem since the 'no-stop' times for such dives are longer than one hour.

To calculate any requirement for a decompression stop you need to know the 'bottom time' i.e. the duration of the dive from leaving the surface to starting the ascent at 15m per minute. If the bottom time is less than the 'no-stop' time you may surface directly at the recommended rate. If the 'bottom time' equals the 'no-stop' time (or is very slightly less a precautionary 'stop' at 5m depth for 5 minutes is recommended. If the 'bottom time' exceeds the 'no-stop' time you must carry out the stops in the tables.

Thus if your 'bottom time' at 30 metres was 23 minutes you carry out the stop tabled for the next time duration after the 'no-stop' time of 20 minutes. The tabled time is 25 minutes but though your time was 23 minutes you obey the 25 minute time. This is the meaning of the rule that you do not interpolate the table. The 25 minute time requires a stop at 10 metres of 5 minutes and then at 5m for 5 minutes. Each stop timing commences as you leave the previous position, i.e. the 10m stop is timed from leaving the bottom, and the 5m stop from leaving the 10m stop. (US practice differs on this point.)

If your dive was of irregular profile you measure your depth for reading the tables as the greatest depth and the bottom time as the time from leaving the surface till ascending above 9m, or starting a 15m per minute ascent. This rule may shorten your 'no-stop' dive durations but gives you a great degree of safety. Disobeying the rule may place you at risk of decompression sickness.

Repetitive diving and dives of irregular profile

Two problems bear forcefully on the amateur diver's practice of decompression. The first is the natural wish to get as much diving as possible when at a site, so that the diver may wish to make several dives a day. The second problem is that the average amateur (and many professional) dive involves a fin swim over quite an area with very variable depths being attained in the course of the dive. What decompression rules should be applied to meet these problems?

The simplest rule for repetitive dives carried out on the same day is that the decompression after the second dive should be based on the sum of times for both dives and on the greatest depth attained in either dive. Thus the tables should be entered at say 60 minutes and 30 metres if both dives were for thirty minutes and the first dive to 30 metres maximum and the second to 19 metres. Obviously this rule becomes unrealistic if the second dive is exceedingly shallow. A simple rule is that if the second dive is to less than 10 metres depth no further decompression need be done after the second dive. A good practice is to ensure that the second dive is shallower (or at least no deeper) than the first. The reason for these rules for repetitive dives is that elimination of excess nitrogen from the body while at the surface may take up to somewhere between 12 to 18 hours in extreme cases. Obviously the simple rules set out above tend to lead to unnecessarily long decompression on occasion but the rules are easy to apply. Repetitive diving tables for decompression have been prepared by the RN and the USN which are fairly easy to follow and which give more realistic decompression times for the second dive. These are available in simplified form from various USA diving manufacturers. These tables take into account the time spent at the surface between dives.

Repetitive diving combined with a failure to observe proper decompression practice has been responsible for an alarmingly large number of serious and fatal bends incidents, both in Britain and elsewhere. Thus the amateur and professional diver populations should clearly give much more attention to following the rules than they have done heretofore.

Dives with an irregular depth-time profile pose serious problems in the accurate estimation of decompression times. Normally the diver has little precise idea of the dive profile and even if he had, the calculation of a decompression time might require advanced mathematical methods. The simple solution is to assume that the diver spent the whole of the dive until the final ascent past 9m depth at maximum depth. Professional diving often requires that the diver spend all his time at one precise depth so that decompression is relatively easy to calculate, but amateur divers have this obvious but unfortunate tendency to move around at varying depths during a dive. Both this problem and that of repetitive dives are partially met by the use of an electronic decompression meter.

The effect of altitude on decompression

If a dive is made into a lake which is considerably above sea-level the underwater pressure increases with depth in nearly the same way as in a lake at sea-level. But after the dive the diver emerges into an atmosphere where the partial pressures of all the gases is much lower than at sea-level. In consequence the supersaturation of nitrogen in his body is relatively greater than it would be after a dive to the same absolute pressure in the sea. Consequently adjustments have to be made to the decompression table and to decompression limits to prevent decompression sickness.

For dives made from water surfaces up to 100 metres above sea-level no adjustment need be made.

If the water surface is between 100 metres and 300 metres add one quarter of the depth to the true depth of the dive and enter the tables at this value.

For surface altitudes from 300 metres to 2000 metres add one third of the depth to the true depth.

Similarly divers should not ascend mountains or fly immediately after diving because the reduced partial pressure of nitrogen at altitude may lead to symptoms of decompression sickness. Aircraft pilots have developed decompression symptoms when they flew shortly after diving. If the dive required no stops the maximum altitude (or effective altitude in a pressurised aircraft) should be 300 metres for the first hour after diving, 1500 metres between 1 and 2 hours afterwards and thereafter there is no limit. If a dive required a stop, altitude should be limited to 300 metres for the first four hours, 1500 metres for the next four hours, 5000 metres from 8 to 24 hours afterwards and thereafter no limit.

PRINCIPLES OF COMPRESSOR OPERATION

This section contains a description of the material or set of facts which underlies compressor operation. If you are about to use a particular compressor, either for the first time, or after any prolonged period in which you have not been operating that particular compressor, refer either to the appropriate Instruction Manual or to a person competent in the operation of that machine.

If you do not know and understand the set of facts set out below, you may still be able to operate the compressor, if you follow the instruction manual, but you will be operating like a robot without any comprehension of just how compressing is taking place. Lack of that basic knowledge may lead you into misjudging, misunderstanding or misinterpreting remarks in the instruction manual.

Compressors of the type used for producing air for the use of divers must be capable of:

1. Producing air up to pressures slightly

above the working pressure of the air cylinders which are to be filled.

2. Producing air of the appropriate degree of purity for breathing.

3. Be fitted with appropriate over-pressure valves (safety valves) or cut-outs so that there is no risk of damaging either the compressor, filling hoses, pipes or cylinders by running the compressor to too high a pressure.

Compressors used for producing breathing air for divers usually operate at maximum pressures of about 250 Bar in the UK. On occasion compressors working up to higher pressures may be found. Usually the main compressor operator will set the maximum pressure to a value 10 to 20 Bar above the working pressure of the type of cylinder he usually fills. So, as a consequence, note that if your cylinder has a maximum working pressure below that for which the compressor is set, you must ensure that the pillar valve is closed when the cylinder reaches its working pressure.

When air, or any other gas, is compressed rapidly it heats up (Charles' Law, see page 41). Thus the air from a compressor would be very hot if it were not cooled by the design features of the machine. Similarly, as a cylinder is filled with compressed air, i.e. its contents are compressed, they warm up. If the air is released from a high pressure cylinder and expanded rapidly to ambient pressure, it cools.

Thus a compressor consists of a number of compressing pistons; each piston, with its associated inlet and outlet valves being called a stage, and interstage cooling pipes. If interstage cooling was not applied the air would be delivered from the compressor at temperatures well above that of boiling water. The pistons are driven from a crankshaft which in turn is rotated by an electric, a petrol, or occasionally a diesel engine.

Typically the first stage might compress the air from ambient pressure to 10 Bar, a tenfold reduction in volume, while the second stage takes the pressure from 10 Bar to 50 Bar and a third stage from 50 Bar to 200 Bar. Four stage compressors take four 'bites' or 'goes' at the same job. There are two reasons for using several stages in compression, (i) the heating of the air that would result from a single compression from ambient to 200 Bar would be dangerous; (ii) it would be mechanically inefficient, and very difficult, to design a piston system that would achieve such a compression ratio.

De-oiling, de-watering and filtering

The air delivered from the final stage of a compressor is, even in the best designed and maintained ones, unsuitable for breathing without further treatment. The air will have picked up a certain amount of oil from the lubrication system for the pistons. It will also contain a large amount of water. The water is derived from the moisture always present in air. If 100 litres of air are compressed into 1/2 litres volume (at 200 Bar) there will be 200 times as much water in that volume as there would be at ambient pressure. Now, although air under pressure can carry more water vapour than air at lower pressures it cannot carry this load. Consequently water mists develop inside parts of the machine as it runs. They tend to occur in the interstage cooling sections where the air is cooled and are most likely to precipitate the moisture as 'mist' or 'rain'. Mechanical traps are used to catch the oil and water mists and these drain into tubes fitted with taps which can be drained off from time to time. Normally such a drain or 'blow-down' valve is fitted after each stage. Provided that these drains are 'bled-off' i.e. allowed to drain, from time to time, very little water and oil will pass beyond the final drain valve towards the filling cylinders. However, if these drain valves are not 'bled off' from time to time the accumulated water and oil will be blown towards the cylinders. As a further precaution a filter bed is fitted to trap the final traces of oil vapour and water.

The filter bed may be packed with activated charcoal which adsorbs oils and other organic vapours. Activated charcoal does not ad- or ab-sorb water. A silica gel filter may be fitted to remove moisture. Silica gel is fairly efficient at trapping oils as well. A third type of filter material is provided by the rather expensive, but effective 'Molecular Sieves' which are artificial zeolites capable of efficient trapping of oil vapour and water. Unfortunately these are expensive: types 10X and perhaps 13X might be used but not types 3X and 6X. Again filters do not last indefinitely and eventually so much of the filter bed becomes saturated with oil and water that it is useless. A regular replacement of the filter bed at a frequency determined by the amount of air compressed and the manufacturer's instructions should be followed.

Usually the filter bed is packed between felts or inside fabric bags, so that there is no risk of filter bed material escaping into the cylinders. If filter bed material does blow through into the filling cylinders, it may damage them or their pillar valves or the first stages of regulators fitted to the cylinders. On occasion, mainly in the past, alumina filter beds were used but these do not seem to have been very effective. It is common practice nowadays to use at least two of the materials listed above, if not three, in one filter system. The effective life of a filter bed can be prolonged by ensuring that the 'drain valves' are bled off frequently, perhaps as often as once every 50 cu.ft. compressed.

It should be noted that once a filter bed does become saturated with oil it is possible for this oil to oxidise rapidly giving rise to carbon monoxide or dioxide. Occasionally air has been found to be heavily contaminated with these gases due to this process. The more usual reason for carbon monoxide contamination is that the air intake for the compressor is close to and downwind of an internal combustion engine, may be the compressor's own driving engine.

Downstream of the filter bed lie in turn a valve, a pressure gauge, a filling valve and one or more filling hoses with 'A' clamps coming off a manifold. Connections to storage cylinders may also be fitted. The pressure gauge allows you to measure the pressure at which the air in the cylinder is, isolated if necessary from the compressor. Thus you can determine what pressure a cylinder has in it when it is brought in for filling, and that it has reached the correct working pressure when filled. Many compressor operators stand the cylinders in fresh water while filling. This cools them down so that there is little pressure drop in the cylinder after filling, which would be appreciable if the cylinder were warm. It also affords a certain measure of protection if a cylinder were to rupture.

Main points of operation

The cardinal points to obey when operating a compressor are:

1. Read the instruction book before attempting operation, or take instruction from a qualified operator.

2. Identify the location of all main operating parts, in particular the controls for the drive (e.g. switch for electric motor), 'blow-down' or 'drain valves' etc.

3. Before starting operation check that the compressor has an adequate fill of the correct type of special compressor oil. Check that the filter bed is still likely to be usable. Check the working pressures and test dates of the cylinders to be filled. Do not fill 'out-of-test' cylinders.

4. Open all 'blow-down' valves (i.e. drain valves). The reason for this is that the compressor should never be started with compressed air inside it, nor should it be switched off (except in emergency) with compressed air inside it.

5. Switch the compressor engine on or start it up.

6. When the compressor engine has come up to speed close the 'blow-down' valves, starting with the one on the first stage and proceeding to later stages in turn. The pressure in the output end can be read on the gauge and as soon as it rises to 20 Bar or 20 Bar more than the pressure in a cylinder which is to be filled, open the valves so that filling begins. The pressure in the compressor should always exceed that in the cylinder.

7. Drain off the blow-down valves frequently and always when one batch of bottles (cylinders) has been filled. If you fail to do this not only will you shorten the life of the filter but you will also probably run the pressure inside the final stage and filter bed up to a value at which a safety valve blows or a cut-out operates. Use of these drain valves allows you to run the compressor on almost 'no load' and without pressure build-up when you open them.

8. When disconnecting cylinders close the pillar valves, shut off the filling hoses, and then blow-down the hoses (or in some better types of equipment just the air space in the 'A' clamp).

9. Before turning the compressor off return it to the state in which the blow-down valves are all open.

10. Log the hours that the compressor has run and the amount of air compressed.

Air purity

If you are in doubt about the purity of air being delivered by your compressor ask a Regional Coach to test the air with one of the test kits he has been issued with. Note that the air should meet the following specification:

Oxygen	21% ± 0.5%
Nitrogen	78% ± 0.5%
Carbon dioxide	0.03% (0.035% permissible)
Carbon monoxide	5 parts per million maximum
Oil	1 mg. per m^3 maximum
Nitrogen dioxide	Under 1 p.p.m.
Water	As dry as possible

Chapter 6

Endorsements

The following endorsements are recommended to all SSAC members who have the prerequisite awards listed for each endorsement. In practice all 3rd Class Divers should hold the ABLJ/Stab Jacket endorsement, the dry suit endorsement if they use a dry suit and the Advanced Lifesaving endorsement if they become BTPs. The Deep Rescue endorsement is intended primarily for the more advanced diver who plans to take the 1st Class Diver Examination. The theoretical knowledge required for these endorsements has been described earlier in this manual.

Examination for the endorsements requires in every case that the candidate be a current member of SSAC.

DRY SUIT ENDORSEMENT

1. The candidate must have completed aqualung training (3rd Class) or at least have started his or her qualifying dives. He or she must hold a current medical.
2. Training may be carried out by any BTP who holds the Dry Suit Endorsement. Assessment (examination) may be carried out by a BDO, or Regional Coach, or Instructor 1 who holds the Endorsement provided that they have not trained the candidate.

DRY SUIT DIVING

Introduction

Dry suits (see also pp. 35-36) have the great advantage that the diver will be warmer in a dry suit, both in and out of the water, than in a wet suit. On the other hand they are rather more difficult to use than wet suits. The reason for this comes from the changes in volume. The foam neoprene type of dry suit shows a second type of change in buoyancy as well as the change due to trapped air. This is due to compression of the foam.

All modern and effective dry suits have a suit inflation system. In the UK this is usually by means of a direct feed which takes air at intermediate pressure from the first stage of the regulator and which can be used, with manual control, to feed air into the suit. A separate air cylinder may be fitted but this is usually of insufficient volume to permit more than a limited amount of inflation of the suit. Some dry suits in other countries rely mainly on oral inflation but this is a slow and time-consuming way of establishing buoyancy.

The air space inside the suit provides a major part of the thermal insulation between the fibres of the thermal undergarment (polar bear or woolly bear) that dry suit divers usually wear. In addition, if you start a dive with little air in the suit and descend without adding further air, two other unpleasant events will occur. First, the suit will start pinching you as increasing pressure reduces the air space even further. Second, you will become negatively buoyant. Thus the main aim of the dry suit diver is to control the amount of air in the suit so that he or she is very close to neutral buoyancy, reasonably warm and in no way pinched by the suit. To do this the diver will need to add air to the suit during a descent and to remove air ('dump' air) during ascent so that he or she does not become over-buoyant during the ascent. Furthermore the diver must ensure that if he has to rescue someone else, at the surface or underwater or to rescue him or herself, that sufficient buoyancy can be safely and securely achieved to do this.

Weighting

The first point to consider is how much weight should be worn with a dry suit. The answer will depend partly on your build and partly on the thickness of undersuit clothing that you choose to wear. However, it is very clear that you should endeavour to keep the weight to as low a value as you can. There are several reasons for this recommendation. First, a very heavy weight belt is awkward to carry and to adjust and don. Second, if your weight belt is close in weight to the lift of an ABLJ/Stab

Jacket it may be impossible to lift a diver who is unable to inflate or retain inflation of his dry suit with his or her ABLJ. Even worse, if you get into trouble and cannot inflate or alternatively retain inflation of your suit, and your buddy is absent, you really need your ABLJ to be able to lift you. If you wear too much weight this may be impossible. You might argue that you would release your weight belt but experience shows that divers are too reluctant to do this, and in any event if you did your ascent would be uncontrolled and very rapid.

So the suggestion is that you should wear less than 30 lbs of weight and preferably around the 7-8 kg (17 lb) recommended by the makers of membrane-type dry suits. Those using foam neoprene dry suits will need rather more weight but it still should be below 14 kg (30 lb). Note that a foam neoprene dry suit will give you no buoyancy, below about 30m depth, arising from the suit itself.

If you wear overmuch weight you will use overmuch air in the suit to offset buoyancy and this will mean that the pressure in the suit, and thus the strain on the seals, is greater than would be the case with less air. Furthermore, having too much air in the suit gives rise to the possible accident of a feet-first ascent floating feet-upwards at the surface. This may be an unlikely event but as you can probably see it is a very undesirable one. Ankle weights, of about ½ kg weight each, may be of some value in helping to prevent feet-first surfacing (inversion), and will also help to give you a better position for finning, especially at the surface. Do not rely on them however.

Valves: inflation and deflation

The second point to consider is the use of the suit inflation and deflation valves (see Fig. 70). If these are positioned on the chest, as in some models which have been on the market for quite a long while, it will be very difficult to use them if an ABLJ is worn as well, unless it is the type of ABLJ designed for dry suit use. It seems probable that the inflation valve should be placed at about waist level and fairly well to the diver's side. The suit deflation valve should be placed high on the arm or just on the shoulder, but clear of any straps that are fitted to the aqualung. If a secondary deflation valve is fitted it might be on the wrist just above the wrist seal. The Viking type deflation valve is, when open, semi-automatic in that it will release any air in excess of a very slight pressure

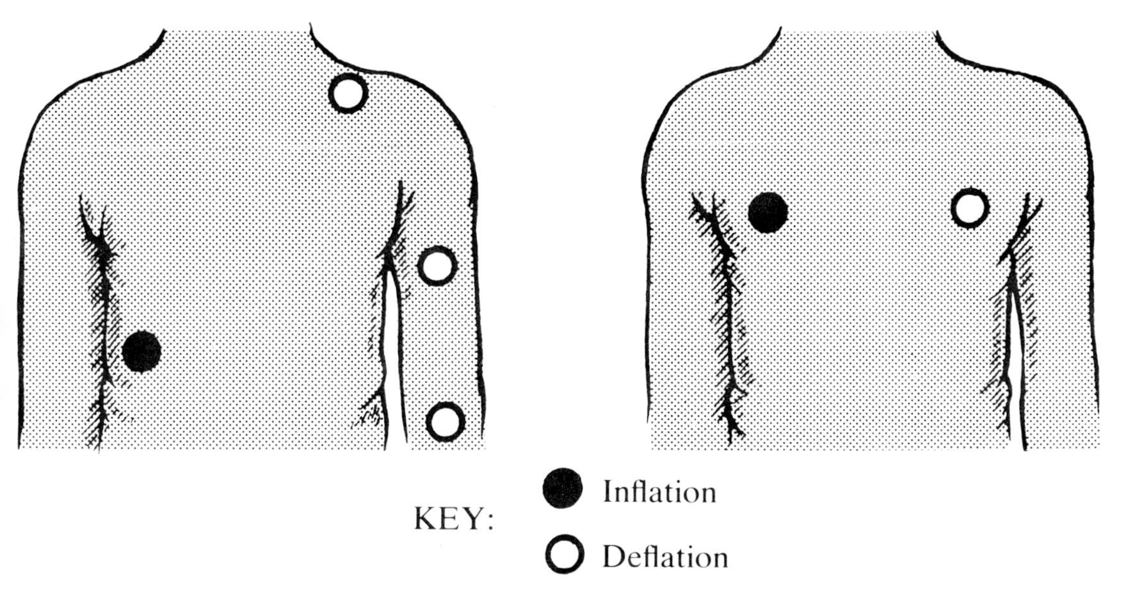

Fig. 70. Positions for dry suit inflation and deflation valves. The left-hand illustration shows positions which are compatible with ABLJs, three alternative positions for the deflation valve being shown. The right-hand illustration shows a layout which is extremely difficult to use with most ABLJs. There is no significance in the left or right-hand placing of the valves, except that this should be related to the side on which your regulator and ABLJ direct feed are fitted.

above ambient, so that as you ascend it will tend to keep the suit with a constant amount of air in it, provided you remember to open it at the start of an ascent. The deflation valves fitted to many other suits require manual operation so that many divers have fitted Draeger valves to their suits in addition. These dump air fairly fast but not as rapidly as the air may be expanding in your suit as you ascend. Moreover, they are not lockable in a closed position so that you may continue to dump air spontaneously at the surface unless you keep that part of your suit bearing the Draeger valve below other parts of your suit. The Viking type valve can, and should be, locked shut on reaching the surface. Inflation, of course, comes from air from the first stage. Reliance on air from a small cylinder is, by itself, undesirable as too little air is available.

You may also consciously or accidentally dump expanding air through cuff seals or a neck seal. If you choose to dump air this way bear in mind that you can only do it if at least one hand is free to pull at the seal. Accidental loss of air, particularly through the neck seal, can be very rapid so that the resulting change in buoyancy is very large. Leaky zips, small tears and holes will leak in water and let air out but their effect on buoyancy control is slight.

Buoyancy control

So the skill in using a dry suit is to ensure that an ascent is controlled and that you can maintain buoyancy at the surface if you have to wait for pick-up or rescue another. The skill in ascent comes mainly from anticipating buoyancy changes because if you leave buoyancy changes too late it may be impossible to dump air as rapidly as the air inside the suit is expanding. In such case you end up in an accelerating ascent and out of control. Maintaining buoyancy at the surface can only be done totally reliably if you wear a lifejacket, though if you are in full command of your faculties and have a good neck seal it should be done with the air in the suit, only using the lifejacket in emergency.

We do not advise you to use both the dry suit and the lifejacket for routine buoyancy control underwater. The combination of two separate sources of buoyancy will be difficult to manage. Since the dry suit will inevitably have air in it, it is too painful not to leave some air in it, it will inevitably have expanding air during an ascent and will need control.

Descent

So in the course of a dive with a dry suit you will start on the surface with some positive buoyancy. To submerge you release sufficient air to enable you to sink by operating your deflation valve, or possibly by holding up the arm with the Draeger valve on it. As soon as you submerge add air through the inflation valve so that you are as close as possible to neutral buoyancy. Obviously you will need to continue to add more air as you descend further (Boyle's Law). Do not let yourself get into the state of marked negative buoyancy. If, despite this warning, you do so you may find that you start sinking faster and faster as the air compresses and that it is difficult to add air fast enough to gain positive buoyancy. This type of incident is more likely the more weight, and thus the larger air volume, in the suit.

Ascent

If you have a Viking-type valve open it fully. If you have a Draeger-type valve be ready to hold that part of the body with the valve on it uppermost. If you only have a manually controlled valve be ready to control it. As you fin up take note of your increasing buoyancy and dump air as appropriate. You will find that whatever system you are using practice is necessary in order to learn how to anticipate the moment at which to dump air. If an ascent begins to get out of control increase the dumping rate, stick your fins out and breathe out. But you may misjudge the amount of air to be dumped in such a situation and end up negatively buoyant. Nevertheless, with practice you can obtain a finer degree of control of buoyancy with a dry suit than by any other method.

On the surface

If the dump valve is lockable lock it and add enough air to the suit to be comfortable. For safety's sake inflate your ABLJ/Stab Jacket slightly in any event, since it is much harder to lose air from the ABLJ than the dry suit by accident. Air loss through a Draeger-type valve or through neck seals at the surface is in fact quite likely so that slight inflation of your ABLJ gives you a real margin of safety. If you have not got a lockable dump valve it is still more imperative that you inflate your ABLJ for surface buoyancy.

Underwater emergency due to loss of buoyancy

If this happens due to tear, neck seal dumping, failure of inflation valve or even more improbably first stage failure, you have two lines of defence. The first is to inflate your ABLJ, the second and final one is to dump your weight belt. Since the main principle in diving is always to have three lines of defence it is clear that you should wear an ABLJ or Stab Jacket with a dry suit. The first line of defence is, of course, the dry suit itself which provides buoyancy.

Surface emergency

The ABLJ/Stab Jacket or even a surface life jacket will give buoyancy on the surface and help another rescuer to hold you in the correct position for EAR if the dry suit does not give the right position by the action of its buoyancy.

Examination syllabus

1. Wearing all equipment normally worn in open water diving including the undersuit normally worn (if any).
2. Demonstrate correct adjustment of buoyancy.
3. Demonstrate the correct operation of inflation and deflation valves to provide good positive buoyancy on the surface and then deflate the suit ready for diving.
4. When the simulated dive test (Part of 3rd Class Award) has not already been carried out then a full simulated dive as for 3rd Class wearing and using the dry suit is to be carried out including recovery from a buoyant 'feet up' position. If the candidate passes this test he or she is credited with passing both the test for this award and the Simulated Dive test for 3rd Class.

If he or she has already passed the Simulated Dive test previously with wet suit then an exercise is to be carried out in which the candidate shows that they can control depth and buoyancy, air sharing, life saving and recovery from the buoyant 'feet up' position.

5. The examiner will flood the candidate's dry suit by opening the entry zip about 30cm. The suit must be allowed to flood as fully as possible. The candidate is then to return to the surface in a controlled manner. The weight belt may be removed if necessary.

OPEN WATER TRAINING AND TESTING

This is only to be carried out when the candidate has successfully completed the pool examination.

1. Fit all diving equipment normally used.
2. Dive to the bottom of a heavy shot line in 10 metres and adjust buoyancy to neutral. The candidate must remain close to the shot so that he or she can take hold of it in case buoyancy becomes too marked.
3. Then the candidate carries out a dive in which the performance and buoyancy control of the diver is tested. The exercise should include several depth/buoyancy adjustments, a simulated decompression stop and a simulated rescue. The depth of the dive is not to exceed 10m.
4. At a depth of not more than 15m dump all air possible from the suit without causing any pain from pinch and establish neutral buoyancy using the candidate's ABLJ or Stab Jacket. Make a controlled ascent.
5. Demonstrate on the surface a recovery from a buoyant 'feet up' position.

ABLJ/STAB JACKET ENDORSEMENT

Minimum requirements

1. The trainee must have progressed at least as far as the qualifying open water dives for 3rd Class and have attended the lectures on buoyancy control and on use of buoyancy aids.

Pool training

1. Revise and consolidate all aspects of ABLJ/Stab Jacket pool training required for 3rd Class training concentrating on buoyancy control so that the diver can float in the water with minimal movement.
2. Carry out controlled buoyant ascents in the pool using each method of inflation and deflation fitted to the jacket. A good performance with the most difficult technique will exempt the trainee from demonstrating simpler techniques.
3. Breathe from the ABLJ or Stab Jacket using air supplied by the direct feed, first resting on the pool bottom and then maintaining position in mid water. This exercise is to be repeated using the emergency cylinder to supply air and the candidate shall then show that he or she can fin at least 25m in midwater breathing from the emergency cylinder.
4. On the surface wearing ABL or Stab Jacket fully inflated disconnect all feeds and remove main cylinder. Help will probably be needed to remove the main cylinder from a Stab Jacket. Hand equipment to an attendant. The candidate is to establish a stable position and fin 25m,

then the candidate removes the weight belt handing it to an attendant and gains a stable position and then to fin 25m. The 25m fin should be 12.5 metres on the front and then a similar distance on the back. The candidate must have his mouth clear of the water.
5. This exercise (4) is to be repeated removing the weight belt before the main cylinder.

OPEN WATER TRAINING

Repeat exercises 2 to 5 above in open water in a depth of no more than 10m.

Open water assessment.

1. Carry out a controlled buoyant ascent without using fins from 15m using all methods of inflation and deflation of the jacket.
2. Carry out a finning ascent breathing air from the emergency cylinder at the recommended rate of ascent from 15m depth.
3. Remove the weight belt and establish a stable position on the surface, refit weight belt, remove main cylinder and establish a stable position, remove the weight belt and establish a stable position. Assistance must be at hand and may be used to hold equipment and help in reaching a stable position. Failure to establish a stable position is not in itself a reason for an unsatisfactory assessment but the candidate must handle such problems with calmness and competence.

The assessment may be carried out by any 2nd Class Diver who is a BTP, and Instructor or Examiner, provided that they hold the award, other than the person who trained the candidate.

ADVANCED LIFESAVING

Prerequisites

1. The candidates must be qualified at least to 3rd Class Award level and hold an RLSS Bronze Medallion or an RLSS Pool Bronze medallion.
2. The candidate must pass a practical assessment on pool work in one session and a theoretical paper. When these are completed successfully the candidate then proceeds to an open water assessment.
3. The assessments are to be carried out by a Club Examiner or Instructor holding the award.
4. Unlike the ABLJ/Stab jacket and Dry suit endorsements application for assessment must be made through your Regional Coach.

Syllabus for training and assessment.

1. Swim 25m fully kitted but without suit at speed to a conscious but weak (simulation) fully kitted diver in difficulties on the surface in water appreciably deeper than the victim and rescuers' heights. Inflate the victim's ABLJ/Stab jacket, drop the weight belt by handing to the examiner, remove the victim's weight belt and cylinder and tow the victim 50m. The subject is to struggle once during the tow and is to be assisted from the water at the deep end of the pool.
2. Fin 50m fully kitted but without suit at speed to a diver simulating unconsciousness on the pool bottom. Bring the casualty to the surface with proper care to prevent possible injury to the victim tow 50m giving EAR in the recommended manner and rate. Demonstrate the effective use of an assistant in an emergency situation. Continue EAR on the poolside. Place the victim in the recovery position and treat as for shock.

The candidate must show an ability to maintain correct buoyancy of himself/herself and victim at all times.

Open water assessment.

1. Surface rescue, the rescuer wearing full snorkel equipment, the victim full diving equipment. Fin 50m to a casualty in deep water, demonstrate three releases, tow the casualty to an entry point 50m distance away, using three methods of tow, during which the victim will struggle once, and assist the victim out of the water.
2. Underwater rescue. The victim will be placed in an area 15m square at a depth of 20m and the candidate is to find the victim, who is simulating unconsciousness. The candidate will lift the victim to the surface in a controlled buoyant ascent. Tow the subject 50m to a boat or shore administering EAR at the recommended rate. The candidate is to give instruction to assistant(s) on the removal of the victim from the water.

Note. Prior to any open water training the candidate is to be encouraged to take part in a discussion on the problems of rescue, removing equipment, finning and towing speeds, the effects of currents and waves, rates of ascent, buoyancy adjustment and control and on removing the victim from the water. The candidate may remove any equipment he or she sees fit to increase speed of rescue but must not compromise safety. The candidate must demonstrate satisfactory care and after-care of the victim. The subject is to be fully briefed on how to behave before the tests, both in pool and openwater. The open water assessment should be carried out in a sea state with wave height of at least 30cm. Training should cover all aspects of the rescue.

Theory assesssment

The candidate is to give oral or written answers to questions on life-saving, water safety and emergency procedures.

If all three sections of the examination are passed the examiner and the NDO shall sign ratification of the result in the candidate's training record.

DEEP RESCUE

The aim of this endorsement is to train and test a diver in raising a negatively buoyant dry-suited diver from 30m depth which simulates the rescue situation from appreciable depth. Rescue of a wet-suited diver would be appreciably easier. The rescuer may be wet-suited or dry-suited. Two methods are used.

Prerequisites.

The candidate shall be a 2nd Class Diver and shall have dived to 30 metres depth within two weeks of the test. Application for test shall be made through the Examination Co-ordinator.

Training

The candidate shall, under the supervision of an Instructor, attempt lifts of the following types:

1. A buoyant lift of a diver simulating inability to fin. The rescuer shall lift the victim to the surface by using inflation and control of the victim's ABLJ or Stab Jacket. The lift must be steady and controlled.
2. The lift of a negatively buoyant diver. The rescuer may adjust his or her buoyancy to neutral at any depth as they normally would but must remember that in lifting a negatively buoyant victim there is an appreciable risk that they pull apart. Thus much of the skill in this lift is holding the victim very firmly. There are basically two techniques, a frontal thigh grip by the rescuer or a frontal chest grip of the victim. Each method has its advantages. Lifts where the rescuer is behind the victim are unlikely to succeed because amongst other things the rescuer has no visual contact with the victim. Since it would be impossibly painful for most dry suited divers to descend from the surface to 30m without suit inflation a compromise is made by asking the victim to dump as much air from dry suit as he or she possibly can when on the bottom at 30m. The rescuer adjusts his or her buoyancy to neutral at 30m. This means that the test is partly one of controlled and sustained use of considerable exertion to raise the victim from 30m to about 15m depth and then control of victim, and of the rescuer himself/herself to the surface.

The main problem is that the trainee may over exert himself and the instructor must guard against this and abort training or testing on the slightest suspicion of this. The instructor must also check that those concerned do not exceed no-decompression stop times.

Tests.

In both tests the candidate leads a dive to 30m with a bottom at this depth. The descent should be reasonably fast but controlled and co-ordinated to 30m. On the bottom, after OK signals have been exchanged, the rescue should be started after the giving of a 'Distress' signal by the rescuer combined with an 'OK' signal to show that the distress is not real.

Rescue 1.

The rescuer inflates the victim's lifejacket or Stab Jacket until ascent starts. Neither rescuer or victim may fin. The rescuer controls the buoyancy of both so that a steady ascent is made at the correct rate pausing at 3m for 1 minute. The rescuer must be in contact with the victim at all times.

Rescue 2.

The victim dumps as much air from his/her dry suit as they can without discomfort at 30m and then gives 'Distress' signal outlined above. The rescuer is at neutral buoyancy. The rescuer lifts the victim by finning until the pair become positively buoyant and then controls the rate of ascent by releasing air from dry suits (and from the rescuer's buoyancy aid if he or she is wet-suited).

One of the two rescues must be completed by an EAR tow of the victim for 50m on the surface and landing of the victim into a boat.

Bibliography

This bibliography mentions only a few of the more recent and accessible books on diving. See the *Advanced Dive Training Manual* for a much fuller bibliography.

Sport Diving. The British Sub-Aqua Club Diving Manual. 11th Edition. 1985 (or later). Stanley Paul, London. ISBN 0 09 163831 3.

A very useful if rather bulky text that takes you most of the way from the most basic features of diving to 1st Class Diver standard. Rather expensive. Very good on basic physics and equipment.

Advanced Sport Diving. 1990. Stanley Paul, London. ISBN 0 09 173828 8. Pp. 160.

Covers much the same material as the second part of the SSAC Training Manual, in much the same detail, though it is more heavily sectionalised. It does, however, contain a small section on UW explosives!

Underwater Diving. Basic techniques. By Peter Dick and David Sisman. 1986. Pelham Books, London. ISBN 0 7207 1664 0.

An introduction to the sport taking you to a level slightly below SSAC 3rd Class. A companion volume *Advanced Diving* is planned. Recommended by the Sub-Aqua Association.

Scuba Diving. The adventure Series. By Anneka Rice. 1988. Robson Books, London. ISBN 0 86051 463 3.

A straightforward guide to elementary aspects of diving. It accompanies a video of the same title.

The complete Scuba Diving Guide. By Dave Saunders. Photography by Mike Portelly. 1987. A. & C. Black, London. ISBN 0 7136 5536 4.

Complete? Pretty nearly for elements of scuba diving!

Index

This index is to both the Introductory and to the Advanced Manual. Page numbers for the Introductory Manual are set in normal type, those to the Advanced Manual in bold type e.g. **126.**

Please note that references to this volume in the index of the *Advanced Dive Training Manual* are not correct because this edition of the *Introductory Manual* supersedes the one in use when the *Advanced Dive Training Manual* was published. Index references in this volume to the *Advanced Dive Training Manual* are correct for the *Advanced Dive Training Manual* 1st Edition.